Writing the

D0627895

Writing the War

*My Ten Months in the
Jungles, Streets and Paddies of
South Vietnam, 1968*

STEPHEN E. ATKINS

McFarland & Company, Inc., Publishers
Jefferson, North Carolina, and London

LIBRARY OF CONGRESS CATALOGUING-IN-PUBLICATION DATA

Atkins, Stephen E.
    Writing the war : my ten months in the jungles, streets and
paddies of South Vietnam, 1968 / Stephen E. Atkins.
      p.   cm.
    Includes index.

    ISBN 978-0-7864-4272-0
    softcover : 50# alkaline paper ∞

    1. Atkins, Stephen E.   2. Vietnam War, 1961–1975 —
Personal narratives, American.   3. Vietnam War, 1961–
1975 — Regimental histories — United States.   4. United
States. Army. Infantry Regiment, 31st. Battalion, 6th.
I. Title.
DS559.5.A86   2010
959.704'342092 — dc22   2009046149
[B]

British Library cataloguing data are available

Cover image ©2010 Shutterstock

Manufactured in the United States of America

McFarland & Company, Inc., Publishers
  Box 611, Jefferson, North Carolina 28640
    www.mcfarlandpub.com

Table of Contents

Introduction   1

1. Background and Training for the Vietnam War   11
2. First Weeks in South Vietnam   25
3. First Blooding   37
4. Operations in the First Weeks of May   45
5. Battle of the Cholon Y Bridge   58
6. Combat in the Mekong Delta   69
7. Adapting to the Rear-Echelon and the Battle of the Plain
   of Reeds Report   82
8. Back at Bearcat and the Thai Presidential Award   101
9. Events at Dong Tam and Special Assignment   114
10. Back at Dong Tam   126
11. Last Months in South Vietnam   139

Conclusion   152
Appendices
A. *Captured Viet Cong Attack Plan*   157
B. *Battle of Saigon, May 1968*   163
C. *After Action Report, Battle of the Plain of Reeds*   165
D. *Evaluation of Intimate Psychological Warfare*   185
E. *Recondo Checkerboard Concept*   188
F. *Psychological Warfare Ground Action, 11 November 1966*   192

G. *Psyop Estimate of INPSYWAR*   195

H. *Air Cushion Vehicle Report*   196

I. *Viet Cong Strength and Combat Effectiveness, 1 August 1968*   202

J. *Viet Cong Order of Battle (9th Infantry Division's Area),*
   September 1968   203

K. *"Form Letter" from the 9th Infantry Division*   206

Index   209

Introduction

It has been nearly thirty-five years since the end of the Vietnam War in 1975, but to many of the veterans of that war it is still a constant reminder of a lost period in our lives. In the past, veterans have considered war as a unique personal experience that has transformed all those who played a role in it. Veterans of other wars have tended to look back to their combat experiences with sadness about the loss of friends, tinged with nostalgia about their youth, and shared experiences. Most Vietnam War veterans have kept the sadness without the nostalgia and no desire to relive the war. Such are my memories about the ten months that I spent in South Vietnam from the spring of 1968 to late January 1969.

My tour of duty in South Vietnam as a member of 3rd Platoon, Company C, 6th Battalion, 31st Infantry, 9th Infantry Division from April 3, 1968, to January 29, 1969, changed my life dramatically. It took me nearly a decade after my return from Vietnam to readjust to civilian life. My wife can testify that it changed my personality from a mild-mannered academic to a person determined to make a success of myself. Although my front-line duty lasted only a little more than six weeks, it was enough to impress me about the frailty of human life. Too many buddies of mine lost their lives during this period. Later, I watched the casualty lists for the fate of my friends. Those of us who survived believe that we were and are now living on borrowed time.

My company participated in three different types of combat: jungle fighting in the south Central Highlands; street fighting in the suburbs of Cholon, and guerrilla warfare in the rice paddies of the Mekong Delta. During the six weeks after two weeks of acclimatization to South Vietnam, my unit averaged a firefight once a week. Casualties were also heavy with more than a dozen deaths and many wounded. My role as a point man for the company, responsibilities as a sniper on ambush patrols, and use of demolitions blowing up bunkers were all dangerous jobs. That I survived had nothing to do with my knowledge or abilities but merely luck.

By a combination of luck and circumstances, a transfer to a rear-echelon unit undoubtedly saved my life. Major Cook, the new commander of the 19th Military History Detachment, arranged my transfer to his unit in late May 1968. What saved my life was a master's degree in history and the ability of a sergeant to work his way through and around army regulations. This sergeant bribed a sergeant in division headquarters with a case of beer to change my military occupational specialty (MOS) from infantry to clerk-typist. Few people can place an exact value on their life. For me, it was a case of beer costing in the PX at that time around $2.50. Later, I learned that my replacement as a point man with my company was killed less than two weeks after my transfer.

From the relatively safe position in the 19th Military History Detachment, I spent the remainder of my tour in South Vietnam serving as a military historian traveling around the 9th Infantry Division's area of operation collecting information on battles, personnel, and information for reports on the conduct of the war. These reports were then forwarded to the Department of Defense for further analysis. This job was still dangerous but not nearly as dangerous as being on point for an infantry unit out looking for Viet Cong fighters.

The combination of my combat experience along with access to various military units during my sojourns gave me a unique opportunity to study military operations of the 9th Infantry Division between April 1968 and January 1969 in its areas of operation in the Mekong Delta, the Plain of Reeds, and around Saigon. Enemy opposition in the area of operation of the 9th Infantry Division was the traditional low-intensity warfare with a mix of local force guerrillas combined with a number of North Vietnamese main force regulars. Viet Cong forces conducted both full-scale military offensives and local guerrilla activity throughout 1968, keeping the 9th Infantry Division busy countering their operations.

It has taken me more than thirty-five years to come to grips with my experiences in the Vietnam War. Several times friends have broached the subject of my writing down my war experiences, but each time a convenient excuse intervened. At first, I was too close to the events to claim objectivity, and, during the first few years, some of my disclosures might have had security complications. Time has solved both of these concerns. What I did do, however, was to begin gathering materials that I had brought back with me from South Vietnam and start writing my experiences. This exercise had a cathartic effect on my adjustment to civilian life and reconciliation with my memories. At the beginning of my writing my Vietnam experiences, I decided to return to working on my dissertation in French history at the University of Iowa. This endeavor occupied all my energies for the next seven years, culminating in my Ph.D. in 1976. In the meantime, there was the birth of my daughter, Stephanie, in 1973, and my son, Jordan, in 1976. Job-hunting and a career change to academic librarianship led to more schooling and a library science degree in 1983. After finding a position at the University of Illinois at Urbana-Champaign Library as a political science subject specialist, the drive to obtain tenure took most of my energies for the next six years. Another job change, this time to Texas A&M University Libraries, followed in 1989. A trip to the Vietnam War Memorial in Washington, D.C., in 1992 brought back memories of those friends and acquaintances who never made it back alive. I had made several trips to Washington, D.C., earlier but I had always avoided the memorial because it was too painful. This 1992 trip renewed my desire to come to grips with the past, but first I had to finish several other publishing commitments. Only after a conversation with my daughter in 2006 did I decide to do something about publishing my Vietnam War experiences. Several bouts with colon and liver cancer informed me that time is passing me by. On top of this, a former member of my platoon contacted me to say that the 6th Battalion was starting to hold reunions and invite me to one in Syracuse, New York. I could not make the reunion, but it reinforced my desire to work on the book on the Vietnam War. Even now, Vietnam veterans are starting to get old and in another decade or so there will be far fewer of us.

Although my memories are still present, I have relied on refreshing my memory with a diary that I kept during most of my stay in South Vietnam. Keeping a diary was a court-martial offense in South Vietnam, but I ignored that prohibition because even as a combat soldier I considered myself a historian viewing the war from below. I also have a number of letters which were written in South Vietnam. Moreover, in my capacity as a military historian, I had access to divisional intelligence reports as well as daily situation reports. My copies of some of these documents may be the only records still available since most of these documents were destroyed when the 9th Infantry Division left South Vietnam in 1971.

Another factor in my decision to write about my experiences in the war is to give insights into the military situation in South Vietnam during most of 1968. It is my contention that 1968 was the pivotal year in the history of American participation in the Vietnam War. It was during this year that American military forces had their last chance to win the war before the politicians finally took over completely. My battalion was the last unit deployed to South Vietnam as part of the Johnston administration's original troop deployment to win the war. When General Westmoreland and the rest of the military commanders decided that it would take nearly double the previously authorized military strength of 550,000 troops to accomplish the pacification of South Vietnam, it was realized that this would mean a commitment of over one million troops. President Johnson realized that the political stakes were too high to tolerate this level of troop commitment, and he decided not to seek reelection to the presidency. News of President Johnson's decision reached my battalion on the eve of our deployment to South Vietnam. A general appeared to talk to my company telling us that President Johnson's announcement would have no impact on our deployment or the combat situation in South Vietnam. He was right, as it had no impact on us whatsoever.

Republicans were able to capitalize on opposition to the war and the public's desire to win the war to gain the presidency for Richard M. Nixon. After Nixon's election, it soon became apparent that his administration was going to depend on Vietnamization to win the war or, alternatively, at least end the South Vietnamese dependency on American troops. By the time this strategy became apparent, those of us in South Vietnam realized what a false panacea this strategy was. Those of us who had fought beside the South Vietnamese Army (ARVN) considered Vietnamization a joke. When the 9th Infantry Division moved into the Mekong Delta area of operations, it was because of the unreliability of ARVN's 25th Division. Rumor had it that an agreement had been reached between the commanders of ARVN's 25th Division and the leadership of the Viet Cong that allowed ARVN forces to operate with impunity during the day and permitted the Viet Cong the same freedom during the night. Confidence was so low about the trustworthiness and fighting capabilities of our South Vietnamese ally that most American units in our area refused to share intelligence information with them. Occasionally, a lack of communication caused embarrassing incidents, such as the time my platoon found itself in the middle of a South Vietnamese Army free-fire zone during an ambush patrol.

Certain myths have abounded about the composition of the American army sent to South Vietnam. While a high percentage of minorities and the less educated segment of the American male population were sent to fight in the infantry in South Vietnam, more college graduates were in the combat arms than is commonly known. Nearly a third of the members of my infantry company had a college education from schools like the Massachusetts Institute of Technology, University of Iowa, University of Michigan, University of Wisconsin, and Virginia Tech, to name only a few. The rest of the battalion had a similar mix.

My career goal in 1966 did not include service in the military. My college record at that time included a B.A. with honors (1963) and an M.S. with honors (1964) in European and French history from the University of Missouri–Columbia, and it was directed towards a career in academia. I had started coursework on a Ph.D. in French history at the University of Iowa in the fall of 1964. My Ph.D. comprehensive examinations had been scheduled for November 1966. That September my draft board in Mexico, Missouri, for Audrain County had begun to run out of warm bodies to draft. A friend of the family, who was also the local draft board clerk, informed my aunt in Mexico, Missouri, that my draft appeals had been exhausted and a draft notice would be forthcoming in the next mailing in November 1966. This news was not totally unexpected: draft boards in rural areas like Audrain County, Missouri, were having trouble filling draft levies because so many of the farm boys were unable to pass the physicals. Too often, these farm boys had lost fingers or hands to farm accidents. Draft boards were becoming desperate, and the army doctors were lowering medical standards. During my draft physical in St. Louis, Missouri, a doctor passed a graduate of the Missouri School for the Blind for service in the military.

Since I had already passed my physical at the huge induction center in St. Louis, Missouri, in the summer of 1966, there was no chance of my avoiding military service. Any effort to join the National Guard or Army Reserves was hampered by the lack of political influence of any member of my family. Shortly after returning from my physical, I began negotiating with the U.S. Army recruiter in Iowa City, Iowa, for a delayed entry into the army in exchange for a two-year enlistment with a guaranteed slot in Officer Candidate School (OCS). My enthusiasm for the military life was muted by the fact that I was already 25 years of age, 50 pounds overweight, and had been married for less than nine months. The delayed enlistment, however, allowed me to finish my Ph.D. comprehensive examinations with flying colors and have a Christmas vacation before entering the army on February 5, 1967, shortly after my 26th birthday.

Part of my lack of enthusiasm for the army was because of a growing skepticism about the aims and conduct of the Vietnam War. While public opinion in the autumn of 1966 was overwhelmingly pro-war, I was still hesitant. A few anti-war rallies had been held in downtown Iowa City, Iowa, but the danger was more that the demonstrators would be harmed by rock-throwing counter-demonstrators than that they would cause property damage or win converts. My sympathy for the demonstrators, however, was not enough for me to demonstrate with them. About this time, the former prime minister of France, Pierre Mendès-France, had a speaking engagement at the University of Iowa. During a reception after his speech, I had the opportunity to ask him several questions about his negotiations with the Viet Minh at Geneva, Switzerland, in 1954. The crux of his answers to my questions was that during the Geneva negotiations Mendès-France believed he was dealing more with Vietnamese nationalists than with international Communists. While I found these remarks informative, my mind was still not made up about the war. I supported the Johnson domestic programs of civil rights and social progress, but I had reservations about his foreign policy of containment of communism in Southeast Asia. Warnings from various experts about the dangers of involving American troops in land warfare on the Asian mainland made sense to me.

These reservations were on my mind when I reported to the army at Fort Dix, New Jersey, in the middle of a massive snowstorm on February 5, 1967. Nothing is as depressing as taking basic training in the middle of a New Jersey winter. My basic training unit was a mix of draftees training for combat in South Vietnam, and National Guard and Army Reservists putting in their six months before returning to their homes. My eight weeks in basic training at Fort Dix was unforgettable except that I had the good fortune to have excellent drill sergeants. Sergeant Mason and Sergeant Williams were both above-average drill instructors, and they were relatively good to the trainees. Both sergeants were African Americans and Fort Dix had the reputation of having the best basic training drill instructors in the U.S. Amy because most of the African American instructors served there. They had the reputation of being fairer to the trainees than the white drill sergeants were. Both made it plain that they had volunteered to go to South Vietnam. Somehow, in all the exercising and training I managed to lose about twenty-five pounds and graduate from basic training. It was at Fort Dix that a lieutenant gave me the nickname of "fatty-four eyes" because of my weight and my glasses. After finishing basic training, my next assignment was Advanced Individual Training (AIT) at Fort McClellan, Alabama. While at Fort Dix, I managed to wrangle a two-day pass to visit New York City. I was lonely but I had so little money that I just walked the streets taking in the city atmosphere.

At my new assignment at Fort McClellan, I stayed on the base the entire six weeks. On my arrival at Anniston, Alabama, the taxi cab driver made it plain that soldiers were not welcome in Anniston, and, if caught there after 9:00 P.M., would be arrested by the police. I felt more welcome later in South Vietnam than in Anniston. Fortunately, I had to spend only six weeks there. Normally Advanced Individual Training took eight weeks, but the army was rushing us through as fast as possible. My most vivid memory of Fort McClellan was avoiding all the rattlesnakes on the rifle range and in the forest there. They were all over the place. I remember noticing six rattlesnakes near the firing line when we took rifle training.

During both basic training and Advanced Individual Training at Fort McClellan, I was too busy adjusting to the army and learning how to handle my weapons to worry much about possible service in South Vietnam. Drill sergeants constantly alluded to South Vietnam in our military training as a way to motivate us, but the training emphasized conventional warfare rather than preparing us for guerrilla fighting in the jungle or rice paddies. The army appeared less eager to indoctrinate us about the war than to teach us how to fight the army way. We did receive several lessons on the Uniform Code of Military Justice, and our obligation as soldiers to disobey an unlawful order.

Although I hated aspects of the military — mostly the lack of privacy and the constant details — what made me most furious was the condescending attitude of the national guardsmen and reservists towards the regular army recruits during training. They made little pretense that we had been suckers for not having opted for safe slots in the Army Reserve or the National Guard. None of them admitted that they had political pull or friends to get them those safe slots. Most of us had inquired about slots in the Army Reserves and National Guard only to be told that it took several years on waiting lists before acceptance. Later, we learned that exceptions were being made all the time for those with the right connections. There were times in South Vietnam that some of us were rooting for the rioters against the National Guard during the 1968 riots.

During the remainder of my stateside military training, the specter of combat in South Vietnam became overwhelming. I learned soon after my arrival in Officer Candidate School (OCS) that it had been a mistake trying to become an officer. My original plan had been to earn a commission in OCS and become an intelligence specialist. Once in OCS, however, I learned that unless an officer candidate had a physical profile (some type of non-serious injury) he would be commissioned in the infantry and sent to South Vietnam as a platoon leader. Early in my career in the army, I concluded that becoming a combat platoon leader was not for me. The low survival rate for a platoon leader was common knowledge. More important was my belief that I had a better survival chance as an enlisted man since I was less confident of survival if I had to be concerned with the safety and conduct of members of a platoon. Finally, I had been a competitive tennis player, but my athletic ability was limited. None of this mattered in the long run because there soon developed a personality conflict between my tactical officer, a former basketball player and college dropout, and myself. I was too old, 27 years of age, insufficiently motivated, and not athletic enough to earn a commission by this route. Although I understood the rationale behind the mental and physical harassment of OCS, I had trouble adjusting to it. Ultimately, the army decided the issue by deciding that it no longer needed so many second lieutenants and began curtailing the OCS program. Emphasis shifted instead to training non-commissioned officers. All these things came together and I left the OCS program after eight weeks. While I had few doubts that the army would send me to a combat unit in South Vietnam as an infantryman, my confidence that I could protect myself better in combat without the responsibility of thirty or so men sustained me. My later experience in combat in South Vietnam only reinforced the wisdom of this decision. Instead of being sent directly there as a replacement, the army sent me to Fort Lewis, Washington, to train with a newly formed infantry unit.

Before I left Fort Benning, Georgia, for my new assignment, I had one lasting personal experience. Working at Fort Benning's Military Museum gave me some free time that I spent with my wife. The movie *The Green Berets* was in production at Fort Benning in the summer of 1967. Army personnel had been assigned to help with the movie and give it some authenticity. One evening I had a weekend pass with my wife, Susan, and we decided to eat out. We went to the Back Angus Restaurant in nearby Columbus. The restaurant was crowded so the headwaiter seated us in a private back room. Soon after ordering, John Wayne and his family walked into the room. Several other actors also showed up, among them Aldo Ray. We sat there slowly consuming our steaks watching John Wayne, his wife Pilar, and his children interacting. It was an experience that neither of us will ever forget. We thought it would be bad manners to approach either John Wayne or any of the other actors so we left them alone. I was also in uniform and it would have been bad news if any of the actors had complained about my conduct. My wife and I left the restaurant without their ever noticing us. Years later, I could recount that I once had dinner with John Wayne. By the way, the movie was terrible. I have never been able to stand watching more than about half of it before becoming too disgusted to watch the other half.

This book is a personal account of my tour of duty in South Vietnam, but I would have never made it back without help from my buddies. For that reason, I want to dedicate this book to the twenty men in my platoon — 3rd Platoon, Company C, 6th Battalion, 31st Infantry — who died in South Vietnam. I have their names engraved in my memory, but a mere listing is not enough. We trained together and became friends. They made the ultimate sacrifice and I want to honor them. Some of their names will appear in the text of the manuscript, but I want to emphasize that they all died honorably for their country.

1

Background and Training
for the Vietnam War

After two days of confinement in the barracks at Fort Lewis, Washington, with armed Military Police as guards, it was with a certain amount of relief that my company boarded the buses for transit to McCord Air Force Base. The occasion was the movement on April 2, 1968, of Company C, 6th Battalion, 31st Infantry from Fort Lewis to points unknown in the Republic of South Vietnam. After more than five months training on the foothills of Mount Rainer, my unit was finally going abroad to that unnamed area of conflict in Southeast Asia.

My company had celebrated April Fools' Day during our confinement, but nobody had been in the mood to find any humor in our situation. Rumors had been circulating that our outfit was destined to join the 196th Light Infantry Brigade, Americal Division, at Chu Lai. A briefing by the Commander of Company C had confirmed the rumor that our battalion had indeed been assigned to the 196th Light Infantry Brigade. Several of us had immediately dashed to a map of South Vietnam and looked up the location of Chu Lai. Chu Lai was not far from the Demilitarized Zone (DMZ) separating South Vietnam from North Vietnam. This fact scared us that we might be conducting military operations so close to North Vietnam. Although the Tet Offensive of January 1968 had been on the national news during the past couple of months, the fragmentary nature of the information about the battle and more recent publicity about the fighting around the DMZ and Khe Sanh made us concerned about landing in a situation where there was heavy fighting. Peace talks in Paris had started a few weeks before, but few of us had any illusions about the prospects of avoiding a full tour in South Vietnam or escaping combat. Each side on the peace talks would use the military situation to try and gain political advantage. Consequently, the men of Company C, 6th Battalion, 31st Infantry, left the continental United States with few illusions and much foreboding.

The 6th Battalion, 31st Infantry had been reorganized on November 1, 1967, and it was one of the last units to train in the United States for Vietnam duty as part of President Johnson's original military buildup. Unit histories informed us that the 31st Infantry Regiment had a checkered military past. Personnel from the 8th, the 13th, and the 15th infantry regiments had been combined by the army in 1916 to form the 31st Infantry Regiment for duty in the Philippines. From late in 1918 to 1920 the 31st Infantry Regiment had the misfortune to draw the assignment to guard the Trans-Siberian Railroad during the Russian Civil War. It was during this duty that the regiment acquired the polar bear as its symbol. Except for brief tours of duty in Japan during the 1923 earthquake and in China during the 1932 Shanghai Incident, the regiment had spent the interwar years in the Philippines. The Japanese invasion of the Philippines in 1941 found the 31st Infantry Regiment opposing it, but the regiment was overwhelmed by superior forces on Bataan. The regimental colors had been destroyed to keep them out of the hands of the Japanese. Its survivors participated in the Bataan Death March where the high death total left few survivors. Most of those that did survive spent the war in Japanese prison camps.

After the regiment's reorganization in 1946, it was stationed in Korea. The regiment was still there when the North Koreans invaded South Korea in 1949. After experiencing the hardships of the first days of the war, the regiment rebounded and participated in almost all of the major battles of the Korean War from the Inchon Landing to Pork Chop Hill. With such a record of foreign service and battle experience, there was no reason why the 31st Infantry should escape duty in South Vietnam. For the first time elements of the 31st Infantry were stationed in the continental United States for training for a deployment in South Vietnam. Those of us assigned to the new unit found the 31st Infantry's nickname of "The American Foreign Legion" ominous at best. Moreover, the symbol of the 6th Battalion, 31st Infantry was a sitting polar bear with a strange expression on its face. We soon dubbed it the "constipated polar bear." Such attempts at humor were attempts to bring normalcy to a situation that we had no control over and were scared to contemplate.

By the spring of 1968, the Vietnam War was in its second year of full-scale American military intervention. Conversion of the army from a peacetime to war footing meant that the army was already having to scrape the bottom of the manpower barrel to form two new infantry battalions. The constant call for replacements in combat units meant that the number of non-commissioned officers was being depleted at a rapid rate. Those NCOs at training facilities suddenly found themselves with orders to units either in South Vietnam or with units training to go to South Vietnam. At Fort Benning, emphasis had shifted from the Officer Candidate School (OCS) to non-commissioned officer training, but the results were slow coming. This meant that two new battalions, the 6th Battalion, 31st Infantry, and the 5th Battalion, 12th Infantry, in training for South Vietnam duty at Fort Lewis received their non-commissioned officers from basic training and other stateside commands. Almost none of these NCOs had previous combat experience.

Personnel issues plagued our battalion from the beginning of training. At full strength, a battalion was authorized to have 852 officers and enlisted men. After nearly five months of field training, my battalion had finally reached this strength two weeks before the battalion started its pre–Vietnam leaves. Part of the reason for this delay in reaching full strength was that the army had tried to pull a fast one over a pre–OCS AIT (Advanced Infantry Training) class. When the army decided to cut back on the OCS program in the summer of 1967, it gave the soldiers in the pre–OCS program the choice of assignments if they would sign releases from the OCS commitment. Many of the men at Fort Dix signed such releases only to find themselves with an infantry MOS (military occupational specialty) and an assignment to an infantry unit bound for South Vietnam. They were furious about this double-cross. A congressional investigation was requested by these men, and, after a two week investigation, these men received the transfers that they had originally requested back at Fort Dix. Their joy was short-lived because almost immediately the army put them on levy for duty in South Vietnam. At least these men avoided the dangers of a combat unit. Most of us remaining in the battalion were also delighted with their good fortune because all of us at one time or another had been lied to or dealt with in bad faith by the army. With the constant shift of men in and out of the battalion, there were hardly enough men to carry out proscribed training.

The army intended the five months of training at Fort Lewis to prepare us for combat in South Vietnam. Although the war had been going on for several years, our battalion had few Vietnam veterans — four company commanders and two sergeants. While several of the senior non-commissioned officers had Korean War combat experience, most of them were career peacetime professionals. They had reluctantly left soft training jobs in basic or advanced infantry training units. Although each of them had previous opportunities for Vietnam duty before being assigned to our battalion, none of them had done so. These peacetime warriors proved to be master politicians, but not good combat leaders. Most became combat casualties or had to be relieved for incompetence once the unit had experienced combat.

The situation was better with officers. Our company commander was Captain William Owen, a West Point graduate. Owen was not loved, but he was a competent company commander. He had also served a prior tour of duty as a line officer in South Vietnam. The platoon leaders were recent graduates of Officer Candidate School and only one of them could boast of having passed 21 years of age. Battalion had few Vietnam veterans — four company commanders and two sergeants. These youthful officers also faced the complication that the initial levy of enlisted men for the unit had been OCS dropouts. Several cases existed where the officers and the enlisted men had been members of the same OCS class, and some of the officers had been instrumental in washing out the enlisted men from OCS.

Command team of Company C., 6th Battalion, 31st Infantry at Fort Lewis, Washington — Captain William Owen, commanding officer; 1st Lieutenant David Wilson, executive officer; 2nd Lieutenant May, and 2nd Lieutenant Ronald Belloli.

They had been members of the infamous class of #50, which produced Lieutenant Calley of My Lai fame. My former class had been #55 and several times my class had been harassed by senior candidates from #50 as they had been approximately eighteen weeks ahead of us in training. Several personality conflicts were carried over from OCS into the new unit. Moreover, the educational level of many of the enlisted men was much higher than that of the platoon officers. This was to change later as the unit was filled by levy from personnel sources other than OCS rejects. The educational level of the battalion, however, always remained higher than in other army units.

The army has always depended upon the OCS program to produce officers in times of war, but the system has had to withstand criticism. Maybe my remarks can been called sour grapes, but I believe many of the criticisms are justified. In theory, the program makes sense: by placing potential officer candidates under severe physical and psychological stress the army can select only those best able to cope with stressful situations. In practice, however, the system tended to produced one-sided officers. College graduates dropped out of OCS in large numbers because they were unwilling to make the total commitment to the army demanded by the tactical officers (TACs), who were recent graduates of the same system and without combat experience. What were left in OCS were either college dropouts desperate to succeed at something, or career army types eager to make the shift from enlisted to officer ranks. Most of the twenty-three weeks of training dealt with technical matters and physical training, but more emphasis was placed on the latter. By making TAC officers so powerful in the OCS system a moral code was perpetuated that insured no matter what methods were employed no questions would be asked as long as the officer accomplished the mission. The result has been to produce technically proficient but morally weak lieutenants with tremendous egos. If these officers had performed at a high level on the battlefield, then there might have been some justification for the OCS program. In the units in my battalion nearly half of the OCS lieutenants were relieved for incompetence or other command defects. In my estimation, OCS officers were a distant third in combat effectiveness to West Point and ROTC graduates.

The personnel in Company C were a diverse group. Although I never had access to the personnel files of my company, a personal canvas of the unit showed that my company had approximately a third college graduates, a third members of minority groups, and a third 67ers. The term 67ers refers to the number prefix on the army identification tags for those unfortunate 100,000, the so-called McNamara's 100,000, who had been drafted into the army although their test scores were below minimum army requirements. Ostensibly, the army was to place these individuals into military technical schools where they could learn a trade, but most of them ultimately drifted into the combat areas. While these soldiers tended to be discipline problems stateside, they proved to be good in combat. My unit's most decorated soldier was a 67er as was the unit's first killed in action.

Battalion training at Fort Lewis can be characterized by noting the absurdity of preparing for combat in Southeast Asia in a Washington winter. Those cold winter nights in the foothills of Mount Rainier reminded some of us of scenes from the World War II movie *Battlefield*. Our enemy was the cold and boredom rather than the harsh weather and the Germans as in the movie. Restrictions on the use of tents compounded our exposure to the cold. My company spent at least 50 percent of the five months in the field with much of our training done at night. Long range night patrolling became second nature to us. There is nothing like moving up and down the hills in the middle of the night over unfamiliar terrain. It

Training in the foothills of Mt. Rainier in the middle of winter prepared us more for a war in Korea than one in South Vietnam.

was this part of the training that proved useful once our unit reached South Vietnam.

Training was hard enough that it began to take a toll. After a lengthy exercise, the unit would return to the barracks and before any free time the weapons had to be cleaned and our gear taken care of. This led to a funny incident. Our platoon sergeant for Company C was pretty good most of the time, but occasionally he would become nasty. After one extremely difficult training session, my platoon returned to barracks. As the men were working on cleaning their weapons, somebody noticed that the sergeant had fallen to sleep on duty. I grabbed a camera and took a picture. Several days later the picture was available, and as a joke I let the sergeant see it. From that time onwards, Sergeant Sanchez was a lot nicer to me. I had no intention of blackmailing him because it was just a joke, but afterwards I believe that he felt that I had something on him.

This fieldwork was considered so essential by the army that our battalion was not allotted a Christmas vacation. I had to buy my way out of kitchen police (KP) to spend Christmas day with my wife in Tacoma. Only an occasional glimpse of Mount Rainer in the early morning relieved the monotony of the fieldwork. Most of the time we marched up and then down the hills of Washington, proving conclusively what most of us had long suspected — our officers could not read maps. My unit also learned

Sergeant Sanchez, platoon sergeant for 3rd Platoon, relaxing in his office after a day of training.

to appreciate those long six to twelve mile forced marches with full pack. What I learned on those marches was which items to dispose of once in South Vietnam. My opinion remains to this day that most of the training was misdirected. Training was almost exclusively in conventional combat tactics rather than in the low-intensity type of warfare taking place in South Vietnam.

A trend in the training began to disturb me as each time a specific type of training was required I was volunteered for it by my platoon sergeant, Sanchez. At first, it was sniper training. I spent a couple of weeks in sniper training with instruction provided by specialists from the U.S. Army's National Match Rifle Team. Fortunately, I was a good shot and qualified easily as a sniper. This was somewhat surprising because I had never been a hunter and my experience with firearms was limited. My sniper team did not train with scopes because the heat and humidity of South Vietnam made them difficult to use.

Next, it was demolition training. Soon I learned to blow up things with C-4 explosives. Blowing up things was not as much fun as sniper training, but it certainly beat details. Finally, it became apparent that I was being trained to be the point man for my platoon. Each time my com-

Rest break for 3rd Platoon, Company C during a forced march at Fort Lewis.

Training as snipers with the National Match Weapons Team at Fort Lewis, Washington, in March 1968.

Having qualified as a sniper, this is me with my National Match M-14 at Fort Lewis, Washington.

pany took place in the front of the battalion, I ended up on point. Even then, I knew the life expectancy of a point man in South Vietnam was short.

In the middle of the unit training a possibility developed that our battalion might be sent to South Korea if hostilities broke out there after the Pueblo Incident. The North Koreans had seized an American intelligence ship, the USS *Pueblo*, in international waters outside of North Korea. Rumors were in vogue in December 1967 that our battalion was on standby for deployment to South Korea in the event of hostilities against North Korea. Our Fort Lewis training would have made the battalion better prepared for the type of combat in Korea than for South Vietnam. In any case, the crisis over the *Pueblo* soon vanished and my battalion continued its pre–Vietnam training in a cold Washington winter.

Morale in the battalion was low from the beginning and nothing the army did improved it. As soon as I arrived in Tacoma, Washington, the taxicab driver informed me that my new outfit was bound for South Vietnam and gave me his estimation of our probable destination. My buddies received identical treatment. Most of us assimilated this information with-

Comrades in training in the 3rd Platoon, Company C — Don Chikuma, Joe DeAngelis, Stan Krosky, and myself.

out difficulty, but then the army decided to play a mind game with us. The official army position was that our unit was being trained for an unknown war zone. Just how many war zones did they think the United States was involved in 1967! Senior officers threatened us with court-martial if any of us mentioned South Vietnam to anybody by phone or in the mail, including relatives. This charade did little to improve morale in my unit

The prospect of South Vietnam loomed ahead of us and it impacted on each of us a different way. Several of the men in my company tried to escape reality through drugs. LSD was in vogue in those days, and a couple of soldiers had bad trips. We had to restrain one soldier from attempting to jump out of a second-story window during a LSD trip. He had flashbacks for several months. None of this drug experimentation had any appeal for me. Others tried to escape reality by denial, or merely ignoring the future. A few became severely depressed enough so that they believed that their deaths were inevitable as soon as they arrived in South Vietnam. This sort of depression affected one soldier enough that it came true. In contrast, my attitude was that I was going to be a survivor.

I made good friends during my five months of training. There was a kind of brotherhood among us because we were experiencing the same training and prospects for the future. Unfortunately, several of my friends failed to make it back alive from South Vietnam. Our first killed in action (KIA) was Donald Hannah, a machine gunner. Another fatality later in the war was Larry Nelson. He was killed in action in a hot LZ (landing zone). His conduct earned him the Distinguished Service Cross for gallantry under fire.

Donald Hannah was a machine gunner in 3rd Platoon, and he was the first member of Company C killed in action (KIA) in South Vietnam.

Few of us wanted to go to South Vietnam. I conducted an unofficial poll of the men in my company on the eve of our departure from Fort Lewis, and only one enlisted soldier was convinced of the righteousness of our cause in South Vietnam. None of us, including the one true believer, had the least desire to fight in South Vietnam. Several late arrivals promptly deserted once they heard of our probable destination. They left before we could even learn their names.

About once a month the company had a public information class in which the men discussed current events. One such session was on American participation in the Vietnam War. Our company commander did not even attempt to justify American intervention in South Vietnam, or the American government's policies towards the war. He emphasized that the battalion was going over there whether we liked it or not. Politics was always a lively topic in my company with most of the soldiers ranking President Johnson low on our popularity list, but hawkish Republicans were no more popular.

My two weeks Vietnam leave was spent with my wife in Tacoma, Washington, and Vancouver, British Columbia. We had rented a small house in Tacoma, where my wife had a job working as a clerk at J.C. Penney's. We were desperate to have a good time before I had to report back to my unit. One week we spent at my uncle Robert Gordon Bragg's home in Bellingham, Washington, and the other we visited Vancouver, British Columbia. Both trips were enjoyable, but the specter of South Vietnam interfered with our pleasure. After the end of the two weeks, I reported back to Fort Lewis for deployment to South Vietnam.

The confinement in barracks was trying on all us. In close confinement with nothing to do but look at each other, tempers soon frayed. No fights broke out but there were numerous arguments. Most of it was because all of us were scared

Larry Nelson was another friend of mine in the platoon, and he was killed in action later in South Vietnam. His conduct earned him the Distinguished Service Cross for gallantry under fire.

beyond belief. The military police surrounding our barracks had been armed so there was no possibility of going anyplace. There was no way of communicating outside of the barracks, as the telephones had been made inoperative. One member of my platoon watched helplessly as his fancy automobile was stolen. He tried to tell the military police, but they would not talk to us. The car thief stole the automobile and the owner was never able to report it stolen even after he arrived in South Vietnam.

My company arrived at McCord Air Force Base early on the morning of April 2 for our scheduled departure. My curiosity about South Vietnam by no means rivaled my fear of going there. Our plane was a charter from Trans-International. After the war, I learned that Trans-International was a CIA-front airline operating out of Oakland, California. It was a bare-bones outfit with only two stewardesses for a planeload of nearly two hundred GIs. A general gave us a pep talk at the air base, but everyone appeared too nervous to listen. Even the band music could not shake our lethargy, nor our fear.

The first stage of our flight was uneventful with a pleasant 45-minute stop at the Hilo Airport in Hawaii. Most of the time the men were busy watching the overworked stewardesses doing their jobs. Our plane arrived in Hilo around 4:00 P.M. Hawaiian time, just in time for it to rain. After a brief rain, both volcanoes at Hilo were encircled with clouds, giving them a halo effect. At our second stop at Guam, however, the plane blew both engines on landing. A seven-hour layover to repair the engines allowed a couple of our sergeants from Guam an opportunity to visit their families after nearly a two year absence. It was a standard joke that each time our sergeants from Guam visited their families there was a new addition nine months later.

It was after takeoff from Guam at 6:00 A.M. Guam time that the executive officer for Company C informed us that our unit had been diverted from the American Division at Chu Lai to the 9th Infantry Division at Bearcat. This last minute change in plans was justified to us on the grounds of security, but none of us was fooled. We were told that this base camp was about 25 miles northwest of Saigon toward War Zone D. While none of us had any idea what to expect at Bearcat, rumors began to circulate that military conditions were bad there. This sudden change did mess up our mail for several weeks. My complementary copy of *The Sporting News* never caught up with me. I hope that whoever received it in Chu Lai for that year was a sports fan because my favorite team the St. Louis Cardinals won this National League pennant that year.

There is evidence that the 6th Battalion, 31st Infantry had been trans-

Ed Bowden was another close friend of mine, and he was able to survive the war.

ferred to the 9th Infantry Division at the last moment. This is the contention of Lieutenant General Julian J. Ewell and Major General Ira A. Hunt in their book *Sharpening the Combat Edge: The Use of Analysis to Reinforce Military Judgment* that appeared in 1974. Lieutenant General Ewell was commander of the Infantry Division in 1968 and 1969, and Major General Hunt was his chief of staff. Gossip was that General Ewell talked General Westmoreland into giving him our battalion because the 9th Infantry Division needed more troops in its push to pacify the Mekong Delta.

As the aircraft flew towards South Vietnam, I was struck by the absurdity of the Vietnam War. My company was so heavily armed that even though it was classified as a light infantry company, it had more firepower than a battalion had in Korea. Yet, the American army had been unable to defeat the Viet Cong in a war lasting for several years. I remembered the adage that guerrilla warfare can neutralize superior forces much as the Viet Minh did to the French in the early 1950s. The question remained whether our forces were going to suffer the same fate as the French. It was thoughts like these that were so disquieting. Conversation was kept at a minimum because nobody had anything worth saying. Each of us was wondering about what to expect in South Vietnam and hoping to return stateside in one piece.

2

First Weeks in South Vietnam

My first glimpse of South Vietnam only increased my apprehension about my tour of duty as helicopter gunships were busy conducting close fire support and Air Force aircraft were delivering air strikes against suspected Viet Cong positions just north of Saigon. As our airliner circled to land at Bien Hoa Air Force Base, my main concern and the preoccupation of my buddies was how long it would take us to unpack our rifles and pass out the ammunition. A rumor had circulated widely around the battalion while at Fort Lewis that our sister battalion, the 5th Battalion, 12th Infantry, which had preceded us to South Vietnam by a couple of weeks, had been ambushed on the way from the airfield to their base camp. Although this rumor was later proved untrue, each member of my company was certain that a Viet Cong soldier lurked behind every obstacle.

Despite our fears, the bus trip through the Long Binh Complex was uneventful. There was evidence of recent bitter fighting during the recent Tet Offensive. Buildings along the perimeter of the base had been destroyed and heavy weapon hits showed on the walls of the surviving structures. It was obvious that the Viet Cong had seriously challenged the U.S. Army in this area. By order of our company commander rifles were available but rifle bolts were kept under lock and key during the twenty-five mile trip to our base camp. This precaution was a wise one, because my unit's nervousness increased with each of the 25 miles or so it took to reach the 9th Infantry Division's Base Camp at Bearcat. Bearcat was almost due east of Bien Hoa.

My first impressions of South Vietnam were of the beauty of the landscape, the attractiveness of the Vietnamese, and the poverty of their surroundings. The landscape resembled a fairyland with odd-looking hills, jungles, and rice paddies. Women were working in the rice fields with cone hats and distinctive dress of flowing materials. It was strange to see

My first impression at Bearcat Base Camp of the 9th Infantry Division was the large number of women laborers.

so many women working as manual laborers. Most of the manual labor had been left in the hands of women. To Americans it was novel to see such tiny women working as manual laborers. Most of the men were either in the South Vietnamese army, or with the Viet Cong. All the young men present were in one type of uniform or the other. Civilian males were either very young or very old.

Buildings appeared to deteriorate rapidly in the climate of heat and humidity of South Vietnam. Even some of the recently built Catholic churches already looked old. The housing looked run down, but beside each house, or hooch, there was some type of vehicle. It was most surprising to see the large number of motorbikes and bicycles traveling all the roads

The battalion's first two weeks in South Vietnam were spent in acclimatizing the troops to the heat, the humidity, the smells, and the 9th Infantry Division's ways of conducting military operations. Although nearly half of the division's forces were on operations in the Mekong Delta, Bearcat remained the divisional headquarters until the middle of the summer of 1968. Bearcat was located northeast of Saigon near Long Thuah in a countryside that was sparsely populated, full of thickets, and heavily wooded with short trees resembling Texas mesquite trees. Trees had grown so close together that along with the thickets it was only passable on narrow trails.

Bearcat Base Camp served as a base of operation for the division's 15,000 troops, and Thailand's contingent, the Queen's Cobras Regiment. The Thai military area of operations was in an area southeast of Bearcat. Except for a stray Viet Cong intelligence gathering team, the region around Bearcat had been pacified for several years. Increasingly more of the division's assets had been diverted to the Mekong Delta so by April 1968 Bearcat was no longer functioning fully as the division's primary base camp.

Lieutenant David Wilson, executive officer of Company C soon after the unit arrived at Bearcat Base Camp in South Vietnam.

Despite the security of Bearcat, the Viet Cong conducted periodic assaults or mortar attacks. One such attack on the perimeter had killed two guards and wounded thirteen others just after our battalion arrived at Bearcat. Then on April 6, a major and his driver were ambushed by a remote control detonated claymore outside the perimeter and killed. These attacks were well publicized throughout the division to alert us to the danger of living in a war zone.

On April 9, General Ewell, the commander of the 9th Infantry Division, welcomed my battalion to the 9th Infantry Division in a short speech. His welcoming speech was as corny as most such speeches are. He did tell us that we would be assigned to the 3rd Brigade in Long An Province, which is south of Saigon. His description of the 3rd Brigade's area of operation was that it was half rice paddy and half swamp. In the meantime, the battalion was to undergo training to prepare us for this assignment.

Divisional services at Bearcat provided most of the conveniences of a stateside military base. Fifteen-cent beer and cigarettes, a large PX (Post Exchange), and a large swimming pool were all provided for the convenience of the rear-echelon soldiers. All the soldiers at Bearcat lacked to make life comfortable for them was a golf course. They issued us ration cards that could be used in the PX, but it was obvious that few of us would ever come close to buying up our quotas because of a simple lack of time. Some soldiers in my unit did buy expensive items, cameras and sound systems, to send back to the States.

After the initial shock of the sights and smells of South Vietnam finally wore off, most of the soldiers in my company began to enjoy the camp's leisure spots. Beer was cheap and plentiful. It was also our first exposure to the beautiful Vietnamese women and their slinky aio di dresses. They walked around the base camp exuding sexuality. Most of the Vietnamese women worked on building and rebuilding the defenses of the base camp, and they were much less sexy.

Prostitution was a problem at Bearcat. The Vietnamese women worked on this base for 80 cents a day, but they could pick up extra money by prostitution. The going rate for a trick was $3. There were plenty of bunkers which the soldiers and the girls could disappear into for a brief interlude of sex. The girls then went back to work as if they had had a rest break. No one paid much attention to these transactions. While these Vietnamese girls were attractive, it was just as certain that many of them had been infected with venereal disease. All of the American troops had been warned about venereal disease, but this warning never stops prostitution.

There were other strange things that new soldiers to South Vietnam had to adapt to without delay. The first was an exposure to the military currency in use in South Vietnam. This currency resembled funny or Monopoly money. Since the American government wanted to control the supply of dollars in the hands of foreign governments and slow down the ever-present black market, all U.S. currency was exchanged for military paper money ranging from the sum of a nickel to dollars. Moreover, soldiers could send home only two hundred dollars a month. This precaution was intended to control black market profits, but for a nominal fee, most soldiers would send home money for a buddy regardless of where he obtained his funds. Several times the military authorities changed the currency while I was in South Vietnam to prevent large-scale holdings of military script. Those caught with large sums of the replaced currency were just out of luck.

Each solder was also introduced to malaria pills. Malaria is endemic to South Vietnam, but there was a different type of malaria between north South Vietnam and south South Vietnam. In south South Vietnam the pill was a big orange one nearly the size of a quarter. Up north, the soldiers took a small white pill daily. The army required each soldier to take a malaria pill every Monday. It took me several weeks before the malaria pill stopped making me sick each time I took it. I had a mini-malaria attack with the fever and chills. As I became acclimated to taking the pills, they made me sick only about once a month.

One indicator of our presence in a war zone was that the army relaxed its prohibition on facial hair. Mustaches were allowed as long as they were well groomed. I started growing a mustache as soon as the company commander gave us permission on April 5, 1968. Beards and long hair were still out of bounds, but the mustache soon became a symbol of independence in my outfit. I still retain my mustache since then because it serves as a symbol of my independence from the restraints of the military.

Almost as strange as the scenery was the ever present smell of human waste disposal. The heat and humidity of South Vietnam made an ideal laboratory for bacteria and fungus. Disposal of human waste was imperative to prevent sickness and the army way was to burn it. Burning shit produced a smell that seemed to permeate the atmosphere. It was everywhere. Open latrines were another familiar sight. Modesty was not possible so nobody bothered with it. Within a few days, American soldiers were as casual towards bodily functions as the Vietnamese.

An event took place in my company soon after our arrival that had long-range implications. My company had a large minority representation —

thirty-five African Americans, five Puerto Ricans, one Peruvian, and one Guamese. Civil rights disturbances were still making news stateside, and the news of outbreaks of violence even reached South Vietnam. Most of the African American soldiers in the company were non-militant, but they were sensitive to happenings in the United States. Few racial problems had surfaced during the training at Fort Lewis and good racial relations appeared to have been extended to South Vietnam. The news of Martin Luther King's assassination reached my unit on April 5 and it showed how deceptive this good racial climate really was. Black soldiers immediately went into deep mourning along with a few white sympathizers while several white senior NCOs held a party. This celebration was not only in bad taste; it showed the depth of the racial problem that the army refused to acknowledge at the time. Long-term bad feelings resulted from this incident although I must admit that it in no way affected the fighting proficiency of the company. Rumors from other battalions indicated that similar incidents had taken place with more serious consequences. It was only a few weeks later that an African American soldier opened fire on his fellow soldiers, killing several of them — both black and white — before he was wounded and disarmed by a black NCO. Everybody hoped that he would die of wounds, but he survived. Later, I learned that he was sentenced to life imprisonment at hard labor.

Peace negotiations were in the news, but these talks were discounted by those of us in South Vietnam. Consensus in my unit was not even to talk about the possibility of peace, because there was no hope that anything would come out of these negotiations while we were in South Vietnam. It was obvious that all of us would pull a full tour in South Vietnam regardless of the progress of the Paris Peace Talks. Events proved our cynicism correct. My assessment at the time was that the fighting would enter its most vicious phase because both sides would want to win concessions based on military advantages gained on the battlefield.

The first few days of the division's acclimatization policy found my company at the Old Reliable Academy. The Old Reliable Academy gained its name from the nickname of the 9th Infantry Division, "The Old Reliables." All replacements up to the rank of captain were sent to the academy to undergo a five-day course in military fundamentals. It existed to acquaint new troops with trends in fighting against the Viet Cong. A sergeant gave us a lecture on the importance of helping the Vietnamese win their country from the Viet Cong, but his snide comments showed his contempt for the backwardness of the Vietnamese. Each of us examined booby-traps and punji stakes, and marveled how ingenious and deadly they were. Instructors warned us that if one of us set off a booby-trap to hope that it was homemade and not American manufactured grenades or explosives. American explosives killed while those of the Viet Cong maimed. Most of us believed that a foot or a leg was an acceptable sacrifice to escape the Vietnam War zone. My biggest fear always was to sustain a brain injury — or worse, to become a basket case (no arms or legs). My most notable contribution at the Old Reliable Academy was falling face first into the water on a training exercise. While our training in the Old Reliable Academy dealt with problems of jungle fighting, we knew already that our battalion was going to be sent to fight in the rice paddies of the Mekong Delta. Little of the training covered this eventuality. First, however, my company had to finish the other phases of our in-country training.

By stages, my unit was exposed to the SOP (standard operating procedures) of the 9th Infantry Division. In rotation, each unit started conducting small-scale patrols around Bearcat. These patrols began lasting only a few hours but later they became all day operations. My first experience as a point man was in a company sweep about a week after our arrival. Fortunately, few Viet Cong units were operating in this region, and booby-traps were rare. About the only contact with the Vietnamese was when one of our units would come across Vietnamese wood gatherers. Several units in my company did report that they believed that they were being shadowed by the Viet Cong, but nothing came of it. On off days, my company was on call in case another unit on a mission made contact with the enemy. In such an eventuality, my company would provide reinforcement for the unit engaged in combat.

These initial operations revealed that some of the personality conflicts in the battalion were still with us. Most of the enlisted men were under the assumption that once the unit arrived in South Vietnam things would change for the better. The battalion and companies would function as a team with mutual cooperation, but this proved not to be the case. Senior sergeants guarded their prerogatives jealously and the gap between the NCOs and the enlisted men continued to grow. One night soon after our arrival at the base camp, the first sergeant called a police call to pick up everything, including sticks. We took almost an hour and a half conducting the police call before the first sergeant gave in. My platoon leader lectured the enlisted men several times about our bad attitude towards the senior NCOs, but little changed on either side. My platoon sergeant also made an appeal for cooperation. Although I had always liked the sergeant, none of the men were too impressed with his and others' remarks because they had the feeling that the lower ranks always get it in the neck in the end. Too many of the senior non-commissioned officers still treated us as if we were in basic training. Only later in combat did the conflict between the ranks end after some of the more obnoxious of the senior NCOs were either relieved for incompetence, wounded, or killed.

Personality conflicts also flared among the officers. Our company commander was in the middle of a feud with the battalion commander and the battalion sergeant major. Evidently, the problem was that battalion high command disliked the independence of Company C. In particular, they disliked the operations of our dayroom that served beer and soft drinks. It was common knowledge that our commander wanted to transfer out of the battalion. His possible transfer worried us because the captain was an able officer and brighter than most. An outcome of these tensions was that the battalion operated sluggishly in our early missions, and several times the division's liaison officers chewed out the chain of command down to the squad leaders. On an early river crossing mission a major severely criticized the platoon leaders, the platoon sergeants, and the squad leaders for not controlling their men. Those of us outside the command structure listened with some amusement at the discomfort of our leaders. The enlisted men had merely followed orders despite the fact that some of the orders had been laughable.

My stateside training as a sniper meant that any new weapon attachment was turned over to me. Besides my single-shot, National Match M-14, I was assigned a starlight scope. A starlight scope was a large light reflector, which utilized available light from the moon and the stars. This scope could be highly effective on clear nights, but less useful on overcast nights. It was a court-martial offense to lose one of these scopes since they were issued in small numbers and at that time still officially secret. A starlight scope cost in the neighborhood of $30,000 so this was another consideration. A rumor floated around that already one starlight scope had been lost in combat. A starlight scope in the hands of an enemy sniper was a terrifying thought. My problem with the scope was that it was another twenty pounds to carry on my back.

My impressions about the Vietnamese began to form during the course of these exercises. On a long-range patrol, my unit made contact with a number of Vietnamese families. They were obviously scared of us. I considered this natural enough, because American soldiers are so much larger and dressed in our battle gear we must have been a scary bunch. Because of all the marching, I am sure that we had a pungent smell. The men always remained impassive during our searches, but the women and girls showed their concern openly. They smiled weakly and nervously. Some of them might have had reasons to be nervous, but it was impossible for us to identify a Viet Cong agent or sympathizer without some overt act, or an intelligence source to finger them. Children seemed delighted to see us and always made a big fuss. While we tried to be as polite as possible during these searches, our appearance in full battle dress had to be intimidating to them.

Another part of the unit's training was education about the dangers of Vietnamese narcotics. Drugs have long been a threat to the military stateside, but it had become an even greater danger in South Vietnam. Army lectures depend on overkill so the lectures on the dangers of marijuana were laughed off because many of the fellows in my unit had used it before entering the army. These soldiers knew fact from fiction, but other information was more interesting to us. Vietnamese drugs were more powerful than those in the United States were and more dangerous. Marijuana was almost unknown in South Vietnam and there was no demand until American troops arrived there. The army claimed that drugs came from Viet Cong controlled provinces, and the Viet Cong used the money to buy arms and ammunition on the black market. While I saw widespread evidence of drug use by American soldiers, I was never tempted to buy drugs. It was simply too dangerous to go about South Vietnam stoned. Out in the field during operations it was too dangerous to be under the influence of drugs because it could get one killed. At base camp in reserve, there was always a possibility of an impromptu operation.

On April 17, my platoon went out on a night ambush patrol. We moved out after dark and it took us over seven hours to make it to our ambush site. Because of the lateness of our setting up the L-shaped ambush, we stayed only around three hours before we started back to Bearcat. The terrain was such dense jungle that we had difficulty making any progress. Several members of the patrol reported that they felt that they were being shadowed by small Viet Cong units. Already all of us were aware that the Viet Cong had the opportunity to initiate contact at their choosing, because our outfits move so slowly and awkwardly through the jungle. The Viet Cong carried much less equipment and moved much better through the same terrain. It was also noticed by the enlisted men that our lieutenants had improved in their handling of their responsibilities from the days of our training in Ft. Lewis.

My squad learned a valuable lesson on taking shortcuts in an active military zone during one of those early patrols around Bearcat. It involved a squad exercise with a senior NCO in charge. Although he had been in the army for more than a decade, this sergeant was both inexperienced and scared. He decided instead of making the four thousand plus meter reconnaissance patrol we would move out about 250 meters beyond the perimeter of Bearcat and find a good place to relax. Members of the squad recognized what he was doing but there were no complaints. False reports were radioed back at intervals to allay suspicion back at company headquarters. Suddenly, a pair of Viet Cong stumbled into our resting place and a brief firefight ensued. Nobody was hit which was fortunate because an air evacuation of wounded at a site several thousand meters from where we were supposed to be would have produced embarrassing questions. Never again would the men in my outfit tolerate such a deception because it was simply too dangerous. Finally, it made us too vulnerable to unpleasant surprises from the Viet Cong. The need for artillery support was too crucial in a firefight. That sergeant lasted only a few weeks before he was transferred to a rear-echelon position

Obtaining intelligence about the Viet Cong was always uncertain. Later, I ran across an intelligence report dating from February 22, 1968, that showed how difficult it was to get good intelligence and how the Viet Cong were able to track our activities around Bearcat. Long Thanh was a small village a couple of miles outside of Bearcat.

> The plantation Manager of Long Thanh Plantation stated the Viet Cong entered Long Thanh Village every evening to hold meetings in the school yard. He stated that each day the US ambush patrols show up at approximately 1500 hours. The small children in the village follow the patrols then report their location to the VC. The VC then use this information in their meetings, pointing out the area of ambush and telling the villagers there the US troops cannot enter the village because of policies. The plantation manager recommends the US send other ambush patrols into the area at approximately 2000H to 2200H, and they would get results. The manager complains that a Captain from the US 9th Infantry Division shows up every day and asks questions. The manager does not like this because it "puts his life in danger." He refuses to give the Captain any information.

One phase of the training was to become accustomed to airmobile operations. Airmobile operations had become essential in fighting the highly mobile Viet Cong, and the 9th Infantry Division prided itself on its conduct on airmobile operations. The standard troop carrying helicopter was a Huey (UH-1D), which had a crew of four (pilot, co-pilot, and two door gunners) and could carry six fully loaded combat troops. Especially nerve-wracking was the fact that to transport and unload its cargo of six soldiers four of them had to sit in open doors with their feet hanging over the sides. To those of us who were unused to peering between our legs down several thousand feet, it was a new thrill. More than once a copter had to make a sudden turn to evade ground fire and soldiers would fall out. An example was the case of a first lieutenant in the 19th Military History Detachment. He fell when a copter turned sharply after receiving gunfire from the ground. His fall was nearly thirty feet into a rice paddy, or else he would have been more seriously hurt. In addition, copters never actually touched the ground so that troops had to jump from two to three feet. During the dry season, this jump made for a hard landing, but the wet season it was doubly dangerous because the depth of the water was difficult to judge. Mud also restricted rapid movement of soldiers away from the immediate zone of fire. For ages, I thought that I had a fear of heights, but within days, my fear evaporated and the copter rides became almost enjoyable. At least I was escaping long marches through the water and mud.

As the final phase of our training ended, the battalion began to conduct company sized operations. Each indoctrination exercise became more realistic. Also, the chances to make contact with the enemy became more likely. On April 18, the captain briefed us on our next operation. He bet his captain's bars that we would make contact with the Viet Cong on the next operation. Our unit was to be airlifted approximately 15,000 meters and dropped in a zone where intelligence reports estimated that there were more than 200 Viet Cong operating there. This mission would be a two-day operation. Because there was a possibility that our company would receive mortar fire, our officers advised us to dig our foxholes so deep that it would take a direct hit to harm us. They gave us permission to build three-man foxholes, which meant more rest and better security. They intended to send with us 90mm recoilless rifles, starlight scopes, and digging equipment. All of this information scared the hell out of us. My response was to write a last will and testament just in case.

On April 19, my company conducted a combat assault, inserting by copters at 0830 in the vicinity of map coordinates YW185898. A reconnaissance in force was the term used to describe these sweeps of suspected enemy locations. My unit maneuvered through bamboo thickets and thorn branches making slow progress. After almost a full day of no contact, Company C received around a dozen incoming rounds of M-79 grenades at 1605. While no casualties resulted from this contact, the company only advanced a few kilometers before establishing a defensive perimeter. At 2015, my company completed an air extraction back to Bearcat. While there had been little of the advertised contact, there was enough that none of us demanded the captain's bars. Each exercise was becoming more realistic, but the lack of casualties made them seem like stateside training.

The most serious problem encountered by my company in this exercise was the lack of water discipline. All of us emptied our water canteens much too fast. Although standard operating procedure was to carry three canteens on operations, men emptied their canteens at a rapid rate. Water conservation always remained a concern in all of our operations in South Vietnam because of the heat and humidity. It was only gradually that members of the unit began to acquire good water discipline. Still most of us were in perpetual dehydration during field operations. Only when we went back in base camp were we able to obtain enough liquids.

Rumors began to circulate in my company on April 23 that our last training exercise before full-scale deployment would be a five day sweep in the jungle due north of Bearcat in an area thought to be relatively clear of enemy activity. Regardless of the assurance that this was a peaceful area, there was considerable nervousness among us about the exercise due mostly to our preconceived ideas about fighting in South Vietnam. Most of us, myself included, still had a TV image of combat. Memories of the Tet Offensive were still recent, and, despite the company's recent successful operations, confidence in our abilities remained low.

A three-day delay in the mission did little to modify my growing mood of depression. Evidently, the delay was in obtaining the necessary air assets to transport us to our area of operation. During this delay, I had a conversation with an artillery officer and he told me that the area that our unit was going to operate in on our next mission contained a base camp full of North Vietnamese regulars. We were to land about 1,500 meters from their base camp. This news did little to cheer me up. Finally, my company packed up in preparation for the three to five day operation. Once the helicopters arrived my nervousness increased, but at least the whole company would be available to counter enemy resistance.

3

First Blooding

The first major operation in South Vietnam was a scheduled three-day sweep in the jungles hundred of kilometers east of Bearcat. Its intent was to root out any Viet Cong forces in the area. Intelligence could give the battalion no idea of Viet Cong strength there, but it suspected that there were considerable Viet Cong assets in the area. There was also the possibility of a North Vietnamese Army (NVA) base camp. Later, I learned that our operation was in Long Thanh Province near a large rubber plantation (Ap Cam-Chau Rubber) around 15,000 meters due east of Bearcat and southwest of Xuan Loc. At the time, however, none of us knew this. All the members of my unit knew was that we were part of a large-scale sweep of a suspected Viet Cong staging area.

My confidence in the operation was not heightened by the intensity of the air force and army fire support at the landing zone. They blasted at everything that could possibly constitute a threat. If my presence had not been so actively engaged as a participant, I would have enjoyed the show. It was better than anything I had witnessed in stateside firepower demonstrations. The helicopters — called slicks — dropped my squad in Landing Zone Grasshopper (YS30785) after about fifteen minutes of prepping fire. My squad was one of the first to land. After establishing a perimeter, our job was to provide security for the troops landing after us. It took almost 45 minutes to deliver the rest of my company because this operation had limited airmobile support and six slicks could deliver only thirty-six soldiers at a time. Since I had been in the first group to land, this unwelcome privilege allowed me an overview of the entire operation. As soon as each shift hit the group, the reinforcement lengthened the defensive perimeter using rice paddy dikes for shelter. Fortunately, only silence greeted us. A recurring nightmare for infantrymen in South Vietnam was to hit a hot landing zone where the Viet Cong could pick us off at their leisure. Hitting a hot landing zone happened on occasion and American casualties could be heavy.

As soon as the company was reunited, the company commander gave orders to move out in a northern direction. Much to my relief my squad had a position in the middle of the company. I was aware that when my squad pulled point duty for the company, my sergeant would put me on point. Since the squad sergeant was a friend of mine since Fort Lewis days, I knew that there was no animosity behind his decision. Somebody had to do one of the most dangerous jobs in a combat zone. Beside the fact that I was one of the brighter members of my platoon, it was my weapon that decided the issue. Although I carried a single shot rifle, a fiberglassed M-14 with a welded selector switch, it was the most accurate and dependable weapon in the company. I considered it ironic that someone trained as a sniper would instead be used on point. From hindsight, however, the irony became less apparent because experience was to show us that the M-16 rifle was not a dependable weapon for jungle fighting. It needed too much cleaning and the cartridges tended to expand in the heat and humidity when chambered. This caused the M-16 to jam. A jammed weapon can be lethal in a firefight. Moreover, patrolling in South Vietnam meant going in and out of water causing that M-16 to sometimes be submerged. A wet buffer assembly could cause the M-16 to explode. This actually happened to our company commander during a firefight a month later. Moreover, it would have been folly to place a soldier with an M-60 machine gun on point. While I heard of units so utilizing M-60s, it always seemed wasteful to endanger a machine gunner in such a hazardous responsibility. In combat, the point man, machine gunner, RTO operator, lieutenant, and medic — and not necessarily in that order — were considered the most dangerous positions in the platoon in a firefight.

The company started its sweep hesitantly with all of us extremely security conscious. Security lessened somewhat when the company moved into heavy thickets. These thickets reminded me of huge briar patches. Thorns ripped at our jungle fatigues and branches snapped into the faces of those following too close behind. Since American soldiers always tended to bunch up, these branches made sure that we spread out. Visual sighting became more difficult and progress was uneven. Flank protection was so weak that the flankers were brought closer in to avoid losing them in the jungle. Occasionally, the company would move out of the jungle into a rice paddy. Each of us soon learned that to step in any kind of water meant to invite leeches. One could almost hear them snapping as your foot hit the water. After leaving the water, each of us had to use a cigarette to burn off the leeches. Fortunately, our C-rations from the Korean War era had unfiltered Lucky Strike and Chesterfield cigarettes. Smoking them was like smoking dried dung, but they were great for getting rid of leeches. Our company searched several small hamlets without finding anything worthy of notice.

Each soldier on the sweep was fully loaded down with eighty pounds of required gear. Intrenching tools, air mattresses, 1000 rounds of ammo, 2 grenades, 3 canteens of water, 3 days of C-rations, and sundry items slowed down our progress. In my case, the starlight scope added to the weight by about twenty pounds. As the day progressed, our packs grew heavier, especially as the company moved into the hillier, triple canopy jungle. The only incident worthy of notice was the location and the destruction of a pressure type mine at around 1030 at YS310858. Water supplies were beginning to run low by noon, as water discipline had been almost non-existent. In the middle of the afternoon, my squad approached a hill stream about ten feet across and three feet deep. Now was the opportunity to fill our three canteens with water and to get rid of excess gear. As I dipped my canteen into the muddy water, my intrenching tool, air mattress and excess C-rations miraculously disappeared into the water. Others were doing the same thing. I would swear that the stream rose at least six inches after the company left it. I disposed of at least twenty unwanted pounds myself. Refreshed by a lightened load and with three canteens of water being treated with purification tablets, my morale was improved immeasurably. Those purification tablets made the water taste funny, but it made the water safe. Even though our boots and pants were soaked, adding some additional weight, the stream had been a lifesaver.

As nightfall approached, a second disturbing incident took place. A fellow in the next squad put a bullet in his right foot. Whether this self-inflicted wound was intentional or not, he had medivaced out by helicopter. The company commander was furious, because this incident meant that our company had to march thousands of meters out of our way to find a medvac-landing zone. It also delayed us making our night destination. Later, I heard that the wounded soldier was court-martialed for shooting himself, but none of us found out about the final verdict. Consensus among those I talked to was that he was going to be serving a lengthy stretch in an army prison. He was a recent addition to the company and nobody seemed to know much about him. Self-mutilation was a common problem in combat units throughout South Vietnam, and this type of incident was only the first of many that I witnessed.

The night passed swiftly and uneventfully. Adrenaline kept most of us awake all night despite having to pull one hour on guard and two hours off. Each squad had been issued a starlight scope to increase visual effectiveness at night. Since I had been assigned the starlight scope for my squad, I always pulled the most dangerous spot on night duty. The night was peaceful, but the starlight scope picked up any type of movement so sometimes I watched little animals scurrying around during most of the night. On one occasion, I watched as a large rat ran towards me and jump and land on my back and bound off. There was nothing I could do because any movement would give the ambush away to the Viet Cong, and my squad could end up being ambushed.

After a brief cold breakfast of C-rations, the battalion sweep continued. My squad was closer to the front of the column making me more concerned about what was to happen next. A new enemy appeared in the form of vicious red ants. Now I am familiar with red ants in Texas and their stinging bite, but they are not worthy of comparison with their Asiatic cousins. These ants lived on the bush leaves and as one moved through the bush they would land on bare flesh and bite. If one succeeded in slapping them off, which is a natural first reaction, their bodies would fall off but not their heads. Their jaws became firmly embedded in flesh; they also seemed to be able to penetrate jungle fatigues. Later, my squad learned that our best ally against these ants was the explosive C-4, which burned at such a high temperature that it toasted the ants. At the time of the sweep, however, most of us considered carrying C-4 a nuisance and avoided doing so at every opportunity. C-4 also was excellent for heating C-rations, but that was something we also learned later. A second day of no contact with any enemy, except the ants, had made us less nervous about this operation. Boredom had replaced anxiety.

The second night found us too tired to worry about the Viet Cong. Two days of constant marching had been wearing us down. Again, my company established a defensive perimeter. Members of each squad alternated guard duty, usually one hour on and one hour off, but the exhausting march and the stress accumulated during the day combined to cause laxness by the second shift. Any Viet Cong activity would have found most of us asleep by midnight. I was no exception.

The third day started out much the same as the previous days except that it was my squad's turn to go on point. As I had anticipated, this meant that I became the point man for the company. As the company moved deeper into triple canopy jungle, progress became slower. Trails wandered here and there, but two days of uneventful marching left us considerably less cautious than previously. The company commander had been pushing

us to make better time in order to make a distant landing zone for resupply, especially water. Marching progress had been so slow the previous two
days that it looked like a fourth day might be necessary to make our objective. Nobody wanted to spend yet another day out in this jungle subject
to contact with the Viet Cong so everybody seemed anxious to make good
time. I did not share this casual attitude because going too fast exposed
me to booby-traps or running into a Viet Cong bunker. Both could be
fatal. Consequently, I moved as slowly as possible. As I moved down well-
worn trails, it slowly dawned on me that the trails showed recent usage.
Foxholes were also present, but they appeared to be old. Finally, towards
the end of the afternoon, I moved into a semi-clearing in the vicinity of
YS328993.

Something told me that this clearing was trouble, but on the surface,
there appeared to be no outward signs of recent occupation. Then I noticed
what looked like fresh diggings around some old foxholes. During summer vacations in college, I had worked as a laborer and I was aware of what
fresh diggings looked like. Some black pajamas were also hanging on a line.
Since the standard uniform of the Viet Cong was black pajamas, I reported
this disturbing information to my platoon leader along with my feelings
of disquiet about the area. He passed this information to the company
commander whose response was to order an advance. I moved gingerly
down the trail until it divided into two paths. Undecided about which path
to take, I finally started slowly down the left path. I had not taken over a
dozen steps when a tremendous explosion took place behind me. Pieces
of dirt and rock dropped around me for several seconds sounding much
like heavy rain. Freezing at the sound of the explosion, I dove into a prone
position to return fire, but nothing could be seen except for motionless
bushes. Then gunfire erupted to my left. In short volleys, the Viet Cong
opened up with their AK-47s. AK-47s have a strange pap sound that is
unforgettable, particularly when you are on the receiving end. A cry for a
medic could be heard almost as soon as the noise of the explosion ceased,
but now more voices were heard shouting orders. Again since I could see
nothing and fearful of hitting friendlies, I refrained from firing to the left.
After the first volleys, maneuver sounds were heard from other platoons.
By the time the maneuvering was completed, the action was over.

My squad had walked into a Viet Cong ambush. It had been a defensive ambush since the Viet Cong fired only one series of volleys after the
claymore had been detonated alongside the path. A claymore had exploded
within a foot or so of the fourth man in the point party — a machine gunner named Hannah. Hannah never knew what hit him. He had taken the

full force of the blast and besides killing him had rendered him into several pieces. Others also received wounds from serious to superficial. Most of the severely wounded here had been hit by gunfire. The medic received three gunshot wounds just below the belt buckle, and he lingered for around ten minutes before dying. Several others had serious wounds, including stomach and head wounds. Sergeant Schroeder, one of the popular NCOs, was also hit and we learned later that he died from a sucking chest wound. The 3rd Platoon sergeant received a shot in the shoulder as well as some shrapnel from the claymore. Another soldier was hit in the back of the head and was blinded.

The captain immediately sent word for a medical evacuation helicopter. The problem was that my unit was in a triple canopy jungle and only two copters in South Vietnam were equipped to handle this type of jungle. After a fifteen-minute or so wait, the copter arrived and started loading the wounded. A quick count showed that ten wounded and two dead needed evacuation. Several of the wounded were in serious condition with sucking chest and abdominal wounds. Midway through the removal the loader line broke. Only six of the wounded had been placed aboard the medvac copter by that time. A quick conference by the officers ended with the conclusion that there was nothing to do but walk to a landing zone. The nearest landing zone was a couple of kilometers away, but the jungle was so thick that progress would be slow. Moreover, it was getting late which meant a night forced march through Viet Cong territory. The company commander expressed his concern that the Viet Cong might regroup and come back to finish the job. Several of us were ordered to inspect the Viet Cong bunker, and, besides a couple of reconditioned M-16s, we found some papers. It was obviously a command bunker. Later we heard a rumor that the documents found here contained plans for the May Offensive against Saigon.

Later, I found the intelligence summary for this ambush in the *26 April 68 Sitrep for 25 April 68*:

> At 1615H vic YS328993 Co. C detonated an unknown type booby trap and received small arms fire resulting in 2 U.S. KIA and 6 WIA (evac.). Co. C found 12 booby traps, 1 Chicom rifle, 2 lbs documents, 2 homemade claymores, 7 electric forging devices, 5 bunkers and extensive tunnel RON vic YS335896 at 2000H.

After policing up the area, which was no easy task since the soldier hit by the claymore had been scattered into several pieces, the company started out for the landing zone about dusk. We ended up placing Hannah's body parts in a poncho. I was still in shock because the ambush seemed so unreal. Others must have felt the same way because everybody just milled around aimlessly. Even the officers seemed affected. I had known the medic well because he had occupied the bunk next to mine at Fort Lewis. He had barely passed his nineteenth birthday when the unit was sent to Vietnam. His first decision out of high school had been to join the army. Since he had been a friend, I volunteered to help carry him to the landing zone. Division policy was never to leave wounded or dead on the battlefield with the threat of a court-martial if this directive was disobeyed. In this case, threats had no import because we had no intention of leaving anybody for the tender mercies of the Viet Cong.

Burdened by the bodies, the wounded, and extra equipment, the night march seemed to last forever. It was then and remains today my idea of hell. Each of us suffered from the heat and the humidity, but nowhere as bad as it did on the bodies. Body juices began to produce that sweet sickly smell of death that I will always associate with South Vietnam. The red ants were still another problem. Daybreak was greeted with enthusiasm because at least we could see our next step. Finally, around noon the company reached a landing zone where the wounded and the dead could be picked up. A mechanized infantry unit was also there for the survivors. My platoon greeted that unit like they were saviors. That night was spent on the outskirts of a former French rubber plantation. They protected us while my unit was resupplied with food, ammunition, and water. The next day the mechanized infantry unit transported us back to Bearcat. All I remember about that trip was the dying vegetation along the road and into the jungle of the application of Agent Orange.

On April 26, 1968, I sent the following letter to my wife.

Well, my platoon was almost wiped out on this last mission. We stumbled into a North Vietnamese regulars base camp by accident while I was on company point. There was little that we could have done to prevent the ambush except possibly to have been more cautious. I had been suspicious of some fresh bunker diggings, but we were in a hurry. I continued down the trail. Suddenly, the earth opened up behind me. They had exploded a claymore in front of Hannah, our machine gunner, which tore him into several pieces. Several men behind him were also wounded — Krosky, Northey, Chikuma, and several others. They called up the medic, Rauber, and as soon as he arrived the Viet Cong opened fire. Rauber was hit three times in the lower abdomen. He lingered for around ten minutes before dying. Sergeant Sanchez received a shot in the shoulder as sell as some shrapnel from the claymore. Sergeant Schroeder received a sunken chest wound, and Chikuma a wound in the stomach region. Simpson was hit in the back of the head, and, if he lives, he will probably be blind. Our platoon is still in a state of shock. Several others received minor wounds. Total dead is two and total wounded is eight.

We have now been told that they were mainline VC and that we stumbled onto one of their major base camps. they are part of a big VC buildup that is taking place now. This buildup is probably a part of their negotiation strategy.

All of us were still in a state of shock when the company finally reached Bearcat. After this debacle, the consensus in our unit was that some down time would be given to us to recover from the ambush and resupply equipment. But the division had other plans for us. This bloodletting just meant that the division considered us veterans ready to assume our place on the battle line. Orders arrived placing our battalion under the control of the 9th Infantry Division's 3rd Brigade, whose area of operation was in the Long An Province of the Mekong Delta just south of Saigon. News of our destination was followed so rapidly by transportation that none of use had a chance to gather up our personal gear. Because our footlockers were left unguarded in our barracks at Bearcat, most of our personal gear was stolen by the time any of us saw the footlockers again. When I finally located my footlocker it had been completely looted. Worse than the loss of personal gear was the shock of losing so many men in combat. My company had been bloodied and never again would it be the same.

4

Operations in the
First Weeks of May

My company's trip to the Mekong Delta was uneventful except for the excitement of passing through Saigon in a military convoy going at a high rate of speed. Military convoys had priority over normal traffic and the trucks barreled through traffic that would have scared a New York taxi driver. Speed was of the essence because it lessened the possibility of a Viet Cong grenade landing in the back of one of the trucks. Drivers had direct orders not to stop for anything. Consequently, it was common for civilians to be involved in accidents with military vehicles during the movement of a convoy through Saigon. Saigon's main avenues ran into cloverleaves, or star circles, in the style of a French city. Each of the squares in the star circle had the statue of a Vietnamese national hero. The standard joke among American GIs was how many new statues would come into existence in the future for fighting against the Americans. For every automobile, there must have been at least ten motor scooters and at least one hundred bicycles. The convergence of so many vehicles of differing sizes and speeds combined with hell-bent-for-leather military convoys made for excitement and accidents. My curiosity about Saigon was piqued by my brief encounter with it as we thundered through it at high speed.

On the trip, the news filtered down to us that our new area of operations was to be the northern sector of Long An Province. Long An Province was the key to the Mekong Delta because not only was it one of South Vietnam's most prosperous agricultural provinces, but it also covered the southern approach to Saigon. Highway QL4 passed through the middle of the province, and the Ben Luc Bridge over the Vam Co Dong River always remained a potential bottleneck if it was blown. The Viet Cong proved the bottleneck potential several times during my stay in the delta by blowing up the bridge. During 1968 alone, the Viet Cong blew the bridge three times, and on each occasion traffic was tied up for several days until the U.S. Army's engineers could repair the damage. In the interval, no agricultural supplies made it into Saigon from the Mekong Delta unless by air or by sea. A captured Viet Cong document in early 1968 showed the depth of planning undertaken by the Viet Cong to blow up this bridge. (See Appendix A.)

My platoon was stationed to guard the Ben Luc Bridge one night in early May 1968. Since this capture of this report was kept secret except to high-ranking officers, we had no idea what to expect. Fortunately, the Viet Cong left the bridge alone that night. If the Viet Cong would have attempted to blow the bridge, there was little my platoon could have done about it. We would have stood there and watched it blow up and begin looking for the Viet Cong saboteurs.

War had been late coming to Long An Province, because of the lax activity of the South Vietnamese military forces. A study of the region by a team of scholars in 1959 and a follow up study in 1964 made it plain that the Viet Cong had an active infrastructure that controlled Long An

Picture showing buildings along the river in Tan An from the bridge, which was often the target of the Viet Cong.

at night. They had conceded control to the South Vietnamese govern- ment during the day in an informal agreement. This study by Gerald Can- non Hickey, *Village in Vietnam*, had appeared in 1964, and there had been little change in political control in the intervening years.

The 9th Infantry Division had been sent to Long An Province to change this situation. It was believed that the commander of ARVN forces, the 25th Division, which was responsible for the defense of Long An, was in collusion with the Viet Cong. He evidently had a longstanding tacit agreement with the Viet Cong that allowed them to operate at night with impunity in exchange for not conducting military operations during the day. It made this commander look good with his superiors without heavy combat losses. Whether there was such an agreement will never be known, but I do know that booby-traps were almost non-existent when my com- pany moved into Long An. I noted this because of my role as a point man. Later when my unit operated in more contested areas the lack of booby- traps in Long An would be fondly remembered. Absence of booby-traps seemed to indicate some kind of a deal. It is interesting to note that the division commander, Lieutenant General Julian Ewell, and Major Gen- eral Ira Hunt claimed in their book *Sharpening the Combat Edge: The Use of Analysis to Reinforce Military Judgment* that Long An was the least pacified province in IV Corps when the 9th Infantry Division commenced oper- ations there.

My company's first mission was to guard an artillery fire support base just off QL4 about 15 kilometers south of Saigon near Bien Chanh. This base camp was the home of an artillery battery which had been operating in this area for several weeks. Guard duty was relaxing after our recent contacts with the enemy. The 3rd Battalion's base camp, Smokey, was about 10 kilometers east of the artillery camp, and it was connected by a narrow dirt road. Base Camp Smokey had been built from scratch in only a couple of days. The battalion's mission was to constitute a blocking force against an expected new Viet Cong offensive against Saigon. Rumor had it that the next offensive might be on May 1 because the Viet Cong liked to tie their offensives with holidays. May Day was always one of their favorites.

It was at Base Camp Smokey that news began to filter in about the dead and wounded at the ambush on April 25. One of my friends had an abdominal wound and ended up losing a kidney. Because of his wound, he was due to be released from the military. My friend was a Japanese- American whose family had lived on the West Coast since the nineteenth century. We had become friends so I was glad that he was going to survive. It appeared that most of the other wounded, except for my friend from Alabama would be returning to the unit. He was undergoing treatment to save his eyesight. Sergeant Schroeder died of his sunken chest wound. Later, the news came down the pipeline that most of the wounded had decided to reenlist in the army and transfer to non-infantry units. Those reupping had the choice of a new military occupational specialty (MOS), but their term of service in the army was increased to four years. They also had to complete their current Vietnam tour of duty. This was the only legal way to transfer out of the infantry and the dreaded 11B MOS. Although I was tempted to try this approach, I did not want to spend two and a half more years in the U.S. Army. Reupping would have meant another year in South Vietnam beyond my current tour.

After a month of living in South Vietnam, I began to gather further impressions about the South Vietnamese, who displayed three distinct attitudes towards us:

1. Most Vietnamese stared at us as we traveled by with no expression whatsoever.
2. Children waved, held out their hands, or made obscene gestures.
3. Sometimes there were outbursts of either friendship or hostility.

I saw old men bow at us and smile, but I also heard a ten-year-old girl tell us to go home in vulgar language. One constant is that they all stopped what they were doing to watch us go by. This reaction probably meant that some of them were busy counting us for Viet Cong intelligence. Our reaction was predictable from wolf whistles directed towards pretty girls, generosity with C-rations for the kids, and non-committal attitudes towards the adults.

For the first few days in May, my company alternated between the artillery battery camp and the battalion base camp. May 1 passed without any significant evidence of enemy activity. The dry season was rapidly coming to an end so the division decided to conduct a coordinated sweep, combining straight-leg infantry, mechanized infantry and armor, of an area 25 kilometers south of the battalion base camp in a suspected Viet Cong staging area. None of this intelligence had made it down the chain of command to my company so our job was to participate in whatever capacity was needed. Huey copters arrived and loaded my platoon on them, and they dropped us in an unknown place. We stayed there for an undetermined amount of time before moving out. Our only inkling of the duration of the mission was that company supply had issued us three days of C-rations and an extra canteen for water. The platoon leader did tell that a resupply of water would reach us during the operation, but most of our water would have to be found during the operation. Further up north finding water was not a problem, but the Mekong Delta was a tidewater delta which meant that salt water backed up the rivers making the water unfit to drink without desalination. Rainwater provided the main supply of drinking water for the Vietnamese, but it was always in short supply towards the end of the dry season. What rainwater could be found was in the private supply of Vietnamese families. Taking their water placed them in danger of not having enough when they needed it.

The three-day sweep proved to be anticlimactic. The only thing livening up the sweep was a display of recon-by-fire by an armored unit. For some reason, probably some sniper fire or an intelligence report, the armored units blasted a deserted hamlet for nearly an hour. My company was stationed less than a kilometer away in full view of the proceedings, which we watched with fascination. Other than obliterating a couple of half-empty hamlets, the sweep produced no results positive or otherwise.

Later, I learned that the sweep had been based on intelligence. An intelligence report on April 28 reported that 150 Viet Cong soldiers and 100 porters were reported in the vicinity of XS622718 and XS626707. Although this report received an evaluation of only F-3, other evidence suggested that the 265th Main Force Battalion had been operating in this area. An F-3 evaluation meant that the reliability of the information was suspect. The scale ran from A to F, and 1–5. An A-1 meant that both the source and the information were ironclad. Something like Ho Chi Minh, the president of North Vietnamese, ordering an offensive in South Vietnam in the presence of an American agent. Another report the same day indicated that there were 80 Viet Cong observed at vicinity of XS 610600. Then on April 29, a further report came in that 80 troops of C315 Local Force Regiment had been sighted in this area. These sightings served as the basis for the three-day sweep from April 28 to April 30, 1968. Our company marched 10 kilometers from woodline to woodline and in and out of water without raising anything but blisters. Even the daily situation report for April 29 was boring.

30 April 68 Sitrep for 29 April
    At O505H vic XS721731 Co. C inserted on LX and conducted Recon in Force operations through vic XS718723 and west to vic XS647714. At 1605H vic XS662709 Co. C found and destroyed 10 bunkers. At 1800H vic XS647723 Co. C established its night position with Co. A/5th-60th Inf. (Mech.).

What my company did learn on the sweep was that mechanized infantry was the best way to travel. Mechanized infantry could haul supplies in their armored personnel carriers (APC) while regular infantry had to carry everything on their backs. There were two drawbacks of mechanized infantry. Riding inside an APC was dangerous because a Viet Cong APC (Armed Propelled Rocket) easily penetrated the light armor making it a death trap. Another disadvantage was the APCs were too heavy to be much use in the Mekong Delta, especially during the monsoon season. The 9th Infantry Division later traded a mechanized infantry unit for a regular straight-leg infantry unit during the summer monsoon season in 1968. Nevertheless, members of our company were enamored with the concept of mechanized infantry. Riding in an APC certainly beat marching through the mud in a rice paddy.

After concluding the sweep, my company returned to the artillery base camp to pull more guard duty. My platoon was pulling maintenance on our weapons when the battalion's sergeant major appeared. He was about 6 feet 5 inches tall and full of his own importance. His first action was to put the company on police call. After three days of constant marching to have to pull police call in an area where none of us had been for three days was enough to tick us off, but then he demanded that we check in our ammunition and grenades. Our collective response was to tell him "to go to hell." After all, what could he do—send us to South Vietnam? He threatened to report us for insubordination, but nothing came of it. Infantrymen were a prime commodity in the division and wasting us like this on such pettiness was insane. At the same time, members of my company were beginning to become a bit cocky, and it became an article of faith that nobody was going to disarm us in the middle of a war zone. Our mission was to protect the base camp and our weapons were necessary to fulfill that mission.

The next day my platoon had another run in with the sergeant major. A Vietnamese prostitute was making the rounds of the perimeter bunkers. She had a small boy soliciting for her and her price was five dollars. I refused her invitation, but I did ask her how many customers she had serviced that day. She answered in good English 41. Just after she left with number 42, the sergeant major charged up breathing fire. He demanded to know where the prostitute was. Several of us had fun misdirecting him to far away bunkers. We heard him fuming for several hours. No harm was done, and, as far as I know, no one came down with venereal disease from his encounter with the hustling prostitute. This was far different from the case of the platoon's officers who contracted the clap from the twenty-dollar call girls on the top floor of the International Hotel a couple of weeks later. My letter of May 3, 1968, explains my attitude at the time.

> Dear Susan,
>
> I am fine. I just returned from a lengthy mission in the Mekong Delta where I still am. I am near Bien Chanh, which is 10 miles south of Saigon. We are supposed to return to Bearcat sometime next week. We were sent all over the delta searching hamlets. We have had no enemy contact yet, although they are around here in about 2 battalion strength. Chikuma is getting out of the service as he lost a kidney as a result of that ambush. The rest will probably return to us except for Simpson who is blind for life. This is a miserable country to fight in, but I do like the people. The countryside has its own type of beauty. As I am writing this letter my bunker is being used by a GI and a Vietnamese girl for you know what reason. This is quite common over here, but you have no reason to worry. The Sergeant-Major is running around trying to protect our morals, but that would be a life time job.

Airmobile operations and night patrols kept my company busy during the first week of May. I averaged only around four hours sleep a night and sometimes my platoon marched all night on patrols. The weather was also beginning to change from the dry to the wet season. Each day around 4:00 P.M. showers began to appear. Between the heat and the humidity, it was hard to move around with any energy. By this time I was beginning to lose weight. Arriving in South Vietnam at a healthy 210 pounds on a 5 foot 11 frame, my weight loss was drastic. Although there was no scale to weigh, I could tell by the fit of my jungle fatigues that I was rapidly losing weight. Part of the problem was that I was so dehydrated most of the time that I had trouble consuming my C-rations except the ones with sauce or fruit juice. I also began eating green pineapples. A side effect of the green pineapples was the runs, but my body needed the liquid.

The most popular tactic used by the 9th Infantry Division in the Mekong Delta during this period was the so-called eagle flights. It also had another name used by the 9th Infantry Division high command: jitterbugging. Units of fifteen to thirty strong would be dropped by Huey copters near suspected Viet Cong positions to flush out enemy activity by serving as live bait. If no contact resulted, copters would be called in to transport the small force to another spot.

If the unit made contact with the enemy, more troops would be ferried in to surround the Viet Cong detachments and annihilate them. This tactic called for outfits to make several drops a day. It was exhausting for

Helicopter slicks waiting to pick up my unit in Tan Tru in May 1968 for an Eagle Flight mission.

the units making the drops and then having to march hundreds of meters to check out bunkers and hooches. At dusk the units would establish a night perimeter. After night fall the units would move several hundred meters away from the previous location. This was to prevent Viet Cong from setting up mortar attacks. Once the nighttime location had been established then squad sized ambush patrols were sent out.

Since my battalion was new and in relatively good shape in comparison with other of the brigade's maneuver battalions, it conducted airmobile operations almost daily for several months. After awhile each company began to develop minor variations in the ways it accommodated to these eagle flights. In Company C, ambush patrols were rotated so that every squad pulled one every third night. After pulling normal daytime operations with as many as six insertions a day and forced marches to objectives, these ambush patrols became snooze patrols. An hour or so after setting up an L-shaped ambush (so-called L-shaped because the formation resembled an L shape) most of the participants were sound asleep. Fear might be a good stimulant, but fatigue proved to be a better drug. Theory had it that each member of the squad was to pull an hour on watch and an hour off for sleep, but by 0100 no one would be awake. Only when it became daylight would the squad wake up. Naturally, our nighttime ambush patrols had limited success.

My platoon's most notable success happened one night when six Viet Cong irregulars literally stepped on a member of one of our sleeping patrols. Fortunately, the Viet Cong were as surprised as our guys, and in the subsequent firefight the enemy suffered two casualties. The company did have a policy never to use a shelter for an ambush site, because the Viet Cong had a nasty habit of throwing bags of high explosives into hooches. In a tightly confirmed space these explosives were lethal. About six weeks later, in the middle of June, another company lost a squad when the Viet Cong deposited a bag of explosives on a patrol asleep in a hooch.

One squad had a memorable ambush patrol. It was ordered to set up an ambush in a factory that manufactured the favorite Vietnamese sauce, Ngoc Maum. This sauce was made out of fermented fish juices and smells like rotted fish. It evidently tastes better with rice, but a strong dose could make one sick. This squad spent the night in this factory, and all members of the squad became deathly sick. The rest of the company had fun with these guys, but they did not think that it was funny at all.

Our first weeks in Long An Province passed without incident. Each day resembled the next with constant patrolling and hamlet searches. The problem with the hamlet searches was that none of us knew just what we were looking for. I suppose weapons, documents, incriminating evidence, Viet Cong supporters, etc. Supposedly division intelligence sent us out on these searches for a purpose, but nobody bothered to tell the searchers anything. My platoon barged into one hooch after another without finding anything suspicious. A poignant moment during one of these searches came when a little old man informed me by sign language that he had lost three sons in the war. Three pictures of young men in ARVN uniforms sat on his Buddhist shrine. Later, I found out that many of the hamlets that my company had searched in during these weeks had been those of dependents of the South Vietnamese government.

Another time my platoon found a sizable rice cache. Division policy was to confiscate large rice caches whenever and wherever they were found, because sooner or later the Viet Cong would gain access to the rice by gift, taxation, or confiscation. We found five tons of rice stored in seven huts. Half of my platoon started loading the rice on copters to take it away, and the other half stood guard. The faces of the local inhabitants were anything but impassive. Suddenly, a copter landed and an American intelligence officer from Saigon demanded to know what was going on. After this officer had been briefed on the situation, he managed to have the orders changed and the rice was carried back to the original storage areas. The villagers were ecstatic, but their hostility towards us was apparent as we marched away. This incident left a bad impression on me, and I wondered then and now how often similar affairs had turned out this well. It

Type of Vietnamese hamlet in Long An Province that my platoon often searched.

also made me doubt that we had the knowledge of the country and its people to win this war.

It was at this time that Company C received its first Tiger Scout. The Tiger Scout Program, or more commonly called the Kit Carson Scout Program, was a way to use former Viet Cong who had defected in the Chieu Hoi Program. They served in front-line units as point men and experts on Viet Cong tactics. My company was late in acquiring a Tiger Scout and language difficulties hampered his effectiveness. Later, this Tiger Scout was killed in action.

Unless in the field on an operation, my platoon alternated base camps every few days. At one of these base camps I first ran into snakes. In our training at the Old Reliable Academy the instructors had warned us about snakes in South Vietnam. They said that there were forty kinds of snakes in South Vietnam, and thirty-nine were poisonous and the other was the python. On my evening trip to the latrine, I walked past approximately fifty snakes. Now I did not stop to identify what kind of snakes they were, but they were probably the kait snake. This snake is deadly poisonous but not aggressive. As long as I had my boots on and with baggy jungle fatigues snake bite was not a problem. Just as long I did not run into a king cobra, which is both highly poisonous and aggressive. Needless to say, I was cautious where I slept that night. Those were the only snakes that I saw in South Vietnam, but I was always aware that one might be close.

Later, I learned more about the enemy that my battalion was facing in Go Cong, Long An and Dinh Tuong provinces. Viet Cong prisoners of war and captured documents showed how the North Vietnamese and Viet Cong infiltrated into these provinces. An intelligence summary of April 1, 1968, gave the history of the Dong Nai Regiment (309the Infiltration Group).

> The following summary is an attempt to present a brief history, to include the current alleged status of the Dong Nai Regiment, compiled from recent captured documents and POWs. The information tends to alter previous OB holdings on the regiment and should not be considered conclusive.
>
> In the spring of 1967, the 568th Regiment, 330th Division, North Vietnamese Army, also known as infiltration group 309, departed North Vietnam and moved south into the Republic of Vietnam via Laos and Cambodia. Its subordinate elements consisted of the 7th Battalion (AKA IG309D), 8TH Battalion (AKA IG309B), 9th Battalion (AKA IG309A), and support units (AKA IG309C). The 568th Regiment reached War Zone D in the Republic of Vietnam in June or July 1967. There it was broken up to form the following units: the HQ, 7th and 8th Battalions and the support elements became the HQ, K2 and K3 Battalions and support elements respectively, of the Dong Nai Regiment; the 9th Battalion became the Phu Loi II Battalion, an independent unit.
>
> To fill out the Dong Nai Regiment, and probably to have at least one subordinate familiar with the AO (Southern War Zone D), the D800 Battalion, a main force unit subordinate to the HQ, Military Region 1 was infused into the Dong Nai Regiment at the K1 Battalion.
>
> Late in the year (December 1967), the K3 Battalion of the recently formed Dong Nai Regiment was detached from the regiment and sent to operate independently in Long An Province. On 10 February 1968 this unit attacked Tan An. It is believed that the Phu Loi I Battalion, formerly an independent unit subordinate to the Thu Dau Mot Province, has replaced the (old) K3 Battalion and, in turn, has been redesignated as the (new) K3 Battalion.
>
> The Phu Loi II Battalion, after operating for some months in Southern War Zone D, was moved (January 1968?) to Long An Province. Since that time the Battalion has operated north of Can Giouc along Highway 5a. Probably one of its companies has been transferred to the 2nd (Independent) Battalion of Long An Province, and, in turn, has infused a number of members of the 2nd (Independent) Battalion into its ranks.

At the same time the 9th Infantry Division was sending more elements into the provinces south of Saigon and into the Mekong Delta the Viet Cong were sending more units into the same area.

Another intelligence report dated April 3, 1968, had further information about how the Viet Cong operated in the 9th Infantry's area of operation.

> 31 March 68, vic XS384460 to XS368433 to XS455453, a 42 member heavy weapons platoon of the Viet Cong 514th Battalion was located in the

vicinity of Long Thanh Hamlet, My Hoa Hamlet, and An Phu Hamlet, Long Dinh District, Dinh Tuong Province. The unit was commanded by Sau Hoang. He was formerly the Executive Officer of the 514th VC Battalion, but since returning from a "mortar and heavy weapons training course" under orders from VC Military Region II, he had taken over as the commander of the heavy weapons in VC My Tho Province. The Viet Cong platoon was armed with 1 120mm mortar mounted on wheels, 2 82mm mortars, 4 U/I light machine guns, 100 rounds of 120mm mortar ammo and 200 rounds of 82mm mortar ammo. Signal equipment include 1 ChiCom high frequency radio and 3 small radios. The Viet Cong wore mostly farmers clothes. The morale of the unit was very high. The unit traveled by foot. The mission of the heavy weapons unit was to continually mortar the Dong Tam Base Camp (vic XS420440) during the "Qui 2" campaign and to inflict as many casualties as possible on the US forces there and to keep them in a defensive position.

The unit had moved from My Hanh Trung Village (NCA;NFI) on 25 March 1968. One element of the Rear Services Group transported the 120mm mortar from Kien Hoa Province, to this heavy weapons element when it was stationed at Bang Long Village (NCA;NFI). The unit had arrived at the above mentioned 3 coordinates on 30 March 1968 at 2130 hours. At that time, the 120mm mortar was emplaced at XS368433, and the 2 82mm mortars were emplaced at XS384460 and XS455453.

At those locations the Viet Cong built secret caves to conceal the weapons. Whenever the Viet Cong were to use the weapons, they were to open the doors to the caves and close them when finished firing. 10 VC troops were assigned to each of the 82 mortars. 22 troops and Sau Hoang himself were assigned to the 120mm mortar position.

The Viet Cong were also utilizing 2 unidentified Vietnamese females who were disguised as prostitutes to work around the Dong Tam Base Camp and make friends with US troops, observe targets and to report to Sau Hoang. The two women were described as Viet Cong members whose sole purpose was to serve as recon and intelligence agents. The 3 mortars described above would be used each time Dong Tam Base Camp was fired upon, and they would be located at the same cave emplacements. In daylight, the Viet Cong were moving the weapons about at times and telling local civilian that the weapons would be used from various positions. But the actually plan was to use the three caves each time. The caves were alleged to be booby trapped and mined.

Throughout April while my unit was in training and beginning to take part in operations, the Viet Cong were busy bringing in supplies and training its fighters. An April 14, 1968, intelligence summary revealed this to be the case.

10 April 1968 vic XS485802, the Viet Cong will attempt to infiltrate supplies and ammo into Long An Province along the Bo Bo Canal, from Cam-

bodia. These supplies will be brought down the canal by sampans in small groups. Between 2300 and 2400 hours, each night, the resupply cadre will rendezvous with Long An Province cadre at the junction of the Bo Bo Canal and the Binh Duc Trail, XS485802. Long An Province cadre will travel by sampan from the Song Vam Co Tay along the Rach Ba Mieu Canal to the Bo Bo Canal. If the Long An Province cadre cannot make the rendezvous the supplies will be concealed beneath the trees in the area. At the same time the Long An Province committee will send small groups of Viet Cont up the Bo Bo Canal to attend training camps in Cambodia. The troops will be escorted by the returning supply cadre.

In hindsight, it was obvious that these supplies and the training were in preparation for the Viet Cong offensive on Saigon in May 1968.

5

Battle of the Cholon Y Bridge

Starting in early May, a rumor started circulating throughout Company C that the Viet Cong might launch an offensive near Ho Chi Minh's birthday on May 9. The Viet Cong had a habit of typing military operations with political events for propaganda reasons. An earlier warning about a possible offense on May 1 had not materialized, but this meant little. The American military was always alert to communist holidays. In the back of everyone's mind was the 1968 Tet Offensive. Saigon remained a tempting Viet Cong target because it was so large that it was difficult to defend. Saigon was easy for the Viet Cong to infiltrate, but it was more difficult to seize and hold. Staging areas for a large Viet Cong offensive were plentiful in areas east and west of Saigon. Besides pacifying the Mekong Delta, the 9th Infantry Division's mission was to guard the southern approaches to Saigon.

The Viet Cong had two large staging areas in our area of operations — the Plain of Reeds, and the Rung Sat Special Zone. Of the two, the Plain of Reeds was the more natural staging area. It was a sea of tall grass too wet for military operations in the wet season and too dry in the dry season. What it did have was direct access to Cambodia via the Parrot's Beak and the Ho Chi Minh Trail. It also had a maze of canals which crisscrossed the Plain of Reeds and which permitted the Viet Cong to send supplies from Cambodia into the Mekong Delta, or to store supplies for an offensive against Saigon.

The Rung Sat Special Zone (also called the Everglades of Vietnam) was a swamp southeast of Saigon. It was a smaller geographical area than the Plain of Reeds, but the swamp made it more impenetrable because of the dense foliage and tidal floods. Because the U.S. military sea supply line to Saigon passed through the Rung Sat Special Zone, it was a place where the Viet Cong could be more than a nuisance to shipping. While its remote location made resupply of a major offense more difficult, the defenses around southeast Saigon were weaker than in other approaches. It was from this direction that the Viet Cong launched the May Offensive on May 7, 1968.

News of a possible Viet Cong offensive against Saigon was leaked to U.S. intelligence, because just before the Viet Cong started the offensive my company moved into a defensive position on the southeast side of Saigon. An intelligence report on May 3, 1968, gave information from a North Vietnamese soldier about a forthcoming attack on Saigon.

On 011400 May 1968, a North Vietnamese soldier rallied at Phu Hoa Dong. He stated that his infiltration group had 600 men when it left North Vietnam, but lost 200 men in movement. The remaining 400 arrived at XT692334 on 23 April 68. The men were assigned to two battalions of Q762 aka 272nd Regiment, 9th VC Division. At 281730 April 1968, the two battalions moved southwest to Highway 14 and then south to XT732231. At 290230 April, they reached the Saigon River at XT29216, but they did not cross due to the absence of boats. On 291700 three sampans ferried the two units across the river during a three hour period. The units moved south and dispersed along a stream from XT723201 to XT727197. At 290400, the soldier left the unit and made his way to Phu Hoa Dong. He did not know where the unit went after he left it. He stated his unit would attack Saigon on an unknown date. At first light on April 7, my company started maneuvering on the northeast fringe of the Rung Sat Special Zone without detecting any enemy movement. Then word reached us that Viet Cong elements were infiltrating into Saigon from our area of responsibility and Company C's mission was to seal off an area near the Y Bridge. The Y Bridge was the connecting bridge from Cholon, the Chinese section of Saigon, to Saigon. Cholon was a priority target for the Viet Cong not only of its population of a million, but because it was, as the Australian communist Wilford Burchett stated in his book *We Will Win,* "the main location of rice-husking mills and therefore the greatest rice storage center in all of South Vietnam." It also had a large number of Viet Cong sympathizers.

Military operations in the area southeast of Saigon were hampered by water and mud. Copters dropped Company C off in an area where the terrain was so heavy and the mud so deep that minimal progress could be made in reaching our assigned blocking position. Several mid-sized streams also proved to be major obstacles. Here is where the company practiced our river crossing techniques that we had learned at Bearcat. During one of the crossings, my company lost another man. Sp.4 Campbell, a native of Georgia and a nephew of Senator Russell, had been one of the more likable individuals in the company. At first, most of us thought that Campbell had merely slipped into the water and had been pulled down by his heavy equipment, but I heard later that when the body was recovered a few days later that he had a lethal gunshot wound. Obviously, a sniper had hit him, but in the noise and excitement of the river crossing, no one had heard the report. His sudden disappearance unnerved all of us. Just about the time the company became situated radio orders arrived transferring our company to yet another blocking position.

After a wait of more than an hour and with evening fast approaching, the slicks finally made their appearance and this time they deposited us in the middle of a swamp. Almost as soon as my squad landed, it started to rain. Raining is an understatement because this was a monsoon type downpour. All night we marched, or rather low-crawled through the water and mud. My canteens of water soon became empty, but all I had to do was to remove my helmet liner and let it fill up with rainwater. I had neglected to clean my helmet liner after shaving the previous day, leaving a residue of shaving lotion. Even with the shaving cream and whiskers, the water tasted delicious. After finally reaching some shelter and our defensive position around 0400, every one was so exhausted that we slept the remaining two hours until daybreak. Fortunately, the Viet Cong left us alone during the night because not only did the company neglect security, but I wager only one in ten M-16s were operable. After waking up, my platoon quickly spot cleaned our rifles with the only cleaning kits left in the platoon. Combat loss of rifle cleaning kits became a real problem in the combat zone. Compounding the problem was that orders had been issued back at Bearcat to take only one cleaning kit per two soldiers. Combat loss resulted in a shortage of cleaning kits within a couple of days. It caused problems because the M-16 had to be kept clean and dry to operate efficiently. In combat, we had trouble keeping the rifle clean and we were always in the water. After eating some C-rations, the company commander directed us to move out towards a river about three kilometers away.

This river was our destination where my company was to link up with other American units to blockade the southeastern approaches to Saigon. It was much easier marching in the daytime, and the company reached the banks of the river by mid-morning. This river was one of the many tributaries running through the delta, but unlike some, it had a nice beach. Orders were given to dig in, but after so many moves in the last couple of days, our enthusiasm for digging foxholes was at low ebb. About this time, one of the M-60 machine gunners requested permission to test fire his weapon. After receiving the go ahead from the company commander, he aimed the weapon in the air towards the north and fired a short burst. No sooner had his the sound of his last round died out when we heard the unpleasant noise of small arms ammo flying over our heads. The whistle of a bullet is unmistakable. Since fire discipline was always a strong point in my company, nobody returned fire. The company commander soon established that the gunfire had come from a sister unit on our left flank.

Once the news reached us that there were American units on both of our flanks everybody in my company relaxed. We felt secure with the knowledge that our unit was not out on a limb dangling in front of Viet Cong forces. Several fellows decided to take a quick dip in the river. No sooner had they entered the water than there were several muffled explosions. It was the sound of mortar shells striking water. All of the men made a mad dash for shore, but one moved faster than the others. One of the bathers had been sprayed with shrapnel. While his multiple back wounds proved to be superficial, it reminded all of us to keep alert. Our initial reaction was that the mortar fire had come from friendlies, and this made us mad. Some of us continued to share this belief until the wounded soldier returned to our unit a few days later and told us that he had talked to the commander of the unit on our right flank; some of his men had been wounded by 60mm mortar fire from the Viet Cong on the same day.

Shortly after receiving the mortar fire, another platoon downstream spotted armed Viet Cong in the open and commenced firing. Since I could see no target, I refrained from joining in the long distance firefight. Part of the reason for my inability to see the Viet Cong firing at us stemmed from the loss of my glasses during the previous night's march. Here I was a trained sniper with a single-shot National Match M-14 with National Match ammo and I could see targets in a distance only as a blur. The army had a policy to find replacement glasses promptly, but since my spare pair was still at Bearcat in my locker, it took nearly two weeks before my replacement pair caught up with me. For the next few weeks, the platoon had a point man and sniper with a distance vision problem. I tried to explain the problem, but nobody would listen.

Early the next morning my company received new orders, along with the other blocking units, to move towards the Y Bridge. My company moved slowly towards the sound of gunfire, but the tempo of movement increased as the volume of gunfire intensified. A friend of mine, who later died of wounds in July 1968, began to advance with me covering him. He then covered for me when I advanced. Building by building the two of us advanced just like in those World War II movies. Suddenly, the two of us were on the banks of a river, probably the Kien Dong Canal, and across the water was a complex of fifty almost new single-story houses. Most the Viet Cong gunfire came from this complex. After the frustrations of the last few weeks, it was almost a pleasure to be able to direct my aggressions towards something inanimate. Since no people were visible, it was almost as if the buildings were the enemy. A feeling of bloodlust seized me and soon I was firing at the windows of these buildings. Without my glasses, I am not sure that I even hit the building let alone the windows. At the same time helicopter gunships were firing rockets at the complex slowly demolishing each dwelling.

In a moment of inspiration I decided to fire my M-72 anti-tank weapon to penetrate the hardened concrete walls. After carrying this weapon for three weeks through all kinds of conditions, it turned out to be a dud. Disgusted, I threw it into the canal with a few choice expletives.

The canal prevented my movement into the suburb which was probably lucky for me since once the firing started I was ready to charge blindly towards the enemy. My intellect warned me of the dangers, but

Bombing run by American gunships in Cholon during the Battle of Saigon on May 9, 1968, near where my company was in action near the Y Bridge.

an adrenaline rush made me want to move forward. Not every member of my company was so foolhardy. It took several hours before my platoon caught up to Nelson and me on the bank of the canal. Few of them had fired their weapons in this engagement and most appeared relieved to see the water separating them from the Viet Cong. Together my platoon watched the gunships completely level the complex with few if any survivors. The official estimate of Viet Cong casualties for the Battle of the Y Bridge came to nearly 1,000. A more accurate report in the 9th Division's magazine *Octofol* placed enemy casualties at 852. My gut estimate of the casualties at this suburb was that at least three civilians died for every Viet Cong killed.

After an uneventful night, my company moved across the Y Bridge the next day. Some street fighting on the outskirts of Cholon was still taking place. My companion and I still worked as a team, maneuvering from building to building and occasionally firing in response to Viet Cong rifle fire in our direction. In the midst of the action, we ran into a Canadian war correspondent. I never learned his name, but he told us that he was covering the action in Saigon for the Canadian Broadcasting Corporation (CBC). We stopped to chat with him behind a strong wall. He informed us that the Viet Cong had been infiltrating Saigon from Cholon for several days and that the fighting had been door to door in this area. Further gunfire distracted us from this conversation, and he stayed behind as we moved forward to investigate the gunfire. Shortly afterward, the fighting ended, and the looting began. The American solider may sometimes be called an indifferent fighter, but as a looter he is superb. The GIs call it souvenir hunting, but it is still looting. So many souvenirs were acquired in the next couple of days that I would wager that each solider carried twenty-five or more pounds leaving Saigon than on entering the battle. All I picked up was a Larousse French-English dictionary that I found in the middle of the street outside of a bombed out dwelling.

The Battle of Saigon was over and most of the participants believed that it had been a major defeat for the Viet Cong. Yet, American military authorities downplayed the victory. Even the division's official version lacks the ring of a resounding victory (see Appendix B). Much has been written about the Tet Offensive and later battles, but little publicity about the May Offensive has been broadcast. This is despite the claim of General Ewell, the commander of the 9th Infantry Division, that the Battle of Saigon was a mini–Tet. Whereas Americans have ignored or belittled this engagement, the Viet Cong and their sympathizers have trumpeted it as a victory. Wilford Burchett made this claim in his book *We Will Win*. His rationale is that the Viet Cong demonstrated their strength by penetrating Saigon against a prepared buildup.

After the fighting ceased, Company C received the order to guard the Y Bridge. This break allowed me to send a letter home explaining to my wife was going on since the last time I had written.

Dear Susan,

They finally have given me a chance to write you. As I indicated from my last note, I have been in almost constant combat for a week. My company was part of the defense of Saigon during the May 7 Viet Cong Offensive. We were in a 4-hour fire fight on May 9 and on May 10 we were hit hard about 5 miles southeast of Saigon. We had one man killed. His name was Russell and he was a newly wed as he got married during his leave. He was shot between the eyes and the Viet Cong then used him for target practice.

I really do like Vietnam, but it is a terrible place to fight in. By the way, I killed somebody in the street fighting. It was not as traumatic as I thought it would be, but I am not happy or proud of it. I am not sure if he was VC but he ran from us and I had no choice. It still bothers me some, but I have to live with it.

It was something pathetic in Saigon watching all the people flee their homes. We talked to a poor woman who had lost 6 children in the war. We shot many innocent people but we had no choice. During the firefight, I know that we shot many innocent people but we had no choice. This was a miserable war as the innocent suffered more than the guilty.

The problem was that I did not know any more about the war than I did back in the States. I had seen Viet Cong prisoners tortured by ARVN (South Vietnamese Army), and yet, most of the ARVN boys I have met, I like. I had no contact with the Vietnamese government, but you could tell that it was corrupt. The people were greedy for necessities. Everybody begged for our C-rations. They used the C-rations to mix with rice. It gave them a protein supplement to their diet.

It had been nearly three weeks without a change of uniform or a clean pair of socks. Because of the nature of the terrain in the Mekong Delta, my platoon had been in and out of water constantly. Our jungle fatigues were rotting off us, and most of us no longer had socks. Because of the heat and humidity none of us wore underwear. We were a pathetic lot guarding the Y Bridge. The bath problem was solved by an ingenious infantryman who fired a .50 caliber round into a water pipe on the Y Bridge. Water cascaded over the bridge making a waterfall shower. Modesty has its place in civilized life, but not after weeks of hygiene neglect. With a shout of glee our company and a few other attached men collectively

Vietnamese families living in concrete pipes after the Battle of Saigon in May 1968.

threw off our disintegrating uniforms, grabbed some soap, and had probably the largest public mass shower in Saigon's history. It was obvious that the Vietnamese women were greatly amused and we heard them laughing and pointing, but in the euphoria of clean water and soap nothing else mattered. After the shower, the company collected our old uniforms and burned them. This meant that supply had to come up with clean uniforms or else my company was going to be the United States' first all nude combat unit. Supply responded by bring us new uniforms. By nightfall, the members of my company almost looked and felt like American soldiers.

After the show and a clean set of jungle fatigues, the fun began. Nobody, officer or enlisted man, seemed worried about the Viet Cong, and, since casualties had been light, all attention turned to the availability of women. A sister unit in the 9th Infantry Division, A Company of the 2nd Battalion, 47th Infantry (Mech.) had been assigned to guard the Y Bridge with us. Members of this unit had pulled such duty before and they knew the location of every whorehouse in Saigon. Orders came down from division for us to conduct ambush patrols around the outskirts of Saigon. Since officers rarely if ever participated in ambush patrols, they headed for Saigon's nightspots. Saigon had been decreed a closed city since the Tet Offensive in January, but the2 Military Police (MPs) were selective about enforcement. Since so many civilians, intelligence agents, and personnel were stationed in Saigon, the MPs stopped enlisted men only in certain sections, mostly along Tu Do Street. Tu Do Street had been the entertainment center of Saigon until the army shut it down by patrols of military police.

The enlisted men of Company C reluctantly began to prepare for night patrolling. As we put on our equipment word came down through the grapevine that the 2nd Battalion, 47th Infantry (Mech.) was to share ambush duty with us. Suddenly most of my squad was on an armored personnel carrier dashing along the streets to Saigon and the nearest whorehouse. I volunteered to go on ambush patrol because the last thing I wanted to bring back from South Vietnam was a case of venereal disease. Ambush patrols were organized and sent out, but the only casualties or victims of that night were those unfortunates who picked up a venereal disease.

During one of those ambush patrols, my squad had an unfortunate experience, which had the potential to produce heavy casualties. My squad moved out at dusk on an ambush patrol along the river southeast of Saigon. After about two kilometers of marching in the dark, we were challenged by an ARVN patrol. They informed us that our squad was in the middle of a South Vietnamese free fire zone, and that no word had been given out to the South Vietnamese of our potential presence in the area. Anyone caught in a free fire zone was subject to immediate termination. Fortunately, no one was hurt, but my squad returned to the Y Bridge with great haste. While this incident was unimportant in its consequences, it is symbolic of communication problems that developed between ARVN and U.S. military commands.

Company level operations continued around Saigon for a couple of days. While no military objectives had been accomplished, the personnel in my company received some down time, which it badly needed. Weapons were cleaned, a supply system was reconstituted, and a respite from a steady diet of C-rations contributed to improved morale in the company. Just to keep the troops from becoming too lackadaisical small patrols were sent out to check out the swamps east of Saigon.

The 9th Infantry Division had a lengthy history of cooperation with the U.S. Navy in mobile riverine operations. Its Second Brigade operated with the navy along the rivers in the Mekong Delta. The next thing my squad knew we were on boats cruising down streams and checking out suspicious sites. It was on one of the checks of suspicious sites that I became stuck in the mud up to my waist. This mud was not the type of mud that sucked one under, but the kind that the more you struggled the deeper you went. There was no danger that I would sink below the mud, but I was in danger of drowning. The reason was that these swamps were in a tidal flat and I had only a couple of hours before the tide was due to come in. At full tide, I would be under at least five feet of water. My patrol was about to radio for a copter to come to pull me out when several guys were able to dig me out. While I was almost completely coated with mud, I was happy to be alive. Every time someone had to be pulled out of the mud by a copter, and it did happen fairly often, the soldier usually had his shoulders dislocated. I communicated this incident to my wife in a letter dated May 19:

> Dear Susan,
>
> I have been stationed here in Saigon for the last few days. I have had no stationery or else I would have written earlier. There is no fighting in Saigon for the present. I am fine but I miss you. We expect Krosky back at any time. They are keeping us busy at the moment because tomorrow some damn general is going to present awards to our unit. My hands are dirty so do not mind the messy letter.
>
> Yesterday we moved through some swamp and I became completely unable to move. It was 45 minutes before they could get me free. I love this life!!!! We are on police all day long because of this general. The one day we could rest we end up doing meaningless details. C'est l'armée! Since I have been in Saigon, I have made several friends and my Vietnamese is getting better. Two engaging young chaps, Kid and Thieu, have been my special friends. These kids are a lot of fun.

This incident marred an otherwise delightful stay in Saigon. Rumors began to fly that Viet Cong activities south of Saigon might make the brigade commit our unit there.

The 9th Infantry Division from the general down to the lowest private first class knew that the Viet Cong had suffered a devastating defeat in the Battle of Saigon. It was not long before intelligence reports surfaced proving this. One proof was the increasing number of Viet Cong deserting their units and becoming Hoi Chanhs. One such Hoi Chanh was Hoi Van Hai.

> INTSUM, 20 May 1968
>
> Hois Van Hai (DOB 41), (POB Da Phuoc Village, Binh Chanh District), rifleman, 2nd Platoon, 2nd Company, 6th Battalion. The Hoi Chanh stated that the mission of their unit was to attack the Chu Y Bridge on 4–5 May 1968. The Battalion stayed in that area until 9 May when it withdrew to XS826818 and XS831855 which is the unit's present location. The Battalion is currently waiting for replacements and upon arrival the unit will

attack Saigon again. The morale of the unit is very low. The old Viet Cong leaders have been replaced by North Vietnamese Army commanders because they were unable to control the battalion. The food supply was very low and the men were hungry. Approximately 40 of the Viet Cong wanted to Chieu Hoi but were being watched too closely by the new North Vietnamese Army commanders. The Hoi Chanh further stated that the unit was engaged with US troop and or about 23 May and they sustained 70 killed and only 20 were left in the company. The Battalion was armed with 4 82mm mortars, 3 .50 caliber machine guns, 3 75mm rockets, and had 1 RPG-2 rocket squad and 1 RPG-7 rocket squad.

There is no way of knowing exactly, but this may have been one of the units that my company clashed with in early May and later in the middle of May.

6

Combat in the Mekong Delta

News of fighting in the Mekong Delta made my company aware of the need to prepare for further combat. Our little vacation was nearly over. Resupply had been accomplished by company supply and now my outfit had freshly clean combat fatigues. Minor injuries and infections had been treated. Finally, weapons had been repaired, cleaned, or replaced. New rifle cleaning kits had been acquired from supply. My unit received these rifle-cleaning kits, because a congressional inquiry team had arrived in South Vietnam to study the effectiveness of the M-16. We spent a full day cleaning our weapons to impress the congressional delegation. It was stop the war to clean our M-16s. While none of us were able to talk to members of the delegation and outline our problems with the M-16, it was nice to have a clean weapon again. Exactly who did talk to these congressional inspectors is anybody guess, but it definitely was not with those in combat units who were having difficulties with the M-16 in the field. In my case, this time meant my M-14 was clean again. I could handle less care about the M-16, but my M-14 still needed only an occasional cleaning. For the first time in several weeks, the unit believed that it was ready to resume full-scale combat.

The hiatus in operations allowed soldiers to trade off weapons. While I still retained my M-14, others were busy exchanging weapons to find the ones that they were most comfortable with in combat. The weapon of choice for many was the M-79 grenade launcher. It was a handy weapon in the Mekong Delta with its capability of lobbying 40mm projectiles nearly 50 meters, but the shotgun shells worked better in the jungles. Many of us would have gladly exchanged our M-16s for captured AK-47s, but division policy would not allow it. Several of us had test-fired captured AK-47s, and the consensus was that we much preferred the AK-47 to the M-16. You could do almost anything with an AK-47 and it would fire. It was a much superior weapon, especially in the hot and humid climate of South Vietnam. While it might have complicated ammo resupply, we were willing to try it. M-16s were too unreliable, and they had a tendency to explode when the buffer assembly group became too wet. To be outgunned in a firefight by an enemy otherwise inferior in firepower was a severe morale factor for American troops. This topic was discussed time and again in informal settings. The tendency of the M-16 to explode if the buffer assembly group became wet particularly annoyed us since we were up to our waists in water all the time.

Throughout our time in the field, the individual soldier had the option of wearing a flak jacket. None of us did so because there was a better chance of dying of heat exhaustion by wearing a flak jacket than being hit by a round. Flak jackets in the Vietnam War era weighed about 20 pounds and stopped little besides an AK-47 round. It made sense for the mechanized infantry to wear them because they rode around all day in APCs, but for those out in the field humping our equipment in the heat and humidity it made no sense to us.

Choppers arrived early on the morning of May 12 and again Company C found itself in the middle of heavy action. A mechanized infantry company had become bogged down along Highway LTL5A outside of Da Phoeuc with heavy casualties including the loss of its commander. Our mission was to clear the countryside surrounding the village of Da Phoeuc. Da Phoeuc had been captured by a Viet Cong unit on the previous day and the American mechanized unit had been ordered to recapture the village before enemy action had stopped it cold.

After the copters landed on the roadway, my company marched down the road between rows of coconut trees and bombed out hooches. It became obvious that heavy fighting had taken place along the road and recently. As my squad passed through the mechanized unit, it appeared to be completely demoralized. Its company commander had received an RPG round in the chest and his stunned men were standing around his body aimlessly. Nobody said anything as we marched by because there was nothing to say. American gunships and air force fighter-bombers were plastering the area north of the village with a vengeance. Still without my glasses, I was on point again. I moved cautiously down the palm tree lined main street of Da Phoeuc. Bodies were scattered along the main thoroughfare, but there was no sign of the enemy. I reported no evidence of enemy activity to my platoon leader, who then ordered me to check out a bunker outside of the village about 150 meters. Despite some verbal objections on my part that it was a suicide mission, the lieutenant insisted that the bunker be secured.

With the rest of the company as interested spectators, another soldier and I searched the bunker. Nothing is as nerve-wracking as entering a former enemy controlled bunker. Booby-traps, wounded enemy, or nervous friendlies make it an extremely dangerous undertaking. Fortunately, the bunker was empty and only a few bloodstains showed it had been occupied earlier. After our company finished securing the village, an ARVN unit relieved us for guard duty. This relief from the ARVN was an unexpected bonus, especially since we had expected to make contact with the Viet Cong at any time. My squad spent the night in a heavily bunkered ARVN compound on the outskirts of Da Phoeuc. After the tensions of the day, I looked forward to a good night's sleep. With a company of South Vietnamese regulars pulling guard duty, my squad relaxed security with only one man on guard and two off every hour. Just after I pulled my 0200 to 0300 shift, the Viet Cong launched a harassment attack on the compound. Nothing infuriates a soldier worse than losing what little sleep he has coming. As soon as I ascertained that the Viet Cong had no intention of assault in the compound and they had no mortars, I went back to sleep with the sounds of gunfire ringing in my ears. For all the sound and the fury during the night, no casualties were suffered by either American or ARVN forces.

The next day Company C started searching the area north of Da Phoeuc looking for the Viet Cong unit that had earlier attacked the village. It was mid-morning when the lead platoon in the company made first contact. My platoon had rear guard duties and the company was in a single file formation moving along a rice paddy dike. Normally battalion policy was to avoid dikes like the plague because of the danger of booby-traps, but the going was so slow through the rice paddies in the Mekong Delta that occasional exceptions were made.

The forward platoon had barely reached a woodline when all hell broke

Sergeant Ray Lehman, my platoon sergeant, in May 1968 after Sergeant Sanchez had been wounded in combat.

loose. Since soldiers on top of rice paddy dikes make for perfect targets, we made a dive for available cover. Water was standing in the rice paddies and the depth of the water appeared to be maybe six to eight inches. Imagine my surprise when I hit the water to find out that on the sheltered side the water was at least six to seven feet deep. It was also salt water. Company SOP (standard operating procedure) on making contact with the enemy was to dump our knapsacks but only after taking cover. After releasing our knapsacks and securing weapons and ammunition, policy was to move towards the sounds of gunfire. Consequently, members of my platoon were heavily loaded when we hit the water. After recovering from the initial shock, I was able to resurface minus my pack and my rifle. Others were also struggling to drop their packs and reach their weapons. Weaponless and in danger from being picked off by sniper fire, I maneuvered slowly towards the woodline. Soon I encountered a small stream at the edge of the woods and found our Tiger Scout wounded in the arm. Sergeant Dominguez and I grabbed the Tiger Scout and together we carried him across the stream. Still unarmed, I started searching for a usable weapon.

Small arms fire was heavy, but I moved into a clearing just in time to witness a medical evacuation. My admiration for medivac copter pilots will always remain high, because they consistently risked both life and their copters to save lives. This clearing was under heavy gunfire and the area barely had the space to permit a chopper to land, but in came the medivac copter anyhow. Since I had nothing better to do, I helped load the wounded. The loading was proceeding smoothly until I heard yelling between the first sergeant and a member of the medivac team. It seemed that our heroic first sergeant had no stomach for fighting, and he desired to board the copter to go elsewhere, anywhere, in a hurry. The medic refused to load an unwounded soldier onto the copter even if this person outranked him. His refusal had the support of the rest of us. After a few threats from us, the first sergeant dashed for cover.

A first sergeant has one of the most demanding jobs in the army, and he receives little love from the rest of the enlisted men. He is the administrative ass-kicker in a company and all the nasty details come through him. At best, a top sergeant is respected for what he can contribute to the company. Sometimes an individual makes that rank who is both useless and a bastard. This was the case with our first sergeant. He had made his rank by politicking at basic training camps. He was the one that always had us on police details. Neither loved nor respected, he had been forced to go into the field by the company commander. He kept a bodyguard with him and in general made of nuisance of himself. His conduct in this affair was the end of his usefulness with the company.

Our company commander heard about this incident later, and, after verbally reprimanding him, he exiled the first sergeant to his paperwork. He had long been a liability to have him around with his bodyguard. Several of the enlisted men were heard to vow that the first sergeant had to go one way or another. The first sergeant had little credit before this incident and none afterwards. Fortunately, the company commander's action solved that problem for us.

After leaving the medivac area, I joined the ammo carriers supplying ammunition to the platoons fighting with the Viet Cong. One of the wounded had given me his M-16 so I was now armed. I started carrying cans of machine gun ammo to the front line. As I headed towards the sound of machine gun fire, I came upon a dozen or so soldiers hiding behind a wall of reinforced concrete. One of them was the company commander. They were like boys at a turkey shoot. One would empty his rifle at an unseen target and then duck behind the wall. Things continued like this for about fifteen minutes when suddenly there was a tremendous explosion. The Viet Cong had fired an anti-tank round, an RPG, at us, and it had blown a huge hole in the wall. Shrapnel had been scattered in all directions. Of all the people behind the wall, only the company commander and I escaped being wounded by the shrapnel. While no one seemed seriously hurt, several soldiers were bleeding badly. The fun had suddenly gone out of the fire and hide practice, and every one started acting like soldiers rather than schoolboys.

A cry for more ammunition caused me to take my cans of machine gun ammo to an M-60 machine gun position on the left flank. I found myself fighting with elements of the first platoon. The firefight continued for several hours with intermittent firing on both sides. Air support had been called in early in the action, and the area in front of us was pulverized for more than an hour. Later, the consensus of opinion among the troops was that the firing of the RPG round was a rear-guard action to keep us occupied while the main body escaped. By the time that we realized that the Viet Cong had left the battlefield, fatigue and hunger prevented us from pursuing them. Instead, a night defensive perimeter was established by the company. Although my company had three dozen wounded, only three were killed in action (KIA). One of the KIAs had been married only a week before he had been shipped to Vietnam. He was a friend of mine, and he was standing near me when he received a bullet squarely between the eyes, killing him instantly.

Throughout the lengthy firefight, I had been active but I had fired nary a shot. After the excitement was over, I glanced at my newly acquired weapon and found that it had shrapnel marks all over its lower side. This damage was extensive enough that the weapon would have probably exploded if I had attempted to fire it. I also believe that the weapon had protected me when the RPG round had hit the concrete wall earlier in the firefight. It saved me from receiving several nasty wounds in my abdomen. Now I had to find another weapon. Several others in the company were also without weapons because of losing their rifles in the fall into the water, or because their weapons exploded after the buffer assembly group became wet. Among those that this happened to was our company commander.

A sweep through the battlefield the next day by another unit found traces of blood, bandages, and damaged weapons in the area across from us. From this meager evidence, the division claimed that our company had killed 31 and wounded 100 Viet Cong. This type of estimating Viet Cong casualties from such slight evidence was a common practice in the 9th Infantry Division. The Viet Cong were skillful in removing their dead and wounded so estimating was the only way that the U.S. Army could justify success in a firefight. We learned in conversations with individuals form other divisions that these units were as generous in the estimations of enemy casualties as the 9th Infantry Division for the same reason.

Despite the lack of identifiable Viet Cong casualties, combat losses for the Viet Cong were heavy during the period between May 4 and May 13, 1968. Intelligence reports began to surface in the middle of May and extending into June that the Viet Cong had suffered heavy dead and wounded in the various firefights. One such report was in a May 15, 1968, intelligence summary. 112100H, vic XS850843, a group of approximately 60 civilian laborers carried 50 wounded Viet Cong from the direction of Cholon to Day Klo Creek. The wounded VC were carried on approximately 30 stretchers. The lightly wounded would sit two per stretcher. Upon arrival at Cay Kho Creek, the wounded VC were transferred to ten small sampans (two to three civilians per sampan). After the wounded were placed on the sampans, the sampans traveled along Cay Kho Creek and other waterways and arrived at Doi Creek, transferred to two large sampans and these two sampans continued to move in a southerly direction. The wounded VC had been wounded for some time, due to the smell of the wounds and the wounds were treated very simply (wrapped with cloth and cotton).

The Doi Creek vic XS865780 is used as a receiving point for wounded VC coming from the Saigon area. During the evening of 11 May 68, ten sampans and a platoon of VC were observed in the area. The wounded

VC would be evacuated to Phuoc Vinh Dong Village vic XS895685, and from this point they would be evacuated to the Rung Sat area for treatment. At approximately 1900 hours on 12 May 68, 5 sampans evacuated 18-wounded VC from the direction of Saigon passing through Tan Nhut, vic XS700843 toward the Ba VC Secret Zone, traveling along Xang Canal. It was learned from the lightly wounded because they could move about easily. It was learned from the wounded VC that all of the wounded had been in the Phu Tho Hoa area during the week of 5 May 68 to 11 May 68. It was also learned that the wounded were forced to hide in local residences until May 68.

Another even more interesting intelligence report showed up in the middle of June 1968. This report discussed a Viet Cong military hospital in the middle of the Rung Sat Special Zone. Several times my company had conducted operations in the Rung Sat Special Zone without finding anything, but evidently it was so well hidden that we simply never found it.

101500H vic XS960630, the "Reception Office" of a Viet Cong military hospital (LBN: GP1-310-K) was located at the intersection of the La Be Canal and the Van Sat River, in the Rung Sat Special Zone. Guarding the "office" are 30 local guerrillas led by Hai Company. Their armament included 2 BARs, 1-RPG-2 and assorted small arms. The office receives wounded VC cadre and soldiers. There is 1 VC nurse at this location who has telephonic communications with the main hospital, which is located deep in the forest over 2000 meters along the Le Be Canal. Say Ly is chief of the reception office. The office is equipped to administer temporary care to wounded while they wait for military and medical cadre to come from the hospital to pick them up. The platoon of guerrillas is always located at XS960630. Some 200 meters east of the mouth of the Rach La Canal, the office is located. There are 5 cadres and 1 nurse permanently stationed there. At the hospital itself are 4 male and 4 female doctors, led by Huynh Ngoc Than, the hospital chief. There are also numerous female nurses and cooks.

At this time there are 70 wounded personnel undergoing treatment at the hospital. Among these are the commander of the Dong Nai Regiment, 2 battalion commanders, 3 battalion executive officers, and many company and platoon leaders wounded in the recent Saigon battles. Important personnel are taken to this hospital because it is equipped with one surgical operation room with ChiCom [Chinese Communist] instruments and medicines.

Inside the perimeter of the hospital area, 2 Viet Cong platoons are responsible for defense. The hospital buildings consist of four huts in the groups of 2 separated by not more than 10 meters. The huts are constructed of local mangrove trees and are hidden under trees to prevent visual recon. Each hut can hold 4 patients. There are passages between the beds (which are made of three branches) so that doctors and nurses can walk between the beds to care for patients. All patients are dressed in long-sleeved black T-shirts and black short pants.

This area is closely guarded by the Viet Cong. Local VC cadre, soldiers and relatives of patients are not allowed to visit the hospital. The patients themselves do not know the hospital's location because of the dense forest around them. Patients being returned from the hospital are taken out by another route. The VC have cached numerous sampans along the swamp in order to move the patients if the area is ever swept. This hospital has allegedly been at this location for a long time.

There is reportedly another hospital located in Ly Nhon Village, RSSZ. Phan is reportedly chief of this 2nd hospital. Reportedly, every day at 1700H 2 sampans and 1 motorboat travel to the mouth of the Vam Sat River to receive food and supplies for the hospital. Only medical cadre are permitted to conduct transport activities between the reception office and the hospital. The VC often send cadre to purchase food from the market in the Kinh Nuoc Man Canal in Can Duoi District, Long An Province.

The engagement on May 13 ended my direct participation in combat in South Vietnam. For the next several days, Company C conducted small unit operations in Long An Province. We were constantly in and out of the water. I bet we crossed a stream once an hour. Many of these streams were more like large creeks with the water sometimes as deep as four feet. Stream crossing were always dangerous, because the Viet Cong like to attack during these crossings.

One of my most unforgettable memories in South Vietnam was one morning watching twenty enlisted men and two officers bare their butts to the world in order to receive their daily penicillin shot. The medic went down the line administering the shots as the sun slowly rose behind them. Those of us not participating in the exercise kept up a running critique of this performance. These shots were their reward for visiting the numerous whorehouses in Cholon and Saigon.

Another incident was my platoon's insertion by copter into a rice paddy near a river. Water was everywhere and only the Vietnamese mausoleums indicated where the river and land began and ended. After landing, my platoon set up an ambush next to the river to interdict Viet Cong river traffic. Because of the proximity of the river, we were warned to sleep on our air mattresses. The next morning my platoon found itself floating in the middle of the river. During the night, the tide had come in and the water level had risen several feet. Fortunately, nobody had fallen off their mattresses because they might have drowned with all the equipment they were wearing. It is a strange sensation waking up floating in the middle of river making perfect targets for any stray Viet Cong happening by. Even then our only guide to returning to land was the presence of the mausoleums.

During the course of the constant patrolling going back to the missions around Bearcat but continuing in the Mekong Delta, I began collecting American propaganda leaflets. The air force dropped tons of propaganda leaflets on South Vietnam each week. Each of these drops had a new weekly theme. I started picking them up and noting where I found them. It was the historian in me. Some of the leaflets were appeals for the Viet Cong to cross over and join American and ARVN forces, but others were warnings what was going to happen to them if they continued to fight. A couple showed Viet Cong atrocities. The military was nervous about the impact of these atrocity leaflets on American public opinion so it was a court-martial offense to take or send these leaflets back to the continental United States. I collected all the different types of these leaflets including the atrocity ones. My wife received the non-controversial leaflets, and I kept the atrocity leaflets hidden in my uniform when I returned to the States.

My leaflet collection has had a curious history. I donated part of the collection to the University of Iowa in 1975. Several years later I inquired about them, and they informed me that my collection had been traded to the Hoover Institute in Palo Alto, California, for some of President Hoover's papers. Whether this collection has been processed or is hidden away in a box somewhere I do not know, but I retained the bulk of the collection, including the atrocity leaflets.

It was about this time that my battalion began to receive replacements. Army units in the 9th Infantry Division usually operated at around 60 percent of authorized strength. After frequent contact with the enemy, units might drop as low as 40 percent. Constant combat between April 25 and May 27, 1968, had reduced the 6th Battalion, 31st Infantry, to less than 60 percent personnel available to conduct operations. Heavy attrition from deaths, wounds, and health problems from infections and trench foot had caused the heavy losses. The first levy of replacements began to arrive in late May. While only a few of these replacements were assigned to my company, one of them made quite an impression. He was a tall, impressive looking African American soldier in his late twenties who was only a PFC (private first class). Since he was older than the normal draftee, I asked him about his situation. He told me that his former rank had been a sergeant, E-6, until he had a run-in with two white non-commissioned officers in a stateside NCO club. They had insulted his pregnant wife and thrown her on the floor while he was in the restroom. After severely wounding the two NCOs with a knife, he had been sentenced to a long prison term at Fort Leavenworth, Kansas. Each sergeant had received several thousand stitches, causing them to be invalided out of the army. The army gave him the option to volunteer as an infantryman in South Vietnam, or serve out his prison term. He picked South Vietnam. I can guarantee nobody looked at him cross-eyed once the story was out. This dumping of soldiers convicted of crimes into infantry units was not uncommon, but it did little to reassure the rest of us of our importance as defenders of South Vietnam's democracy.

Just before I left the field news came down to the unit that some general in the division was on a temperance kick. Part of the daily resupply of units in the field was an allotment of two cans of beer. The beer allotment was a mixture of American, Australian, and Korean brands. This beer allotment was popular and it also helped replenish our body's liquids after long hikes through the boonies. Often my mouth was so dry that I was unable to eat by C-rations except for the fruit and its syrup. Some damn general decided that it looked bad for troops in the field to be drinking beer on duty so he banned further supplies. No order during my stay in South Vietnam was more unpopular than this one. The cursing from all ranks over the cutoff of beer was loud and threatening. Impromptu decisions like this one from top ranking officers with little or no knowledge of combat operations hurt morale badly among the enlisted soldiers in South Vietnam.

South Vietnam was the first rock and roll war. Almost every soldier in the field had a portable transistor radio by the summer of 1968. Armed Forces Radio played a steady diet of rock and roll music. Soul music was particularly popular with James Brown the most popular soul singer. Consequently, my unit could be heard from a distance of several hundred meters as we walked along on patrol. It gave the Viet Cong warning we were coming, but we did not give a damn. I carried my transistor radio in my hatband so it would not get wet during river crossings. At night, the radios went off. Noise carried so far at night that the sound might give the Viet Cong our nighttime position. We loved our music, but not at the expense of a mortar attack.

After all the treatment about firefights and patrols, the question may be asked how the soldiers in the field handled personal hygiene. The answer is that we did not. Our frequent stays at base camps allowed us to shave, brush our teeth, and get somewhat presentable. In the field none of that was possible. We never had the time. There was not a time-out to go to the bathroom. You did it on the run, and since most of us had diarrhea that was the actual truth. Fortunately, we were in and out of the water and these frequent emersions cleaned us up somewhat. The problem was that most of the streams were heavily polluted because the Vietnamese used them for human waste disposal. Because of the lack of personal hygiene, soldiers came down with infections and some of them had to be hospitalized.

My career as an infantry was coming to an end because, unbeknown to me, the commander of the 19th Military History Detachment had initiated a search for a historian. For once my advanced degree in history stood me in good stead. On May 28, word filtered down that I was to report to Bearcat for some sort of interview. Dog tired, dirty, and confused, I traveled back to Bearcat on May 29 and had my first meeting with the

Major Cook, commander of the 19th Military History Detachment, at Bearcat Base Camp in June 1968.

commander of the 19th Military History Detachment. Although I am certain that I made a poor physical impression with my dirty fatigues and two week old beard, the major informed me than he needed somebody with an advanced degree in history to collect battlefield materials and to write his reports for the Department of Defense on the conduct of the war. I informed him that military history was one of my lifelong interests. Evidently my answers impressed him, because the major indicated that he would try to arrange my transfer. Army regulations made it difficult to change from an infantry MOS so he could make no promises. I realized this difficulty. Enthusiastic about the possibility of leaving the infantry but fatalistic about the outcome, I returned to my company still at Smokey Base Camp. Nobody knew the reason for my trip to Bearcat and I kept my mouth shut.

An order followed me back to the company that I was too valuable for further combat duty. This order intrigued the company commander, and he commented that he did not understand the order. Nevertheless, he gave the order to assign me to temporary company supply duty. For the next several days I worked at company supply awaiting developments. It was nice to sleep for eight hours or longer without the interruption of guard duty. Several other soldiers were also in limbo with most of them recovering from foot diseases caused by prolonged exposure to water. None of them was any more enthusiastic about returning to combat duty than I was. I witnessed one soldier from Georgia attempt to break his foot with an ammo box to avoid going back to the field. After our recent combat experiences, I could share his feelings of despair, but I could never take such drastic action.

Finally, my orders came through to report to the 19th Military History Detachment in Bearcat. Since the company was out on an operation with the mobile riverine force deep in the Mekong Delta, I was unable to say goodbye to my friends. Besides what could I say to them except that I would try to arrange transfers for them if it came within my power. Several times I tried to persuade them to apply for positions outside of the infantry with limited success. I was also aware that my transfer had altered my chances of survival from nearly zero to 95 percent. My career as a straight-leg infantryman had come to an end and none too soon for me.

Combat does strange things to people. Throughout training back in the States, I was one of the least motivated soldiers in my outfit. My doubts about American intervention in South Vietnam were part of it, but the transformation from a budding scholar to a combat soldier was difficult for me. Besides that I was probably the least athletic soldier in my battalion. Whenever there was some physically demanding exercise, I was always the last to finish.

Once in South Vietnam, however, I adjusted to combat too readily. I began to take too many chances. It would have been only a matter of time before I suffered some kind of a wound. While the loss of my buddies bothered me, it was the thought of mutilation that frightened me more than death. In three major firefights covering almost ten hours I never did see the enemy up close, but the high number of casualties in my company always let me know that the Viet Cong were around. My move to a rear-echelon unit was welcomed, but I did miss the comradery of my company. I never saw members of my old company again without some feelings of guilt. My access to division intelligence reports in my new unit allowed me to follow the fate of my old company. In a conversation with one of my buddies a few weeks later, I found out that my replacement on point was killed less than two weeks after I left the unit. He stepped on top of a Viet Cong bunker and was shot at point blank range. It could easily have been me except for my lucky transfer.

After I left my old unit, I began to think about the differences in mental attitude and how this affected the survival rate. Several of my buddies were fatalistic about not surviving the war. In almost every instance, they were right. I had lengthy conversations with each of them and I emphasized that they were going to make it. They were even more adamant that they would not. In contrast, I tried every way possible to insure that I would return home. Early in South Vietnam I decided that I had to be aggressive rather than passive. While the fatal bullet, shell, or booby-trap was always possible and survival a matter of luck, I do believe that a positive mental approach helps with survival in combat. At least it worked for me.

7

Adapting to the Rear-Echelon and the Battle of the Plain of Reeds Report

My new colleagues in the 19th Military History Detachment at Bearcat quickly noticed my relief in escaping a combat unit. I had the look of a refugee from a deserted island. My last haircut had been stateside several months before and my mustache had not been trimmed for nearly two months. Most of my social graces had been transformed by the trauma of my constant exposure to combat. I was surly and mistrustful of authority and scared of making friendships. The loss of a dozen buddies that I had trained with in the States made me reluctant to open myself up to new friends. Moreover, I had arrived in South Vietnam weighing in around 210 pounds. When I came out of the infantry, I weighed less than 145 pounds. The last time that I had been at that weight was in 8th grade in Fort Worth, Texas. It was the constant exercise of marching to and fro, and the inability to eat because of the lack of liquids that caused my loss of sixty-five pounds. Because of the shortage of water, I had developed a taste for green pineapples because of their high liquid content. A side effect of green pineapples was a bad case of diarrhea. A constant diet of C-rations and diarrhea will cause anybody to lose weight. I called it the Vietnam diet. A picture taken of me shortly after my arrival in the 19th Military History Detachment shows a lean, dark figure with a lop-sided grin beneath a mustache. The glazed look in my eye tells me that the shock of combat still remained.

A plentiful supply of good food and all the liquids that I needed soon made me feel at home in my new environment. The nightly badminton matches also helped me adjust to the unit. In high school and at the

University of Missouri–Columbia I had played competitive tennis so badminton was easy for me to pick up and I enjoyed playing it. It only took me a couple of days to learn my new duties and know that they were going to be fun and not demanding. My work schedule of seven ten hour days might be considered a hardship, but it was less time than I had been used to in the infantry. Now I actually had some free time. I considered myself in the lap of luxury, if one counted a tent, wooden floors, a canvas bed, and three warms meals a day as luxury. Nightly access to a shower was also highly appreciated. Another luxury was being able to sleep a night without having to pull security shifts.

Shortly afterwards, however, I began to experience the boredom of rear-echelon service. Whereas boredom is ever present with the combat soldier, the episodes of the terror of firefights made boredom something to be cherished. Boredom produced no such feelings among the non-combat types. Although we worked seventy hours a week, the free time promoted restlessness. To me this provides the best explanation why rear-echelon soldiers abused drugs and caused so many discipline problems. Fortunately, members of my new detachment were not into drugs, but discipline problems remained endemic. Part of the problem was the army since basic training had threatened us with going to South Vietnam as a punishment and now we were there. No punishment short of imprisonment made much of an impression on us.

An explanation of how the idea of a military history detachment originated is necessary before my activities in it can be explained. Colonel S.L.A. Marshall's research in World War II taught him the importance of after-action interviews on military performance. He had interviewed soldiers after a military engagement to reconstruct what happened to each soldier and his unit during a battle. In this way, Colonel Marshall could reconstruct what actually happened and why the engagement was successful or not. Subsequent use of this technique during the Korean War again proved beneficial for both the individual units and higher command. By this time, Marshall had been promoted to brigadier general, and he was instrumental in persuading the army to adopt the military history detachment concept. The theory was to have small detachments of specialists gather pertinent documents before they were disposed of after combat and interview participants in the engagements before the details were lost forever. To make sure that this oral testimony could be preserved comments by officers and enlisted men were recorded and the tapes sent to the Military History Office in the Pentagon. Also, why not have these same individuals gather information on the development of new tactics and the performance of new equipment? Their reports could be studied by experts at the Pentagon and help them understand what was happening on the ground. The idea was excellent, and a number of military history detachments were formed in South Vietnam.

To insure that unbiased reports were transmitted to the Department of Defense, the military history detachments were not placed in the normal army chain of command. The command structure placed the commander of the detachment responsible only to the commander of the Military History Office of the Department of Defense in Washington, D.C. Sometimes this command structure caused difficulties within a larger unit, because a higher-ranking officer would try to pull rank to suppress

Specialist Schumacher was a member of the Combat Art Team in July 1968.

something unpleasant. Such incidents happened several times during my stay in the 19th Military History Detachment, but these officers found that their powers to change things were limited by this command structure. Each detachment had a commanding officer, normally a major, a lieutenant, a staff sergeant, and at least two enlisted men, possibly more. Each detachment attached to a division differed slightly in size and in approach. My detachment also had a combat art team.

The combat art team was a popular addition to the 19th Military History Detachment. The mission of the combat art team was to go out into the field and gather impressions of the 9th Infantry Division's operations. These impressions, often in the form of photographs, were to provide the inspiration for the artists to paint combat art. The concept for this program had been borrowed from a similar type program in the German army in World War II. Pictures of German soldiers in action or in heroic poses made for good propaganda. These artworks had been seized by the U.S. Army after the war and released back to the German government only in the early 1970s. In South Vietnam, high-ranking officers

Specialist Patlan was a member of the Combat Art Team in July 1968.

Photographs used by the Combat Art Team for ideas for their paintings.

often appeared in the detachment to look at the paintings and drawings, and they would suggest other topics to paint. The combat art team had just published a collection of their works, which had been sponsored by the division.

The detachment's combat art team consisted of five artists of varying artistic abilities. Since I am not an art critic, it was not my position to judge their abilities. These positions in the combat art team were highly coveted, especially by those in harm's way in the rice paddies of the Mekong Delta. Applications poured in for consideration, but the detachment commander was reluctant to consider but a few of the candidates. It was amusing to see military officers trying to judge the artistic merits of a candidate's portfolio.

The personnel of the 19th Military History Detachment was a curious mix. The commander was a short, stocky, sandy-haired career intelligence officer who felt lost as the commander of the military history detachment. He had a solid knowledge of military history, but he specialized in distrusting the motives of all members of his unit. Perhaps this was the consequence of his long experience in military intelligence units. Somehow, the major had become stuck in this motley unit the mission of which he had mixed feelings about but some sympathy. He had an undergraduate degree from the University of Virginia where he had obtained an ROTC commission. Much of his energy in the early summer of 1968 was spent finding a way to transfer back to a military intelligence unit.

The detachment's lieutenant was a quiet, sad-faced, poker-playing fiend from Chicago, Illinois. His father was a professional gambler, and the lieutenant had inherited his father's love of poker. His appearance was deceiving as I have never seen anyone that appeared so much like a

Top: Painting by Shumacher of an American combat soldier. *Bottom:* Painting by Specialist Rohrbach, another member of the Combat Art Team.

Painting by Patlan of an American soldier in combat.

sucker with his soft manners and slow deliberate speech, but his poker playing associates soon learned that his appearance and manners hid the soul
of a card shark. He was rumored to have won several thousand dollars off
of a newspaper correspondent during R&R (rest and relaxation leave) in
Japan. I know for a fact that he accumulated large sums of money from
gambling because I sent to his address in Chicago two hundred dollars
a month in exchange for my receiving five dollars. Since I was always broke,
this money came in handy. Two hundred dollars was the maximum
that could be sent back to the States in a month. The lieutenant's role
in the detachment was to oversee the output of the military history and
combat art teams, but he was always more successful at the nightly gambling tables. He never placed any pressure on anyone to play with him,
but if you were willing, he would take your money. He asked me only
once if I played poker. Since I never had any money, I was not interested.
His interest in military history was marginal at best, but he was a good
sport about it.

1st Lieutenant Kutscheid was in charge of the Combat Art Team and the Military History Section in the 19th Military History Detachment.

The staffing sergeant was a 300-pound plus dynamo of secretarial and administrative efficiency. My presence in the detachment was the result of his contacts in division personnel. A personnel sergeant owed him a favor so Sgt. Stevens traded a case of beer for documents changing my military occupational specialty from infantryman to clerk-typist. This action was a court-martial offense, but obviously, it had been done before. Since a case of beer cost around $2.50 at the base PX, I have surmised since then that my life was worth no more than $2.50 in 1968 dollars. Inflation since then has increased the value of a case of beer, but it is still a sharp realization about the value one can put on a life. He was highly efficient, and his typing was a wonder to behold.

The two members of the military history section of the detachment at the time that I joined it both talked better performances than they produced. An ongoing problem at the time of my arrival in the detachment was that nothing of lasting value was coming out of the military history wing. The major obviously thought the same, because he brought me into the detachment to do something about this. Since my presence constituted a threat to both the incumbents, they were rather cool towards me. Both of them had only a short time to go before they returned to the States so I generally ignored them.

Sergeant Stevens was the staff sergeant at the Military History Detachment and a superb typist.

My adjustment to the new unit was barely completed when news came to the detachment of a major engagement by the division in the Mekong Delta. The major returned, excited, from a division briefing at Bearcat on June 3. He ordered me to proceed immediately to the 9th Infantry Division's new base camp at Dong Tam and find out all available information on the just completed Battle of the Plain of Reeds. One of the veteran sergeants was to accompany me and show me the ends and outs of the trade. He proved to be of little use except to arrange transportation. My military rank at this time was Specialist E-4, which had no impact at all in the military hierarchy. The major realized this and made

Major Cook congratulating Sergeant Cooke on his leaving South Vietnam in July 1968.

me an acting jack, sergeant E-5. Rank may have its privileges, but at the level of E-5, the privileges were few indeed. It did allow me access to the NCO club, but I managed to avoid that privilege. After a short briefing by an officer at Bearcat on conditions at Dong Tam, I climbed aboard a copter for a ride to Dong Tam. The flight from Bearcat to Dong Tam took about 45 minutes, but the realization that for once I would not end the copter trip in a rice paddy with my rifle looking for trouble made the trip enjoyable.

Dong Tam was shortly to become the division headquarters for the 9th Infantry Division, replacing the one at Bearcat. In June 1968, it was

Vietnamese boy on his water buffalo in the rice paddies of Dinh Tuong Province near the 9th Infantry Division's base camp at Dong Tam.

still under construction in Dinh Truong Province. Dinh Truong Province was heavily controlled by the Viet Cong. In his book *Sharpening the Edge* General Ewell described the reasons for the choice of Dong Tam for division's operations in the Mekong Delta, but the essential one was that the base camp had to be deep within Viet Cong territory to allow maximum disruption of enemy operations. At the time, any travel to Dong Tam except by air was risky. The roads to and from Dong Tam ran through Viet Cong controlled territory and ambushes were common.

After arriving at Dong Tam around midday, I wandered around until I finally ended up at 1st Brigade Headquarters. Since a low ranking enlisted man had little clout at brigade headquarters, I received the customary lack of interest and the typical buck-passing by people who believed that they were too busy to be bothered. I soon learned that the priority of my mission to the brigade rivaled that of the nightly shit burning details. Finally, I found a jeep to ride out in to the brigade's field headquarters — the infamous Pink Palace. The Pink Palace was a term of derision describing a large house alongside Highway QL4. It received the name Pink Palace because it had been painted pink. As an isolated target in the middle of Viet Cong controlled territory, it stood as a prominent target for nightly mortar attacks. Only constant night patrolling by several companies kept

Pink Palace, headquarters of the 1st Brigade of the 9th Infantry Division during the Battle of the Plain of Reeds.

the Pink Palace secure and in one piece. The setup reminded me of a small medieval castle complete with walls and a keep.

It was at the Pink Palace that the plans for the Battle of the Plain of Reeds had originated. Colonel Emerson, codename "Gunfighter," was the brigade commander. Colonel Emerson had the mannerisms of General George Patton without the mystique. A number of commanders in South Vietnam exhibited extreme macho tendencies, and he was one of them. His appearance, however, was against him, because he looked more like an armed clerk-typist than a field leader. Since no one paid any attention to my presence, I wandered around the compound with my tape recorder, camera, rifle, and flak jacket asking questions about the recent operation. This low profile turned out to be an advantage, because I was not considered important enough for the typical snow job intended for outsiders. Most officers above the rank of captain would have been insulted to have to charm a mere sergeant. Everyone was willing to talk except for those enlisted men too spaced out on alcohol or drugs.

The Battle of the Plain of Reeds seems to have been forgotten in the aftermath of the ending of the Vietnam War, but at the time, it was seen by U.S. Army Command as a model for airmobile operations. While my

A closer view of the Pink Palace.

final report is available in its entirety in Appendix C, I believe some background is needed to understand the battle. The engagement took place in a marshy plains east-southeast of Saigon in an area which had long been a staging grounds for Viet Cong operations. This area had served the enemy well as a place for base camps complete with hospitals, POW camps, ammo dumps, training camps, and staging areas. Word had come through intelligence sources that more Viet Cong activity than usual was present in the Plain of Reeds.

The Plain of Reeds had long had the reputation that no U.S. or ARVN unit ventured into it unless that unit was willing for a major engagement with North Vietnamese regulars or main force Viet Cong. Since the entry of the 9th Infantry Division into the Mekong Delta, the level of enemy activity had lowered in the key provinces of Long An and Dinh Truong. Constant patrolling combined with search and destroy operations had caused these provinces to appear on the surface to be pacified, but the major staging areas of the Rung Sat Special Zone and the Plain of Reeds were still untouched. Of the two, the Plain of Reeds was the more tempting target for a large-scale American operation. Another significant factor was the Plains of Reeds bordered on Cambodia and the infamous Parrot's

Picture from the air of the waterways in the Plain of Reeds where the Battle of the Plain of Reeds took place in June 1968.

Beak. Control of this area had the possibility of closing off this avenue of supply for Viet Cong operations in the Mekong Delta. Intelligence sources also indicated that the May Offensive against Saigon had received its supplies through the Plain of Reeds. The decision was made at the division level to conduct a three-day brigade level operation in the Plain of Reeds. First Brigade received this assignment.

Initial results from insertion on May 31, 1968, produced disappointing returns. After locating artillery support bases in the northern section of the Plain of Reeds to provide artillery support, units were landed at spots where intelligence suspected enemy activity. One location after the other proved to be dry holes. The first day of operations had little to show for it. Early the next day a people sniffing team located an area where there was evidence of recent occupation by a large body of troops.

The people sniffing technique was a new innovation introduced by the army in South Vietnam. A device was mounted to a UH-1 helicopter and connected by a flexible hose to a air scoop mounted to the underside of the aircraft. This device sampled air passing through it for the presence of carbon and ammonia emitted by man and other sources. It also sampled compound sigma, which was an emission peculiar solely to man. Readings on a graduated dial could indicate the presence of personnel in an area. The only problem was that the emission could last for several hours, making reports on human activity less than totally reliable. To be certain infantry troops had to be inserted to check out the findings.

Because of this characteristic, the enemy had disappeared before American troops could make contact. Now brigade leadership knew that a major enemy unit was nearby. On June 1, elements of the 1st Brigade made contact with at least a Viet Cong battalion. A running battle ensued with casualties on both sides. After losing contact during the night, American infantry units were inserted in various places on June 2. These Viet Cong forces were finally found near a canal on the southern edge of the Plain of Reeds on June 3. How the brigade finally made initial contact turned into a source of dispute between the involved units and the battalion commander, Lieutenant Colonel Leggett, with me in the middle.

Most of the disagreement concerned the use of the airmobile tactic of the eagle flight. The age-old difficulty of making contact with a guerrilla force in low-intensity warfare except on its own terms had led the 9th Infantry Division to adopt the tactic of dropping small units close to suspected enemy concentrations in order to initiate contact. Units might be inserted as many as five or six times a day. Once contact would be established with the enemy then reinforcements were to be airlifted to surround and annihilate the enemy. A morale problem existed among the infantry units, because the small unit which initially landed risked the danger of being wiped out before reinforcements arrived. Sometimes the necessary air transportation was not available at that particular time. Availability of air assets was always a problem. Any number of things can go wrong to delay reinforcements, which can produce dire consequences for the committed unit.

What happened on June 3 was that Company A, 2nd Battalion, 39th Infantry, landed approximately 100 meters from a woodline to conduct a sweep towards a second woodline along a canal. Almost as soon as the company landed, it became pinned down by heavy automatic weapons fire. During the next several hours, this unit was trapped in an open rice paddy while machine guns and snipers slowly picked off the men one by one. The few survivors were bitter about the whole affair and all of them complained about constantly having their company inserted in landing zones almost on top of suspected Viet Cong enemy positions. This criticism was repeated by others in different units, including by several junior grade officers. My attitude towards these remarks was that these feelings should be reported in my analysis of the battle. There was an issue of resupply the previous night with some soldiers not receiving a resupply of water.

My inclusion of these critical remarks had severe repercussions several months later. A new first lieutenant had entered the detachment in the meantime. He read my preliminary analysis and several points in it bothered him. His response was to submit my preliminary version to the lieutenant colonel in command of the 1st Brigade for review. Several days later in early September 1968, the first lieutenant and I went to see the lieutenant colonel and the reception was openly hostile. After bracing us at attention, he preceded to chew out the lieutenant for permitting my mustache to exceed division guidelines. A few more cutting remarks about my general appearance to show who was boss followed Then the lieutenant colonel preceded to point out what he considered errors in the report. It became apparent that as soon as he had received the report, the lieutenant colonel had ordered a copter and traced troop movements for all three days. His reward was that he discovered that I had misinterpreted the direction in which the Viet Cong had moved on the second day. This was good information improving the accuracy of the final report. I lacked the resources to check the accuracy of my report so his input was valuable. He was more incensed, however, about the criticism of troops landing too close to possible enemy locations. Finally, he insisted that the units had been resupplied with food, ammunition and water on the night of June 2. After thanking him for his contributions, we left his office.

The final report included his new information and his disclaimers about landing troops too close to the enemy in the sense of fair play. I also included his remarks on resupply. As far as I am aware, he never saw the final version. My judgment at the time was that the lieutenant colonel believed this report might hurt his military career, but any criticism by a mere sergeant in an obscure report headed for the Military History Section of the Department of Defense would probably not be too damaging. His attitude, however, struck me as reflective of one of the problems of higher-ranking officers in South Vietnam. It was the so-called "Copter in the Sky" syndrome.

One of the benefits of airmobile operations was that higher-ranking commanders had copters at their disposal to direct operations from the air. While this type of contact may have been a boon to their command and control functions, it proved to be a curse to the troops on the ground. What must have seemed like a short distance to the commander comfortable in the air often turned into a nightmare of sloughing through mud and water, and other types of rough terrain. Occasionally, soldiers would get so frustrated that they would shoot at the command copters. This type of frustration appeared among the reactions of survivors of the Battle of the Plain of Reeds.

A clear dichotomy of views between the participants in the battle appeared early in the interviews. Officers at and above the rank of captain were confident that the battle had been a rousing success. Others, including the lieutenants and lower ranking enlisted men, were less sure. Morale was nowhere as high as it was described in my report. My morale statement was another compromise insisted upon by the lieutenant colonel. While troops were rotated back to the Pink Palace after operations, casualties and wastage from jungle rot and malaria served as a depressant. Drugs and alcohol were resorted to by some soldiers during their down time. I witnessed some of this activity during my stay with several of the units.

Some of the higher-ranking officers came in for some criticism by the enlisted men. Another criticism was unreasonable orders. Company A, 2nd Battalion, 60th Infantry, had been airlifted in during the late afternoon to block off one of the approaches of possible enemy escape. The battalion's executive officer assumed control of these blocking troops, Task Force Joseph, and he ordered a night assault on the canal woodline. His orders were simply ignored by everyone. None of the troops moved out and the assault never took place. My conversations with junior grade officers and the enlisted men indicated that the men believed that the proposed assault would have been foolish and suicidal. The issue of refusal to follow a direct order faded away, because nobody wanted to press the issue.

My final problem in writing the Plain of Reeds report concerned the number of casualties. Exaggeration of enemy body count numbers was a common problem in South Vietnam. The 9th Infantry Division earned a dubious reputation for general body count figures. Rumor had it that General Ewell, the division commander, had approved this policy. Word had filtered down that rewards and punishments would be predicated on body count totals. An elaborate charade existed or otherwise military careers could be ruined by failure to compile large enemy body counts. Standard operating procedure (SOP) was one Viet Cong weapon counted for two killed in action (KIAs), and each piece of a body meant a separate KIA. Naturally these practices reflected well on the division and its commanders, but those unsophisticated souls with their computer in Washington, D.C., should have recognized the fact — much as the German air command did in the Battle of Britain — that towards the end the potential enemy force had been annihilated several times over.

While I had expected trouble over enemy casualties, I was surprised when a problem developed over American casualties. The official count was 12 KIA and 24 KIA for June 1 and June 3 respectively, but when I visited the individual units the combined totals of casualties nearly doubled that of the official count — 19 KIA and 40 KIA respectively. Unable to reconcile the totals through official or unofficial channels, I put both figures in my final report.

During my stay at the Pink Palace, I took the opportunity to go out on a psychological operation with the psyops team of the 1st Brigade. On the evening of June 8, I joined the team and we moved to a village near the Pink Palace. The lieutenant in charge of the team knew little about psychological operations and his assistants knew less. They could, however, run a movie projector. Three movies were shown on alternate nights. Of the three movies for this night Walt Disney's movie showing Snow White and the Seven Dwarfs declaring war on mosquitoes and malaria was the most popular. The other movies emphasized the dangers and hardships of serving with the Viet Cong. While I could not tell the villagers' opinions of these last two movies, they appeared to like the combat scenes. These movies were fun for the Vietnamese, but it was impossible to gauge the effectiveness of them as part of a psychological operation. It should be noted that the division devoted almost no resources to psyops operations in comparison to the resources available to destroy Viet Cong units. It was also dangerous to operate at night on these types of operations. I carried a Stein automatic pistol with only two clips that night so I was glad that the Viet Cong left us alone.

Later, I ran across a 9th Infantry Division report on a specialized psychological operation that it had experimented with before my unit's arrival in South Vietnam. It was the Intimate Psychological Warfare operation. In this plan (INPSYWAR) a unit of the 9th Infantry Division would target an area and began a massive bombardment. This bombardment would be alternated with an appeal to the Viet Cong to surrender by using a small, portable, public address system to convince them of the benefits of surrendering to the South Vietnamese government. This tactic also used the Recondo Checkerboard tactical concept that is also explained in the report (see Appendix D). Evidently this type of psychological warfare had been found lacking because I never heard of any such operation during my ten-month stay in South Vietnam. It had obviously worked up north with the 101st Airborne, but this situation was different in the Mekong Delta.

It was during my stay at the Pink Palace that I experienced one of those embarrassing moments in life. Not unlike any other compounds, the

toilet facilities were in the open at the Pink Palace. The urinals were bar-
rels planted in the ground. I was using one of these urinals when a copter
arrived discharging Vicky Lawrence and another starlet. There was nothing for me to do but finish what I was doing and wave at them as they
passed by. I have no idea what the officer in charge told them, but it was
certainly an embarrassing moment for me.

It was while still had the Pink Palace that news arrived of the assassination of Robert Kennedy. This assassination shook my unit up coming
so soon after the death of Martin Luther King. Although I had never been
much of a fan of Robert Kennedy, my feeling at that time was that it was
a tragic waste of a good man. Many of us in South Vietnam wondered
what we were fighting for if there was so much chaos in the United States.
I was so disgusted that I vented my feelings in a letter to my wife.

8

Back at Bearcat and the Thai Presidential Award

Now that my material on the Battle of the Plain of Reeds had been gathered my return to Bearcat was necessary to prepare the report and resume my duties in the detachment. One of my new assignments in the detachment was to serve as a driver for the detachment's commander. The major arranged time for me to gain a military driver's license. This duty meant several trips into Saigon. The traffic and excitement gave me a migraine headache on my first trip to Saigon, because as the major put it, "The Vietnamese drive like they have Buddha on their side." On one of these trips, I saw the huge sewer pipes where the refugees from the may Battle of Saigon were living. I could not resist taking a picture of a family living in a large sewer pipe. On another trip, I became acquainted with two of the cutest little con artists — two girls, age 11 and 9, who could talk a saint into hell.

My most difficult trip to Saigon, however, was the time the major took time to reprimand two military police for driving too fast. Those MPs followed me for hours, checking on my driving and looking for an excuse to give me a ticket. Fortunately, the MPs found no excuses because the ticket would have been on my record, not on the major's record.

In late June, I received news about my old company's engagement in which a couple of friends of mine had been seriously wounded. They had suffered severe head wounds in a firefight near Ben Luc. At this time, most of the casualties in the 9th Infantry Division had been head injuries. The difficult thing about this type of injury is that it is both painful and difficult to control the bleeding. Nobody seemed at the time to know how either of them was recovering from their wounds, and I never found out their fate. They were both outstanding young men and good soldiers. One was

Company C, 6th Battalion, 31st Infantry en route to another base camp in June 1968.

married with a six-month-old child. I remember talking with him back at Fort Lewis and how often he expressed his feelings that he had no desire to come to South Vietnam and save the world for LBJ.

My next assignment in July was to research and write a draft for a presidential unit citation for the Royal Thai Volunteer Regiment — the Queen's Cobras. This regiment had been attached to the 9th Infantry Division at Bearcat. It had almost finished its one-year tour of duty in South Vietnam and orders had been issued for the regiment to return to Thailand. Rumor had it that the suggestion for this award had come to General Ewell from General Abrams. A hint from the commander of U.S. military forces in South Vietnam had the force of law. This award was also forthcoming because the relationship between the Americans and the Thais was excellent. The Thai regiment was an all-volunteer unit whose term of service ended when the regiment returned to Thailand.

Although the Queen's Cobras were considered one of the elite regiments of the Thai Army, a problem surfaced immediately because this regiment had been deployed in a relatively safe district. The Thai regiment had been in only one significant engagement during its tour in South Vietnam. After studying the preliminary details, I reached the conclusion that politics more than battle honors was involved in the decision to make this award. A larger Thai contingent, the Black Panthers, was in the process of recruitment and training for its deployment in South Vietnam. Nothing was to be done to discourage Thai military involvement and especially that deployment.

Lieutenant Colonel Chawalit, 1st Lieutenant Kutscheid, and myself (writing) are shown at work on the Thai Presidential Unit Citation Award on July 23, 1968.

These political concerns were restraints in my working on the Thai's presidential unit citation with much enthusiasm. Nevertheless, I had no choice but to write the report justifying the award. The lieutenant and I had conversations with Colonel Sanan, commander of the Queen's Cobras, and Lieutenant Colonel Chawalit, deputy commander, about an engagement during the night of December 20 and 21, 1967, when a Viet Cong force estimated at around 500 attacked 180 Thais near Phouc Tho in Bien Hoa Province. Hand to hand fighting resulted in 86 Viet Cong KIAs as compared to Thai losses of 4 KIA and 8 WIA. From the beginning, a series of misunderstandings complicated the writing of the narrative portion of the citation. Lieutenant Colonel Chawalit was always cheerful and cooperative, but anytime I brought up a point of interpretation or presented my view on the events he never argued the point. Only by specific questions on seemingly minor points did he admit that the facts differed between my narrative and what happened. He was afraid that I would lose face, but my only objective was to get the facts correct. This difference in philosophy between the two of us was never solved to my satisfaction. I found it hard to comprehend why it was important that a low ranking American soldier had to save face. Notwithstanding these difficulties my narrative was submitted along with a recommendation for a presidential unit citation for the Queen's Cobras. The granting of this citation made everybody happy, especially the Thais. My dealings with the Thais extended to contact with soldiers in several of their platoons. Thai enlisted men were eager to please and associate with American soldiers. Friendships sprung up between some of us. Several times members of my detachment would go over and visit with the Thais. They would prepare food for us, but they toned down the spices because they knew our systems could not handle such spicy food.

During one of these sessions, I had a lengthy conversation with one of the Thais, Corporal Yoodhana. He was around 22 years of age in 1968

Lieutenant Goldfarb was Lieutenant Kutscheid's replacement.

with four years in the army. His father was a peasant from around Bangkok. Before entering the army, Yoodhana had gone to school for ten years (four years elementary and six years high school). On joining the army, he had to pass rigorous physical and mental tests to get into the 21st Regiment Queen's Guard. After passing these tests, Yoodhana spent a year at an infantry school. He then volunteered for duty in Vietnam. The Thai pay scale is $45 a month for private first class (PFC), $60 for corporal, $70 for sergeant, and officers begin at $100. The Thais told us that they could live well on this pay scale, but they also admitted that inflation had become increasingly bad in the last couple of years. While most of the Thais were Buddhists, I ran into several who were Catholics. They were looking forward to returning to Thailand and rejoining their regiments. Yoodhana said that he did not like or trust the Vietnamese. He also stated that he might volunteer to come back to South Vietnam sometime if another unit was to be organized to fight there.

In the middle of my dealing with the Thais in early August an incident between an American unit and the Queen's Cobras threatened this good relationship. A unit of the 2nd Battalion, 47th Infantry (Mechanized) fired on and killed two Thais of the 1st Company of the Queen's Cobras. Despite the fact that it was dark, the Thais did not fire back. The Thai officers and men were upset not so much about the incident as the fact that the leadership of the 2nd Battalion, 47th Infantry (Mechanized) tried to evade responsibility. These types of incidents can cloud relationships between allies, but cooler heads soon prevailed in this case.

What helped reestablish good relations between the Americans and the Thais were the feelings of mutual respect and confidence. This lack of mutual respect and confidence was missing between the U.S. military and the Vietnamese. Part of the problem with the Vietnamese was ARVN units had inferior weapons. It was past time in 1968 for the ARVN forces to be armed with our most modern weapons. The Thais had as good of weapons as the U.S. Army. They do not, however, carry the same ammo load that American troops carry. Thais carry only seven magazines of eighteen rounds each as a standard load in comparison to the ten magazines of eighteen rounds each for American infantryman.

During an interlude in working on my narrative for the Thais, I spent a day interviewing personnel of the Special Forces Camp at My Phuoc Tay about their role in the Battle of the Plain of Reeds. After covering their activities as a blocking force on June 3, they began to talk to me about their operations in Dinh Tuong Province. They informed me that they were making little progress in Dinh Tuong Province, because of the protection given to the Viet Cong by South Vietnamese government officials. The Viet Cong controlled Dinh Tuong Province because every time American or ARVN troops moved into the area called the Triangle they could expect Viet Cong contact. To challenge this control a plan was devised to move the dependents of the Viet Cong from an area 3,500 meters east of My Phuoc Tay, the Triangle, to a new settlement camp outside the Special Forces camp. Approval and funds had been obtained through army channels, but the necessary approval was not forthcoming from the Vietnamese province chief. Consequently, the plan was stillborn much to the unhappiness of the Special Forces advisors. Compounding their bitterness was the fact that the Battle of the Plain of Reeds had taken place in the Triangle. My conversations with the Special Forces advisors suggested that they believed that they were being underutilized in the war.

Regular army involvement since 1967 had superceded Special Forces activity, and they had become second-class citizens in the war effort.

A friend gave me some information about the chaplain that I met at Firebase Mohawk on June 12. His name was Major Evangelisto. He was one of the most unforgettable characters that I ran across in South Vietnam. He was a massive man with a magnificent beer belly covered by a mass of thick curly hair. Evangelisto was a gruff man, and he considered himself the friend of the enlisted man. He tolerated officers as a necessary evil. His language was as crude as his manners. He was also extremely militant, but the enlisted men loved him. No church other than the Catholic Church would have tolerated his eccentricities.

Major General Julian Ewell, commander of the 9th Infantry Division, at an award ceremony at Dong Tam Base Camp in the summer of 1968.

One of the burdensome tasks assigned to the military detachments in South Vietnam was to compile a report on lessons learned and a progress report from the division. This was the infamous Operational Report of Lessons Learned (ORLL). Every three months, the army required an ORLL. Information would come to us from all segments of the division, and our job was to put it together and send it back up the chain of command. Members of the detachment had to drop everything and spend two solid weeks working on it day and night. Most often, I pulled the night shift, working all night. It was hell for those weeks as information for the ORLL dribbled in late and sometimes the information was incomplete. These ORLL would ultimately make it back to the Pentagon so the high command of the 9th Infantry Division was always nervous about them. These reports helped make or break military careers.

News reached Bearcat that the Viet Cong had been shooting up our helicopters at an accelerating rate. It became commonplace for them to shoot at our command and control copters. The division lost a brigade commander, Lieutenant Colonel Van Duesen, in early July. His copter crashed into a river after receiving heavy ground fire. He was the son-in-law of General Westmoreland. Several other commanders had their copters badly damaged by similar type ground fire. This tactic was unsettling, because it neutralized the commander's ability to order troop insertions. It also made high-ranking officers nervous as their casualty rates increased.

Despite a lull in enemy operations, intelligence reports in late July indicated that the Viet Cong were still active in the countryside. Several intelligence sources mentioned the possibility of an attack on Tan An. Nothing in these intelligence reports hinted about any operations directed at about Saigon. Saigon appeared to be normal to a casual observer. Saigon had been escaping Viet Cong attention except for a few 122mm rockets landing there in mid–July. Despite the apparent lull in enemy activity, many U.S. personnel felt that Saigon was not safe for Americans.

Several of the division's intelligence reports were intriguing and showed that the Viet Cong were in the process of rebuilding their fighting strength. One such report was on June 21, 1968.

At 1400H on 18 June 1968, an enemy soldier stated that his unit was designated the "Thai Quan" Division. At 0300H on 20 June 1968, an enemy soldier stated that his unit was designated the "Thai Quan" Division. He also stated that most of the division was composed of men between the ages of 18 and 26 years from the Thai Binh Province, North Vietnam. He also stated that his division had been transported by airplanes from North Vietnam into Cambodia about 2 months ago and had moved north. He said that his commanders had stated that they were going to move into the Khe Sanh area. About a month ago, the division started heading south and had been continually on the march up until the present. He also states that he had been a student abroad in France and had been called back to fulfill his military obligation. An enemy soldier also stated that political officers of his unit had told them that they were reinforcements for units attacking Saigon. The political officers had stated that the annihilation of Saigon was the only way to end the war in Vietnam. The enemy soldier stated that he personally felt that they would fail in taking Saigon.

The capture of Captain Pham Trong, a political officer, in July 1968 was an intelligence coup because of his lengthy history first in the Viet Minh and then in the Viet Cong.

Pham Trong, Captain/Political Officer, 2nd Infantry Battalion, joined the Viet Cong village forces in April 1950 and worked in the public information section of the Xuan Phuoc (V) until 1952 when he joined the Regular VC forces and was assigned as a commo section messenger of the 84th Regiment, 5th Region of Binh Dinh Province. He held this position for 3 months when he was promoted to platoon leader of Recon and Commo Platoon of 84th Regiment Headquarters. He remained at this position until July 1954 when he was taken to North Vietnam for training in tactics and strategy. He had 1½ years of training at Son Tay Province North Vietnam at the Officer Training School. Upon completion of his training he remained at the school as the political officer of a company of officer candidates until December 1963. He was then assigned to the 50th North Vietnamese Army Regiment in the Do Son area, Hai Phong Province as political officer of the 4th Company, 7th Battalion. He remained in this position until February 1964 when he attended a one month course in the South Vietnam political and economical situation. From March 1964 to June 1964, he awaited orders to infiltrate to South Vietnam. In June 1964 he was led along the Truong Son Mountains with 100 cadremen who had been in North Vietnam for training. The trip took until approximately November 1964 when the group reached Tay Ninh Province. He stayed in Tay Ninh until April 1965 at a replacement center for cadremen. He was then assigned to the 165th Regiment Training Headquarters in the jungles of Tay Ninh as political officer of the 6th Battalion (AKA 5th Battalion) until November 1965, when the 6th Battalion was transferred to Nha Be District. He was reassigned to the propaganda and education section of the Nha Be District. He remained there until November 1967. He had a one-month leave at Nha Be and at the end of December 1967 he was assigned to the 2nd Independent Battalion Long An as Battalion Political Officer. The Battalion was located at this time in Tan Phuoc Village, Tan Tru District. In January 1968 he contracted malaria and stayed in a hospital in Binh Phuoc District, Tan Tru District. He was released from the hospital in late February 1968. He rejoined his Battalion in Hung Long Village after they had attacked Saigon and withdrawn with approximately 34 KIA and 95 WIA. The Battalion moved directly to Da Phuoc Village, Nha Be District where they have remained in this general vicinity until the present when they moved to the vicinity of Tan Phuoc Tay Village, Tan Tru District. The prisoner of war stated that his Battalion moves daily and that he had left the Battalion 2 days ago to attend a meeting at Thuan Battalion commander on 7 July. The strength of the Battalion should be 450 but the present strength is 80 men. The Battalion has been promised replacements but has not received any. The Battalion is currently in a rest period. The Battalion supplies by local purchases and ammo is supplied by local forces where the Battalion happens to be located.

Phan Trong stated (9 July 1968) that the North Vietnamese Army troops had not been prohibited from reading psychological warfare leaflets or listening to loudspeaker broadcasts. Some of the troops had been affected by them and had changed their way of thinking and their morale was lowered. The leaflets should be written in simplified sentences and targeted at family relationships or family feelings since the NVA are not authorized passes or leaves. The leaflets should hit hard at the VC's shortage of medicine and supplies and build up airstrikes because the troops are already scared of airstrikes. The prisoner of war stated that the troops did not understand the Chieu Hoi Program and were afraid to defect. The troops believed that a person that defected received the worst treatment possible. This intelligence report has special significance to me because my former company had been in the Da Phoeuc area at the same time as the prisoner. It explained that we were fighting North Vietnamese regulars instead of main or local force Viet Cong. At the time of the battle, both sides were equally matched with 80 to 90 combatants on each side.

Towards the middle of July, it became apparent that the 19th Military History Detachment was going to be one of the last units transferred from Bearcat to Dong Tam. Everything had to be packed and ready to be moved on twenty-four hours notice. Such sudden notification was usual so that the Viet Cong could not time a departure for ambush. Our standard of living began to drop as more units disappeared. Several times Major Cook drafted me to drive him to Saigon. These daylong trips allowed me to become acquainted with city life in Saigon. Saigon was off-limits to American personnel unless stationed there or on a mission. Most of the time during my stay in Saigon my movements were restricted, but once I was able to eat at the Continental Hotel, famous from Graham Greene's novel *The Quiet American*. I had Chateaubriand and it was excellent. On another occasion I spent some time in a couple of bars on Tu Do Street. Saigon street life was exciting, and the young Vietnamese women were operators. They could talk you out of anything. On one of my trips, I had a camera stolen, and on another occasion, my back pocket with my billfold was picked. Despite these difficulties, I enjoyed these frequent trips into Saigon. These trips ceased abruptly when the detachment finally moved to Dong Tam.

In the midst of the uncertainty, my free time was devoted to a new hobby: photography. Shortly before one of the sergeants returned to the States, I bought his Petri FT camera for $40. Although the Petri was not in the same league as a Nikon or Leica, it was good enough for a novice like me. For the remainder of my tour in South Vietnam, I snapped pictures until I filled five albums with photos. Even having my Petri stolen in Saigon did not prevent me from acquiring another Petri.

Our lieutenant pulled all the strings possible to leave South Vietnam before the detachment's move to Dong Tam. He did not want to risk going down to Dong Tam because it was in a less secured area. I cannot believe that he graduated from Infantry OCS and then became a tactical officer there. He was so different from my tactical officer at Ft. Benning.

A new first lieutenant came in late July to apply for the open position with the detachment. His combat experience was as an officer with Company C, 2nd Battalion, 39th Infantry. He arrived in country a few days after the Battle of the Plain of Reeds in early June. Unlike his predecessor, the lieutenant had two years work on a master's degree in history. His availability was assured because he had a physical profile. In an operation in the Plain of Reeds, his copter changed directions suddenly, reacting to ground fire, and he fell nearly ten feet to the ground. His injuries included a bad shoulder and two fingers on his left hand paralyzed.

From my conversation with the lieutenant I learned that he knew my old basic training drill instructor — Sergeant Williams. I remembered Sergeant Williams vividly from Fort Dix basic training because he was the most popular instructor at that base. Most of the African American drill sergeants had been stationed at Fort Dix, and he was one of the best, treating all of us equally. Williams was an outstanding NCO in the lieutenant's company. The battalion wanted to give him a direct commission, but he had only an 8th grade education. He had three silver stars before being killed in combat later in the year. What a waste of a good soldier!

Shortly before the detachment left for Dong Tam, the major left to join an intelligence unit. For a couple of days, it appeared that new lieutenant in the detachment might be the new commander. The major, however, had reservations about him so the major lobbied headquarters for a senior officer to replace him. A new major was appointed to command the 19th Military History Detachment on August 9. He was by training an artillery officer, who by a perverse stroke of luck ended up commanding our unit. While he had a B.A. in chemistry and a M.A. in education from

Here I model a French submachine gun from our gun collection in the detachment.

Seton Hall University, the new major knew nothing about a military history detachment. He lasted only three months until December 10, but it was a pleasure working for him during this time. The major was popular because he treated both the officers and the enlisted men equally well.

In early August came news that my old company had suffered heavy casualties landing in a hot landing zone. Eleven friends from my old company were killed. Two of the dead, Allen Pretner and Paul Savacool, had been trying to get out of Company C ever since the battalion had arrived in South Vietnam because they had felt that eventually they would be killed. I knew others who were among the dead. One of my good friends received seven wounds with the most serious wound in the jaw. Almost

Specialist Moore (right) and me burning confidential documents at Bearcat before our move to Dong Tam.

all the injuries were head injuries. The company had been on an eagle flight mission and it had landed in the middle of two Viet Cong companies. Both sides had heavy casualties with the final count of 11 KIA from my old company. The new company commander had also been wounded. I tried to persuade the major to let me cover this engagement, but he decided to send somebody else. He told me that my objectivity might be suspect in covering a combat action involving my former company. Instead, my job was to write four awards decorations for those leaving the detachment.

On the eve of the move to Dong Tam, the controversy over whether or not the Americans knew in advance about Tet reignited. The army high command claimed that he had intelligence about Tet and had reacted accordingly. I decided to research the 9th Infantry Division's intelligence summaries for the month of January 1968. With the advantage of hindsight, I noted all reports that indicated that there might be enemy activity around Tet. There was a report on January 16 that the Viet Cong's 274th Regiment had been training for an offensive during the Tet holiday. Other reports on enemy activity identified targets against cities in the Mekong Delta, but these types of reports are not at all unusual. Because so many of these intelligence reports proved to be unreliable, all of them had been examined with much skepticism. My conclusion was at the time that there were indeed hints about a possible Tet offensive, but the intelligence reports were not compelling enough for full-scale preparations to counter it.

The movement of the 19th Military History Detachment from Bearcat to Dong Tam took place on August 15, 1968. We had been on alert for the move and had destroyed confidential documents to avoid moving them. A convoy of about sixty trucks left

Bearcat on 0700 and arrived at Dong Tam on 1500. While the trip passed through areas where I had previously been in the infantry, we moved so fast that I hardly recognized the places. The trip was without incident.

9

Events at Dong Tam
and Special Assignments

The 19th Military History Detachment's first task was moving into unfinished quarters in the northern sector of Dong Tam Base Camp. This base was along the Mekong River just west of My Tho. Our first look at our new quarters made it a certainty that carpentry would be our first assigned task. Since my carpentry skills were almost nil, I tried to help in other ways by rounding up materials and transporting them to the detachment area. Within a couple of weeks, we were able to resume a regular workday.

Dong Tam was in a much less secured area than Bearcat and mortar attacks were commonplace before our unit arrived. Colonel Hunt refused to allow units to build bunkers near places of work so during mortar attacks we would have to run great distances in the open before reaching our assigned bunkers. Since our living quarters were close to the offices, these dashes in the middle of the night often produced more injuries than the mortar attacks. The lack of concern by Colonel Hunt resulted in much muttering in the ranks. Hunt was notorious for his taking unpopular stands with enlisted personnel.

It was not long after our arrival that the Viet Cong initiated us to nightly mortar attacks. On August 21, the Viet Cong harassed us with two mortar attacks: at 0300 and again at 0430. I slept through the second attack as I simply collapsed at around 0330. No one was hurt in these attacks, but much to our amusement the brigade sergeant-major had his hooch destroyed. Again, on August 24 a heavy rocket and mortar attack took place with 23 rounds landing within the Dong Tam perimeter. There was considerable damage to facilities and five engineers were among the six wounded. On August 25, the same story repeated itself with yet another

View of Dong Tam Base Camp from the air on September 30, 1968.

attack in the early morning, but this time the officer's mess was hit. To prevent further attacks perimeter patrols were intensified. The enlisted men muttered that it took a hit on the officer's mess before all out attempts were undertaken to control the mortar attacks. Thereafter, the mortar attacks became more infrequent until they started again in December.

My attitude towards these mortar attacks changed during the course of my stay at Dong Tam. At first, I was rather contemptuous of them. After all, I had been in the field in combat where it was much more dangerous. The odds of our detachment's barracks receiving a hit was rather remote but possible. Other members of the detachment, however, took these attacks seriously to the point of making mad dashes to the shelters. Gradually, I became more concerned as I would read the casualty reports the next day and note the number of wounded and killed. Towards the end of my tour, as it became more apparent that I had a chance to return to the States, my attitude changed. I became almost as panic-stricken as the rest of the members of my detachment.

Shortly after my unit arrived in Dong Tam, the division's intelligence summary on August 15, 1968, reported a Viet Cong prison camp that contained ARVN prisoners and an American soldier.

27 July 1968, the Vinh Long Viet Cong Prisoner of War Camp #6 is located along the Xa Khanh Canal, Tan Quoi Village E, Binh Long Province, on the boundary of Binh Minh District of Vinh Long Province and

Duc Ton District of Sa Dec Province, coordinates unknown. Held captive is one US prisoner and an undetermined number of ARVN prisoners. The US prisoner is described as approximately 40 years old, blond hair, medium build and tall. The camp has two buildings for the prisoners, each 50 meters by 3½ meters and 2¼ meters high. They have thatched roofs, which reach to the ground. The 2 buildings are approximately 30 meters apart. Between the two buildings, but to one side, is a concrete underground bunker, which is covered by earth and vegetation. The prisoners are taken to this bunker during airstrikes in the area. Located in the camp are numerous foxholes, which are used if there is insufficient time to reach the concrete bunker. Also inside of the camp is one latrine and one small pond. The camp is surrounded by barbed wire, booby traps, mine fields and punji pits, except for 2 paths into the camp. Outside of the barbed wire and approximately 50 meters from it, is another underground bunker where prisoners would be taken should the camp come under ground attack. This bunker is 3 meters long by 1½ meters wide and has a bamboo roof, which covered with grass and other vegetation. This roof is the only access to the bunker. The US prisoner is not hidden here, but somewhere in the immediate vicinity. Guarding the security is one VC squad inside the camp and one VC guerrilla platoon which is used for security in the surrounding area. This platoon has a strength of 34 men and is not allowed to enter the camp. The VC are armed with 2 BARs, grenade launchers and assorted small arms. Local VC cadre will occasionally come to the camp to conduct liaison with the camp officials. The US prisoner is usually accompanied by a guard when he is allowed to exercise during the day. At night he is tied to two ARVN prisoners. Source reports that during the last year one US negro soldier was executed when the camp was surrounded by allied soldiers.

This report was disturbing because American prisoners were rarely taken in the 9th Infantry Division's area of operation. I never heard the outcome of this intelligence report. It was obvious that the American prisoner of war would be killed if American troops came close to the POW camp.

My first work assignment at Dong Tam was to investigate the military potential of the air cushioned vehicle (ACV). The lieutenant and I met with the major in charge of the ACV detachment with the 9th Infantry Division on August 28. He gave us permission to go out on a training mission on the ACV. While the ACV's ability to operate on water and land makes it appear to be ideal for large-scale use in the Mekong Delta, our investigation indicated that its range, mechanical reliability, and vulnerability to even small arms fire limited its usefulness. The major allowed us assess to his After Action Report on an engagement in July in an operation in Dinh Truong's Triangle region (see Appendix D). This report is a good source on the strengths and weaknesses of the ACV in combat. It

A view of an air cushioned vehicle (ACV) that was used in combat in the Plain of Reeds.

was fun, however, to ride on the ACV and see the countryside despite its noisiness. I was less confident in the protection offered in case of a firefight. It relied on speed of 70 to 80 knots rather than armaments and armor.

Countering our reservations, the major showed himself to be an articulate advocate for the air cushioned vehicle in combat. He believed that the military potential of the ACV was unlimited. While he conceded the results of their first four months in the Mekong Delta had not been spectacular, he maintained it was because of the limited number of the ACVs deployed. Only three of them were in South Vietnam. His view was that the air cushioned vehicle concept had the same potential as the track and vehicles. And in the watery environment of the Mekong Delta, it had a chance for a better record. He envisaged a machine with the choice of wheels, tracks, or air cushions. Perhaps the major became carried away by his enthusiasm, but the concept had possibilities.

The slowdown of enemy activity in the late summer and early autumn of 1968 became so noticeable that it became of topic of speculation throughout the division. Viet Cong activity had been constant since Tet throughout the 9th Infantry Division's area of responsibility. This lack of enemy activity was so totally unexpected that the division's intelligence sources were unable to come up with an explanation except that the Viet Cong were regrouping after its heavy losses earlier. In the first six months of 1968 Viet Cong units initiated operations in nearly half of the contacts with the units of the 9th Infantry Division. From July to December 1968, almost all of the contacts were made by the division in efforts to ferret out the enemy in areas known to be controlled by the Viet Cong. This lack of Viet Cong activity was finally attributed to their heavy losses in the previous six months (See Appendix E). This was the intelligence assessment issued on August 1 noting that a large number of the Viet Cong units of regimental or battalion size were either not combat effective or only marginally combat effective.

Another explanation was that the Viet Cong were also experiencing morale problems. I read in the division's intelligence summary for September 4, 1968, that prisoners of war kept repeating stories about low morale among Viet Cong units. A captured Viet Cong captain from Dong Thap and the 1st Regiment stated that units of his regiment (261A and 267 Main Force Battalions) were unable to launch effective attacks because of casualties, desertions, and the general lack of personnel. He maintained that American successes were driving the Viet Cong further away from urban to rural areas.

The lack of enemy activity led the division to reevaluate possible enemy strength. Intelligence produced an order of battle of Viet Cong units in the 9th Infantry Division's area of operations for September 1968. Estimated strength of all enemy forces both main force and local force was 11,782 (See Appendix F). Each Viet Cong unit's estimated strength and area of operations were traced in this document. Since the enemy had at its disposal approximately the same number of fighting forces as the 9th Infantry Division, division intelligence refused to accept the explanation that the Viet Cong was too weak to launch offensive operations.

An unexpected bonus in the move to Dong Tam was running into my old college roommate. I knew from an earlier publication that he was in my division, but I doubted that I would ever see him. He was a captain in Military Intelligence at Dong Tam. Come to find out his office was in the next building over from where my detachment was located. At the University of Missouri-Columbia, he was a political science major, and he had obtained his commission through ROTC. In college, the captain was so thin that in a strong wind I sometimes thought he might blow away. When I saw him again at Dong Tam, he had gained some weight over the years, and he looked much better. I had heard a rumor that he had been relieved of his position as head of interrogation because of so-called mistreatment of prisoners, but I never believed this. In a short conversation, he did reveal that he was bitter about his treatment by the army.

At the time, he said that he was considering leaving the army as soon as possible. Since the captain was an army brat and he had always been pro-military, this was quite a change in attitude. His problem was that he had been fighting with his superiors since he had arrived in South Vietnam. He was disillusioned by the inability of his superiors to grasp the nature of the war in South Vietnam.

Soon after I had my conversations with my old college roommate, I again ran into the ways of the military. The major ordered me to avoid contact with him. The army discouraged comradery between officers and enlisted men and even taught a course in ROTC summer camp to new officers in how to avoid contact with pre-military friends. While I found this policy absurd, I could not ignore a direct order. Although the major was apologetic about his order, I still resented it. Soon afterwards, my friend left South Vietnam to head back to graduate school. He was considering attending the University of Kansas, which I found ironic because he had been such a big University of Missouri fan. It was not until years later that I learned he stayed in the army and the last I heard he had reached the rank of colonel.

There was considerable unhappiness between senior and junior officers. Officers below the rank of major led a different life from those of majors and above. The lower ranked officers shared the life and frustrations of the enlisted men. Because of sympathy between those sharing the same experiences, examples of fragging were almost non-existent in the 9th Infantry Division in 1968. Examples of captains and lieutenants being relieved because they disagreed with higher-ranking officers on tactics or policies was, however, commonplace. Too often the lower ranks felt that promotions and medals were more important to the senior officers than the welfare of the soldiers under their command. While this belief may have been unfair to the majority of senior officers, there was enough truth in this assertion to create severe morale problems for those in the ranks of captain and below.

One of the projects that the former lieutenant had left for me to finish was a report on an ambush of the 3rd Battalion, 5th cavalry convoy escort in December 1967. The convoy escort left its base camp in Phuoc Tuy Province early in the morning of December 31 and proceeded along LTL2 to pick up a convoy. Supposedly, this was a secret mission, but somehow the Viet Cong found out about it. Several miles down the road the Viet Cong planted several tank mines and set up an ambush. The combination of exploding mines and point-blank firing of RPG rounds resulted in the destruction of two tanks, five APCs, and one mortar track. U.S. losses were 7 killed in action, 3 later died of wounds, 29 wounded in action, and 3 missing in action. Later, I talked to a lieutenant at the chief of staff's office who participated in the investigation of the ambush. He told me that it took six weeks to identify some of the bodies. While Viet Cong casualties remained unknown, an intelligence report several weeks later disclosed that the Viet Cong had also experienced heavy losses. Nevertheless, it was a bad defeat, and a postmortem of the ambush revealed that some of the equipment on the tanks, especially the infrared lights, was defective. This ambush proved a high price for an equipment resupply problem.

Part of my job was to go out on operations and evaluate a unit's effectiveness. In late September, I traveled to Long Binh to interview personnel and write a report on the operations of Troop A, 3rd-17th Air Cavalry. They were based with the 199th Light Infantry Brigade. This unit had been recommended because of its outstanding combat record. My reception with this unit was as cordial as most of my contacts with infantry units were cold. I had an interview with the commander of A Troop. While he gave me complete freedom of the unit's area, he was lukewarm about my going out on a mission. He warned me that it was extremely dangerous, as his ship had been shot down only three days before. I refused to let him talk me out of going out on a mission, because it was the main purpose of this assignment. After all, how could I evaluate the unit without some experience with its operations.

The air cavalry concept was an experiment in the Vietnam War and it depended on having enough air assets. Troop A had 27 copters of which 10 were Cayuses, six were Cobra gunships, two were Bubbles, and the other nine Hueys. Several of the ships were not combat ready because of battle damage. On September 26, 3 Cayuses, 2 Cobras, and 1 Huey were being worked on for various battle damage and maintenance problems The troop also had available one platoon of infantry to do pick up work on the ground.

My mission was scheduled for September 27. The commander told me to report to Operations by 0600 because the pilots usually checked in by 0615. I was there at 0550 and everything was closed up. The pilots arrived at 0625 and I was scheduled to go out with a people sniffer team. The mission commander was a captain and a warrant officer was the pilot. I was totally ignored for the most part as everyone was busy checking out the ships. Part of the mission was to ferry five cavalry infantrymen and a couple of armament specialists to Tan An Airfield. The infantrymen were to be on ready alert for the day in case of a downed copter. This part of the mission only took about an hour.

This is the crew and the helicopter in which I went on the people sniffing mission in the Mekong Delta on September 27, 1968.

Our copter, a Huey, then preceded from Tan An Airfield to Tan Tru to receive a briefing on the mission. Troop A operated with the 2nd Battalion, 60th Infantry almost exclusively. Our mission was to cover three areas. The first was the canals almost directly east of An Nhut Tan. I went out with the light team, which had 2 Cobras, 2 Locusts, and a Huey sniffer ship as opposed to the heavy team of 4 Cobras, 4 Locusts, a command and control Huey, and a people sniffer Huey ship. The sniffer machine was provided and operated by the chemical team of the 9th Infantry Division from Dong Tam. Our people sniffer operator was a specialist E-6 from Headquarters Company, 9th Infantry Division.

The procedure was for the sniffer ship to make pattern runs along the woodline of streams until something was spotted or else a high reading was recorded on the machine. In either case, the Locust would drop to tree level and move slowly around to see what was down there. Because of this approach, cavalry units commonly had those ships shot up. The nerve of these pilots was tremendous because they operated often within 25 meters of suspected Viet Cong positions, daring the Viet Cong to shoot at them. If the Viet Cong were foolish enough to shoot at the Locusts, the

Terrain in the Plain of Reeds that the people sniffing mission investigated.

Cobras would come down to make them regret this indiscretion. Members of the team told me later that there were sometimes variation on this theme as the Locusts would go in before the sniffer.

Although no significant contact was made during the morning, several bunkers and at least one Viet Cong soldier were noted. We searched some heavy wood lines southeast of Tan An. Maximum readings of 5.0 were noted four times between 1225 and 1345. A mechanized unit was within 500 meters so it was ordered in to check these readings out. I remember thinking about the times when my old unit would have had to check out such sites. While noting these activities, I was also taking numerous pictures with my camera.

After refueling in the middle of the afternoon, we shifted our area of operation. Our group moved southwest of Tan An to the wood lines on the edge of the Plain of Reeds. There at around 1500 three sampans and two men were spotted hiding. We maneuvered around some more without significant results although several troop insertions took place to where we had been operating. I continued to take pictures, especially of the Plain of Reeds.

Our copters returned to Tan An to refuel. Because my ship was needed

Type of sampan used in the Plain of Reeds by the Viet Cong.

to carry some troops I stayed at Tan An to be picked up with the cavalry's infantry. Evidently the slicks of the 9th Aviation had been released for further duty after the insertions of elements of the 2nd Battalion, 60th Infantry, and they needed our ship to ferry troops back to Tan Tru. Only two ships were available so this ferrying took some time. A bad storm moved in, soaking us at Tan An. Our copter returned at about 1930, but it was soon grounded by the storm. At 2145, we finally left for Long Binh. A soaked and thoroughly miserable bunch of soldiers arrived at Long Binh at about 2215. This ended my adventure with the air cavalry.

I spent the next several days interviewing personnel in Troop A. The first day I talked to the pilots. Those interviewed were a first lieutenant who was a Locust pilot, and a warrant officer 2 who was a Huey pilot. The first lieutenant had been one of the two Locust pilots who had gone out with me the previous day. He was the one who did the spotting on the action southeast of Tan An. I learned from him that the Locust pilots were all volunteers, and he told me that the casualty rate was high.

The warrant officer was the more talkative of the two pilots. He had

One of the hooches about 10 miles southeast of Tan An that we checked out for Viet Cong activity.

served ten years as a mechanic before he went to flight school. His frustration about the war showed in his belief that a total military commitment might end the war. He also felt that the aviation branch of the army was approaching the point where the air force and the army parted ways in 1947. He expressed the view that warrant officers were discontent with their lot and needed more special treatment than they were presently getting.

Both pilots verbalized their feelings that copters had been sent out on missions when the copters was not ready for operations. They also complained about damage to copters in low level strafing attacks. The pilots explained that it is necessary to drop below the 1,000-meter safety zone bursting level of their weapon systems in order to give close support to infantry under fire. Several times copters had been shot down by shrapnel from their own weapons, or had sustained heavy damage. I did express to them my appreciation for such low level strafing since I had been a beneficiary of such tactics several times when I was in the infantry.

The next afternoon I interviewed the unit's commander. He expanded his remarks about the tactics used by the air cavalry. The mission of the air cavalry was reconnaissance as the striking power of the unit had its limits. While it had the firepower of the Cobra gunships, it lacked the infantry to mix it up with the Viet Cong. Consequently, the enemy moved out when major infantry units were finally committed. He stressed that he had much difficulty training scouts as so much was expected of them. It could take as long as three months to train a scout.

My interviews with the maintenance and armament sections of the air cavalry took up most of the rest of the afternoon. Both sections suffered from the lack of an adequate supply system for spare parts and the lack of qualified personnel to make the repairs. The practice of cannibalization of copters for spare parts was common. These interviews ended my stay with Troop A. I also conducted informal talks with some of the enlisted men to fill in some of the gaps. What I did notice that the 2/17th Cavalry lived better in Long Binh than we did at Dong Tam. They had Vietnamese girl house cleaners to clean the barracks and pick up after them. Other conveniences (showers, junk food, etc.) were much more in evidence there than at Dong Tam.

As I returned to Dong Tam, I remembered the story about how important forms were to obtain parts. Allegedly, there was an aviation unit deep in the Mekong Delta whose supply forms had been destroyed in a mortar attack. They tried to order parts without the necessary forms, and the requests were returned. When the unit explained the problem they were told to send the form to request forms. Noting that this form had also been destroyed an impasse developed. This is where the story ends, probably as a myth, but it did both then and now have an element of truth in it.

10

Back at Dong Tam

By October, the detachment had finally settled into Dong Tam. Enemy activity around the base camp was much more active than at Bearcat, but members of the detachment made adjustments. Mortar attacks were infrequent but often enough that once every week or so our sleep was interrupted by a mad dash to a bomb shelter. Each time we made the run, we were cursing Colonel Hunt and his refusal to have the bomb shelters close to our barracks.

It was rare that soldiers in South Vietnam paid much attention to news taking place outside of South Vietnam, but the rumor of an imminent pause in the bombing in North Vietnam attracted our attention. The wisdom of this action was widely debated in the detachment with opinion being evenly divided. My argument was that such an action would not significantly alter the military situation, particularly in our area of operations. Bombing in North Vietnam had been more a nuisance value for the North Vietnamese than militarily effective. Remembering my historical studies, I recalled that bombing had always been overrated as a means of obtaining military objectives. This had been proven repeatedly in the Second World War and in the Korean War. When the news finally arrived of a bombing pause effective November 1, none of us was surprised, or encouraged.

A minor event took place on October 21, but it had nationwide repercussions in South Vietnam. Once a year or so the U. S. military authorities ordered the old military pay script (MPC) to be exchanged for a new pay script. This was an effort to control the black market among both the military and Vietnamese civilians. The Vietnamese black market was everywhere, and American military supplies could be bought at wholesale prices. Almost anything was for sale from medicine to weapons. Later it was learned that many senior non-commissioned officers in the American army

126

became wealthy dealing in the black market. The consensus in the detachment was that the big black market operators were not hurt by the exchange as they had prepared for the eventuality, but that the middlemen were hurt badly. Currency speculation had been bad with the old MPCs and counterfeit money had appeared in several places so this action was not unexpected.

In early October, General Curtis LeMay made his appearance in South Vietnam. "Old bomb them back to the Stone Age LeMay" spent four days in country talking to high ranking officers and making public statements that the morale of the field troops was good. My reaction was these high-ranking officers had little contact with the enlisted men in the field; consequently, how in the hell did they know what the morale of the troops was? LeMay was another one of those instant experts on the Vietnam War pontificating about the conduct of the war with little knowledge of what was going on in the war.

Once my completed Battle of the Plain of Reeds report was circulated around the division, it became in great demand. I also became infamous as the lowly enlisted man that had taken on the division's high command. The detachment also received a request from the War College in Pennsylvania for information about the battle. Major Hooper wanted them to receive the report through military history channels so nothing happened about this request.

My attachment to my old unit caused me to follow its career. In late October, news reached the detachment that elements of the 6th Battalion, 31st Infantry, had mutinied. A meeting was held on the morning of October 25 with General Ewell, the division commander, to hush the whole matter up. At the time, I did not know the details of the story, but I knew that units within the battalion were having trouble because of racial feelings in the ranks.

Rumors had been circulating for months in the 9th Infantry Division that there had been racial fights up north. Some resentment had been expressed by white soldiers that the Vietnamese liked the African American soldiers and communicated with them better than they did with the white soldiers. Many of the Vietnamese identified the white soldiers with their former colonial masters, the French. The Vietnamese were more receptive toward the black soldiers because American black troops resembled the Senegalese, who were popular with the Vietnamese during the French occupation.

Later, more news surfaced about the mutiny in the 6th Battalion, 31st Infantry. About a week after hearing about the mutiny, a former member of my old company told me that there had been numerous cases of members of the battalion refusing to go back into the field. Approximately 20 men had been court-martialed for this offense. Several days later, another friend informed me that the trouble in the battalion started out over a racial incident. There were a couple of stabbings in which one soldier was seriously injured. These incidents were followed by numerous instances of men refusing to go back to the field. I saw other friends, but they were closemouthed about the mutiny. I bet that they had received orders not to discuss it. By this time, rumors were flying all over Dong Tam about the incidents in the 6th Battalion, 31st Infantry.

Here I am working on a military history report at Dong Tam in December 1968.

Part of the problem with the 6th Battalion, 31st Infantry, was the constant turnover of personnel. By the end of September, almost 80 percent of the battalion had been replaced either through attrition of disease, wounds, death, or transfers. It had also been overused as a maneuver battalion in the previous five months because the brigade high command considered it a fresh unit. By the beginning of September, the battalion was only a shell of its previous strength. As the battalion was misused, morale began to suffer. I experienced some of the same feelings of low morale before my transfer.

Other incidents involving U.S. troops and Vietnamese soldiers also took place about the same time. The army began placing almost all civilian establishments off limits. My Tho was a town on the Mekong River next to where the 9th Infantry Division built Dong Tam Base Camp. After a fight broke out between U.S. troops and the ARVN troops during which a couple of ARVN soldiers were killed, My Tho was placed off limits.

Resentment by American soldiers for having to fight in South Vietnam and their contempt towards the Vietnamese Army began to bear fruit.

About this time, disturbing rumors began to surface in the division that some American troops had been caught collaborating with the enemy. The 19th Military History Detachment had the additional duty of serving as the storage depot for captured enemy weapons for future display in a museum. The weapons were housed in several large Conex boxes — huge metal containers for storage and transport. It was one of our duties to inventory and clean the weapons. Several of us liked to open the Conexes and handle the weapons before cleaning them. Often we had fun taking pictures handling the weapons. Sometime in September, our Conexes were broken into and rifles, submachine guns, and machine guns were stolen. Members of the detachment thought little about this theft until we learned that the detachment's commander began to serve on court-martial boards. He was tight lipped about the subject of the court-martials, but slowly the news spread around that a small group of American soldiers, around twelve members, had stolen weapons and reconditioned them before giving them to the Viet Cong. It seems that these individuals had become romantically entangled with young Vietnamese women who persuaded them to do this. This tactic was called a honey trap, but it was merely sex and treason.

In late October, the division began a crackdown on uniform appearance. Colonel Ira Hunt, chief of staff of the 9th Infantry Division, ordered the crackdown with the threat that he was going to make an example of the first couple of soldiers that he ran across who were sloppy. It was this type of harassment that lowered morale among both the rear-echelon and combat soldiers. In actuality, it had little impact, but this type of action reminded me that the army wants parade ground soldiers who are good fighters. The problem is that the best combat soldiers are rarely good spit-shine soldiers and vice versa. General Stone in the 4th Infantry Division started the same type of campaign, but he received orders from above to end it.

Late fall of 1968 can be characterized as a period when enemy activity began to increase again and my willingness to take changes decreased. I continued to work on special projects and spent considerable time studying intelligence reports. It had been obvious that the Viet Cong had retrenched their operations in the previous three months, but eventually the unofficial truce was going to end. Like most veterans, I was hoping to make it out of Vietnam before the next major Viet Cong offensive. At first, it looked like the next major Viet Cong target would be Saigon in the middle of November, but to my relief nothing happened in November.

As my tour of duty in South Vietnam was winding down, I began to examine certain topics. Rotation policy was one of these topics, and it was controversial then and continues to be so now. Since I benefited from the one-year limit on a tour of duty in a war zone, perhaps I should not criticize it. But it did have unintended side effects. American soldiers tended to lose their aggressiveness during the last half of their Vietnam tour. Constant changes of personnel in combat units can be expected, but the loss of experienced officers and NCOs seriously affected the combat effectiveness of a unit. With six months of its arrival in South Vietnam, my battalion had witnessed a turnover of almost 80 percent. I hardly recognized anybody from my old company in August. This constant turnover has been criticized by others. A later critic has accused it of promoting incompetence and amateurism. I must admit that I saw both during my tour of duty in South Vietnam.

In early November, the commanding general's new mess hall was opened in Dong Tam. This fact was not a newsworthy item except that it became a topic of conversation among the enlisted men. I talked to a friend of mine in headquarters company, and he told me that the furnishings for the mess cost around $60,000. If trips to Bangkok and Hong Kong by junior officers to acquire furniture were included, the cost of the mess increased to around $100,000. It took nine half-ton air-conditioners to cool 27 eligible high-ranking officers to eat there. I believed then and now such a structure was not necessary for the war effort. It also constituted a morale factor for the enlisted men.

Another incident, on a more positive note, also took place in early November. On November 4, our office person did not show up for work. A member of the Combat Art Team found out that her hooch had been blown up during the Viet Cong attack on My Tho the previous night. Although her English was poor, we also learned that both her husband and baby were wounded in the attack. Their wounds proved to be minor. After talking it over in the office, we decided to check with G-5 to see if our detachment could help her and her friends rebuild their dwelling. The advice from G-5 was to take lumber and cement to My Tho and let the people build their own homes. A bunch of us decided to go into My Tho to deliver the materials. I made two trips to My Tho to deliver cement. We received some static from an army captain who told us that the Saigon government would rebuild the area and the people would sell our cement. While the captain may have been right, the Saigon government was slow and it had probably more red tape than did the U.S. government. Besides, it was a positive gesture on our part. The Vietnamese could do what they wanted

Damage from a Viet Cong 120mm mortar in a December attack on My Tho.

with the cement because the Saigon government did not replace lost personal belongings. Also, the cement was going to waste at Dong Tam. It took us almost an hour to find cement that had not been ruined by careless storage.

Shortly after this incident, I learned something about internal divisions among the Vietnamese. I met Captain Tien, the ARVN liaison officer with the 9th Infantry Division. He was originally from Hanoi, and he had fought with the Viet Minh from 1949 to 1953. His job with the Viet Minh was as a reconnaissance specialist preparing attacks against the French. As a staunch Catholic, Tien moved to the south in the exodus of Catholics after the Geneva Accords of 1954. Tien had been a captain for fourteen years, and he claimed that his lack of promotion was due to his outspoken nature. As a critic of both General Thieu and General Ky, Tien admitted that he had been an admirer of Diem. Although Diem had run a dictatorship in South Vietnam, he had been a strong leader for his country. Tien recounted that he had spent an enjoyable year at the Armor School at Ft. Knox, Kentucky.

My conversation with Tien and with other Vietnamese showed me that there was resentment between northern-born and southern-born Vietnamese. This feeling corresponded closely to the same type of attitude

between northerners and southerners in the United States. Vietnamese
stereotypes were that northern Vietnamese were too pushy and ambitious,
and correspondingly, the southerners were lazy and slow. Vietnamese also
had speech differences in the tonal sounds, which compounded their feelings of hostility. I became aware of the intensity of this feeling when our
office helper expressed her dislike of Captain Tien. She indicated that he

Mia Tiet was the maid employed by the 19th Military History Detachment
in Dong Tam.

was a northerner and therefore she distrusted him. I asked her how she knew this and she replied in her uncertain English that he used an extra tone in his words. She also shared that this feeling of distrust was also directed to Vietnamese of Cambodian extraction. These attitudes and stereotypes affected the selection of officers and the performances of certain ARVN units.

The 1968 presidential election was a source of excitement for several weeks in late October and early November. Most members of the detachment were pro–Hubert Humphrey. Besides liking Humphrey personally, a segment of the detachment, including myself, never trusted Richard Nixon. I also had strong misgivings about Spiro Agnew. It was with sadness that we learned the results of the election.

The potential of a November surprise from a Viet Cong offensive attracted the attention of the top brass in the division. Memories of the Tet Offensive were still fresh. On October 24, 1968, a meeting of all the commanders of the units in the division took place. The general consensus was that there was an attack by the Viet Cong was probable in the Mekong Delta that might impact the election. They estimated that the offensive would occur sometime between October 28 and November 2. Areas of responsibility were assigned to the three brigades. These precautions had little impact because the weeks before the election were quiet in the division's area of operation.

In the middle of November, I ran across a fascinating assessment of the Vietnam War from the Viet Cong perspective. American forces captured a Viet Cong notebook on November 6 with an interesting perspective. The writer stated that the United States wanted a political settlement so there would be a bombing halt. A cease-fire proposal would follow shortly thereafter. A puppet government would be established in order to crush communism. Therefore, the National Liberation Front forces must have a strong position before the peace. This could be accomplished only by an all out offensive greater than Tet. Half of the cities must be liberated and the others destroyed. The writer claimed that units were already in position for such attacks. The strength of the North Vietnamese Army and National Liberation Front was greater now than before Tet, but poor morale and deficient leadership was hindering the war effort. A third phase political reorientation program was to start on October 30 and continue until December 31. While this offensive never materialized, the analysis is still important as a sample of thinking among the Viet Cong leadership.

Another interesting intelligence report was from a captured Viet Cong

medic. Besides commenting on the Viet Cong medical treatment, he talked
about improved morale among the Viet Cong.

> La Than Son (XS685594), 26 years of age, Catholic, Medic, 8th Com-
> pany, 3rd Artillery Battalion. He was born in Cambodia and studied medi-
> cine for 5 years under his father. He joined the unit in February 1968 in Ba
> Thu, Cambodia and had no training of any kind. Most of the unit was
> made up of North Vietnamese Army personnel. The 8th Company consisted
> of 21 men. In February 1968 they entered South Vietnam. 8 companies in
> 3rd Artillery. Once a month the Battalion resupplied his company. Medicine
> was scarce but of good quality. He believed the medicine was brought in
> South Vietnam. It usually consisted of malaria pills, Novocain, and general
> sickness medicine. He had no knowledge of any hospitals or aid stations.
> His unit would move only at night and only on orders from the Political
> Officer of his Company, who in turn received orders from the Battalion
> Political Officer. The morale of his unit was very high because of Viet Cong
> propaganda stating the Americans were weakening and that the Viet Cong
> would win the war in the near future.

Several incidents with racial overtones were in the news in late
November. It seems that the command sergeant major directed a racial
slur towards one of the black soldiers. This soldier filed charges against
him. I never found out the result of these charges, but the sergeant major
had antagonized all of his subordinates by his rantings and ravings. Another
story was about a black soldier in Saigon named "Smokey," who told an
absent without leave (AWOL) black soldier that for $15,000 Vietnamese
money he could be smuggled to Cambodia. If he did not have the money,
the soldier could work off the sum with the Cambodian government. Evidently, this offer was open only to black soldiers.

Saigon had long been off limits to enlisted men, but the military
police did not always strictly enforce this policy. On November 25, several of us, including an old friend from 3rd Platoon, Company C, went
into Saigon on a lark. First, we went to a Saigon restaurant on Tu Do Street.
After a satisfactory meal of steak at a not unreasonable price of $2.50, the
five of us went to a Tu Do Street bar. I had always been curious about
Saigon bar girls. Of course, one short visit does not make one an expert,
and I felt out of place in this environment. My drinking companion was
both an attractive young lady and quiet. She said that her father was an
ARVN captain. I did not doubt her story, because most of the bar girls
showed good manners and breeding. They did make it plain that they
would stay and talk only as long as one paid $2.00 a jigger for tea or coke.
I bought one jigger in order to talk. Our conversation was sporadic and
not very informative. I did find out that these girls were not prostitutes.

They made enough money that theoretically all of them could be virgins as they raked in around $100 a night. Consequently, most of them did not need the $20 for sex. Of course, the ambitious girls could rake in major dough by prostituting themselves. My friend claimed that he had met several extremely intelligent girls at Tu Do bars since some of them were putting themselves through school by the money they earned as bar girls. It was getting late and we needed to get back to Dong Tam so we left early.

Several intelligence sources appeared in the middle of November that proved intriguing. In a November 18 report it was noted that the Viet Cong tax collections had increased from 35 percent of total income to 79 percent plus a supplemental insurrection tax. Punitive actions were to be taken by the Viet Cong against delinquents. Exactly how the Viet Cong expected the Vietnamese to live on what was left to them is beyond me.

In a November 19 report there was mentioned the possibility of a big offensive by the Viet Cong between December 20 and 31.

Another report from November 22 stated that the new Viet Cong offensive would be from 1 to 20 December. There would be three objectives: (1) to make evident the strength of the Viet Cong to Allied and ARVN forces, both to the world, and especially to the negotiators at the Paris Peace Talks; (2) to stir up political resentment among pacifists in South Vietnam and the United States; and (3) to support Nguyen Thi Binh, the National Liberation Front representative in Paris, and to make Americans eager to set up a coalition government in South Vietnam.

Here is a picture of me with my camera and the detachment jeep during one of my infrequent trips to Saigon.

Members of the detachment found this analysis fascinating and we had a lively discussion over it. It was so obvious to us that the South Vietnamese government was in a stalling campaign with the American government. General Thieu wanted to work with Nixon rather than Johnson, because of Nixon's more hard line position. After all that the Johnson administration had done for General Thieu, it only proved that there is no such thing as gratitude in politics.

Members of the detachment sometimes tried to perform good deeds. On the afternoon of November 30, several members of the detachment went out to the Dong Hoa orphanage near Vinh Thanh. It was run by a Vietnamese Catholic father and it is part of a Catholic self-help organization. The children had lost their parents because the parents had been killed by either American or ARVN forces. There were 280 children living in the side rooms of the church. They ranged from 3 to 13 years of age. The boys worked in the fields and the girls sewed to sell clothes.

When an American soldier arrived at the church, the children mobbed him. I tried to take pictures of their living quarters and the kids, but I had limited success. We had gone out there to check on what the children needed for a Christmas party. Since the father had a command of neither French nor English, we had language difficulties. He found one of his parishioners who had a limited knowledge of French. With my Americanized French and his Vietnamized French, we were able to communicate in a fashion. We learned that the children needed clothes and school equipment. While the area where the church was located was in heavily controlled Viet Cong territory, we were not sniped at by the Viet Cong.

On another occasion, however, three of the members of the detachment, including myself, had a scary experience. Our mission on December 6, 1968, was to deliver a friend of the detachment commander to the 90th Replacement Unit at Long Binh. His position in the 3rd Brigade had been as supply officer of Headquarters Company. His educational background was a degree from Maine University where he had participated in its ROTC program. The lieutenant was popular among the enlisted men because of his outspoken dislike for the army and the army way of life.

After dropping off the lieutenant off, we spent some time driving around Saigon. It was getting late so we headed back towards Dong Tam. On the way back in an area called Ambush Alley we saw a dead ARVN soldier who had been horribly mutilated. We also heard some gunfire, mostly M-16 gunfire. This sound of combat made us nervous and the jeep driver picked up speed. Shortly afterwards we had to slow down as a detachment of about 60 black clothed infantrymen with rubber soled

Here is my attempt to communicate in French the plans for the Christmas party with the priest at Dong Hoa Orphanage.

footwear and M-16 weapons crossed our path. There was no doubt then and now that this unit was a main force Viet Cong company. They waved and smiled at us. We politely waved and smiled back until they passed by. Each of us had an M-16 with a limited amount of ammunition, but we were no match for a heavily armed Viet Cong company. The jeep seemed to fly as we raced the last remaining miles to Dong Tam. This incident scared the hell out of us. We were so appreciative of surviving that none of us mentioned this incident to our military superiors.

11

Last Months in South Vietnam

The 19th Military History Detachment was constantly undergoing changes as personnel came and left at regular intervals. In early December, the detachment commander announced that he had finally been successful in obtaining a transfer to an artillery unit. He had been a successful commander of the 19th Military History Detachment, but his first love was artillery. On December 10, he left to report to the 1st Battery, 79th Artillery at Can Tho. While the major had not been happy in the detachment, the members were sorry to see him go. I liked him personally and he had recommended me for the Army Commendation Medal for my report on the Battle of the Plain of Reeds.

Big news in the division was the prospect of another Viet Cong offensive. A warning based on intelligence information came from division headquarters on December 12, 1968, that the offensive would take place in several days. Several of us from the 19th Military History Detachment attached ourselves to the 3rd Brigade. Major Curran, Brigade S-2, explained the reasoning for the warning. He said that there were three sources for the belief in an eminent Viet Cong offensive. First, there were numerous intelligence reports of increased Viet Cong activity. Second, heavy troop movements of Viet Cong had been spotted by radar along rivers and streams. Finally, there had been numerous secondary explosion from American artillery and air strike missions. All of these developments coupled with a strange lull in enemy activity fit past Viet Cong behavior before a big offense. Like so many other warnings, this offensive failed to materialize with the Viet Cong continuing to evade 9th Infantry Division's efforts to locate and destroy them.

In the middle of December, several of us from the detachment went out to the 4th Battalion, 39th Infantry to track down a story about a snatch operation. A snatch operation was the picking up of one person or

Major Hooper, Supply Officer of HHQ Company, 9th Infantry Division, and
a friend of Major Hooper.

a small group after receiving intelligence information about these individuals as possible Viet Cong operatives. Between December 8 and 14, units of the 4th Battalion, 39th Infantry conducted a series of these operations. The initial lead for the most successful snatch operation came from a defector from the Viet Cong, a Chieu Hoi, from around the Long Dinh–Vinh Kim area. He had stated that his next-door neighbor was a bigwig in the Viet Cong infrastructure since high ranking Viet Cong took orders from him. Several days later, he was picked up by the military. At first from his appearance, he seemed to be a harmless man of 50 years of age, who appeared to be almost scared to death by the soldiers. It was only after interrogation that it was discovered that he was a district chief and a member of the policy-making committee in Dinh Tuong Province. Moreover, he had long operated as double-agent, giving information through the ARVN intelligence agent chain. It appeared, however, that his main allegiance had always remained with the Viet Cong.

The captured district chief talked enough to the interrogation team that another raid was made on December 12 to pick up another high official. A firefight ensued during the snatch operation with ten Viet Cong soldiers being killed. American soldiers were able to capture another four, including a couple of girl agents. These girl agents were used to seduce American and ARVN soldiers to gain intelligence information or to turn them into Viet Cong supporters. Each girl was from 15 to 18 years of age and quite attractive. They wore white scarves around their necks as a sign of identification. The target of this snatch operation escaped from the trap as his bodyguard covered for him.

On December 17, the detachment had its jeep stolen. Since jeeps were easy to steal but also easy to recover, this news did not unduly disturb us in the detachment. The next day the Criminal Investigation Division (CID) informed us that they had found our jeep abandoned in front of the enlisted men's club. It seemed that the jeep had broken down and the thief had abandoned it. It was obvious that the thief intended to take the jeep to My Tho and sell it on the black market as he had erased the bumper numbers. The recovery saved somebody a $26,000 bill.

In the midst of the jeep investigation, the Military Police reported that it had recovered some of our stolen weapons. This was a surprise to the detachment because none of us was aware of any missing weapons. After an inventory, the detachment confirmed that it was missing weapons stored in one of our Conex containers. Later we learned that a twelve-member group of GIs or ex–GIs had stolen the weapons to turn over to the Viet Cong. The Criminal Investigation Detachment (CID) agents captured

Lieutenant Shalek, Supply Officer of HHQ Company, 9th Infantry Division, and a friend of Major Hooper.

a member of this group. After his capture, he claimed to be married to a Viet Cong woman, and that he had renounced his American citizenship. I never heard the results of his court-martial, but I am sure that he received a long sentence.

Several intelligence reports revealed information about how the Viet Cong operated in and around the 9th Infantry Division's area of operation. First was information given in early December 1968 by a Viet Cong defector. He told how the Viet Cong selected soldiers for military duties.

100755H, vic XS171412, approximately 3 kilometers of Cai Be, a Hoi Chang/VC rallied to 9th Infantry. Bo Van Hai, Hiep Duc Village Guerrillas. He joined the guerrilla force on 3 December 1968. He received 3 days of training at Hiep Duc. New recruits are given this train-ing camp at an unknown location for 2 to 3 months. The men who are rated "good soldiers" are then assigned to the 514 or 261 Battalions. The other men, including those who have not accepted VC propaganda, are sent to the Central Highlands. The VC told him that North Vietnam and South Viet-nam would soon be at peace because of the Paris Peace Talks. The training leader was Sau Nganh and the platoon leaders was Hai Sau. The subject decided to rally upon discovering that he would be assigned to a Main Force unit after completion of training. He wanted to remain a guerrilla and stay with his family. He stated that he would lead US troops to the training area, but that the VC knew of US units in the area and had probably left the training center.

My old platoon sergeant dropped by the detachment on December 21, 1968. He had been promoted to platoon sergeant in May while I was still in the infantry. Although he had always given me the most dangerous assignments, we had become friends. His transfer to a Military Police unit had been made possible because of his increasing loss of hearing from gunfire in combat. Even the limited time in combat had affected my hearing in my left ear. The feared "artillery ear" was not a serious injury but it was progressive, leading to deafness.

It was about this time that I ran across the most diabolical Viet Cong plot to injure American soldiers. The following report was taken from the official log for the 2nd Battalion, 47th Infantry (Mech.) on February 24, 1968.

> 1700 hours, B Co., Commanding Officer reported a WIA, YS132963 — an enlisted man was having sexual intercourse with a Vietnamese Boom Boom Girl. She had something in her vagina which produced a cut on his penis. MP's brought the WIA enlisted man back to Bearcat along with the Boom Boom Girl for very thorough questioning.

SNATCH-TRAP

Ends wrapped with adhesive tape
Strip of tape   This end first
Straight edge razor

This device produced the above casualty. It slices one's penis lengthwise. Moral: *Fingers First!*

I have never seen a more effective display to control one's sexual impulses.

The Christmas Party at the Dong Hoa Orphanage proved to be a success. Children had a ball with their presents and the candy. I wager that we had as much fun as they did, taking pictures of them with their gifts. There must have been 40 American soldiers and about seven or eight units represented at the party. In fact, I understand that there was not an orphanage in South Vietnam that was not besieged by Americans bearing gifts. Christmas was great, but it was the rest of the year that the kids in these orphanages needed help.

One of the members of the Combat Art Team was the driving spirit behind our detachment's participation. He had conned his way into the Combat Art Team to avoid further combat duty. While he could not draw worth a damn, his other contributions made him a valuable member of the team. He was a curious mixture of cynicism and thoughtfulness. An exceptionally bright individual, his razor-sharp tongue did not always endear him to others, especially when his observations were too close to the truth.

Dong Hoa Orphanage in Long Dinh District, Dinh Tuong Province, where we had a Christmas party.

Two days after Christmas, the Bob Hope Show made its appearance for the 9th Infantry Division. Army security was such that little advance warning was given for his arrival. We heard through the grapevine that he would be in Dong Tam at around 1200. Several of us went over to the outdoor theater at about 1100. Since the army reserved most of the space for personnel from infantry units, our seats were poor. That did not bother us because the infantrymen were doing most of the fighting. About seven or eight thousand soldiers were at the show. The show started promptly at 1230. While I had heard most of Bob Hope's jokes on TV before, it was still fun. Hope depended heavily on cue cards, but someone had obviously briefed him about local personnel because some of his jokes were directed towards them. The acts were good, but not spectacular. Undoubtedly, the show would look much better on TV after segments could be cut and others added from other shows.

Daily my reading of the division's intelligence summaries was for information on how the war was progressing. On December 29, a volunteer source gave the proposed Viet Cong itinerary for the 1968 and 1969 Winter–Spring Offensive and this is how it appeared in the Intsum.

Long range view of the Bob Hope Show in late December 1968.

(a) Phase I (28 December 1968 to 28 January 1969) — During phase the itinerary calls for increasing the pressure on U.S. and Government of Vietnam (GVN) outposts in the form of surrounding and destroying said outposts. These victories can then be exploited for propaganda purposes and can be added to the political victories which can be expected at the Paris Peace Talks.

(b) Phase II (28 January 1969 to 28 February 1969) — This phase is designed to wrest control of the densely populated areas from the Government of Vietnam, i.e. the outskirts of Saigon, Cholon, Gia Dinh, etc. This phase of operations, in conjunction with the Phase I, is designed to impress upon the minds of the people of South Vietnam the overwhelming strength of the National Liberation Front for South Vietnam (NLFSVN). It should cause the people to appreciate the fine soldiers of the National Liberation Front (NLF) and to lend their full support to Phase II of the Winter/Spring Offensive.

(c) Phase III (28 February 1969 to 29 March 1969) — During this phase the general population will rise in support of the NLF and the General Military Offensive with the end result, being a coalition government labeled the "Peace Democratic." This government will mean real and lasting peace to the Vietnamese people.

The intelligence analyst gave this report a middling rating, but he did relate that the information in this report coincided with the strategic objectives outlined in captured documents which originated at COSVN HQ. Reports of this nature were not uncommon. The Viet Cong often set up such timetables, but they were rarely successful in carrying them out. While the Viet Cong had intelligence leaks, they also had good sources within ARVN and the South Vietnamese government so they soon learned about the capture of their planning documents.

Somehow, I survived the New Year's Eve celebration. GIs go berserk when they combine alcohol and a national holiday. There was enough ammunition expended that night to supply the Viet Cong for another major offensive. It was beautiful as all sorts of colored flares exploded in the heavens. Racer rounds provided an addition to the show. It did make several of us a little concerned about the aims of our drunken buddies.

The appearance of our new commander on January 1 changed the lifestyle of the detachment almost immediately. Major Keely had been the original replacement for the previous commander, but he fell ill in the United States. When the major finally made it to South Vietnam, he was assigned to G-2. His undergraduate degree was in philosophy and he claimed no expertise in history. After a brief orientation period, he began to tighten up procedures in the unit. While this tightening up was not unexpected, it was not necessarily appreciated.

Intelligence reports continued to surface that indicated unhappiness in the ranks of the Viet Cong. In the middle of January, one such report was especially intriguing. A young Viet Cong rallied to Company C, 4th Battalion, 39th Infantry. He had been an informer for Team A Assassination Squad. This squad of twelve men had been operating in the Vinh Kim Village Area for approximately two years. He had served as an informer for one and half months. His unit's weapons were 6 M-16s, 6 Ak-47s, 1 RPG-7, and 1 RPG-2. Uniforms were green jungle fatigues (ARVN), red scarves, and green hats. They resembled ARVN soldiers except for a square blue patch on the collar. Two young women also served as informers. They sold sodas to soldiers near Vinh Kim and report information to the squad. A young boy also belonged to the unit. Their function was to warn the squad leader, Ba Dien, before U.S. troops entered the area. If enemy troops entered the area, then squad members would hide in Vinh Hoa.

My time was coming to a close in South Vietnam. My diary is full of calculations about how many days, hours and minutes were left for me in the army. At any opportunity, I could quote the exact figures. Like so many others before me, I became more cautious. Short-timers were notorious for avoiding work, details, and taking as few chances as possible. The change in command in the detachment made me even more anxious to avoid trouble.

My last action in the detachment was to go over to Company C, 4th Battalion, 39th Infantry, to check on an ambush patrol which had been almost annihilated a few days earlier. I took over several new members of the detachment and we talked to a sergeant who had visited the only survivor in good enough condition to talk. According to this individual, the patrol had set up in a hooch when his world exploded. Evidently, a satchel charge of high explosives had been thrown into the hooch. Final casualties were 7 KIA and 3 WIA with one expected not to survive. It was standard operating procedure in my old unit never to set up operations in an enclosed area because it was too easy for the enemy to do what it did on this occasion.

Another intelligence report on how the Viet Cong mortared Dong Tam in early January 1969 was also fascinating reading. This time the defecting Viet Cong soldiers confirmed that the Viet Cong had spotters marking the targets and informing the mortar site on accuracy of the rounds.

05143H, vic XS379455, approximately 4 kilometers northwest of Dong Tam, Nguyen Van Chinh rallied to Company 3, 4th Battalion, 39th Infantry. Subsequent interview revealed the following information: Position: Ammo-bearer; Unit: 1st Squad, 3r Platoon, 263 Mortar Company. He joined the unit early in 1968. It is a separate Main Force battery that is attached to any unit which needs support. Armament is 82mm mortars. He left the unit on 20 May 1968 to return to school. During TET (1968) the 263 Company mortared My Tho City and Dong Tam Base. The commanding officer of the unit was Chien and the executive officer was Bay Luc. During mortar attacks, reports were received concerning effects of the shelling. He did not know who furnished these reports. Six men usually moved to the mortar site, leaving the base are approximately 2 hours prior to the attack. 4 laborers were taken to help carry the weapons and see whether the rounds were located. The crew normally fired 20 rounds and waited to see whether the rounds were located. If not, another 20 rounds were fired. Guerrillas from nearby hamlet furnished security for the crew. If counter-mortar was fired, the VC hid in the area and then departed when the firing ceased. He believes that the units' ammo is kept in Ban Long and that his squad's mortar is hidden in Long Thuan A Hamlet. The mortar site used to mortar Dong Tam on 20 May 1968 was located vicinity XS399451.

During the last week of my stay in South Vietnam, it became apparent that the Viet Cong were increasing pressure on American forces in the Mekong Delta. A base camp at Cai Be in Dinh Tuong Province was attacked with heavy casualties for Company D, 6th Battalion, 31st Infantry. American losses were 8 KIA and 22 WIA. Then Can Tho was hit the next day again with heavy U.S. casualties — 8 KIA. The weekly casualty report indicated that U.S. casualties were up all over South Vietnam this week. What was more significant was that these actions had been initiated by the Viet Cong.

As my time ran out in South Vietnam, my only regret was leaving the unit mascot. Our mascot was T.C., or Tom Cat, a nondescript gray striped cat. The unit had adopted him when it arrived in Dong Tam. He slept in the detachment quarters, and he kept us company on the nights when we had to type reports. I was fond of him, and he prospered with us. Several times he got into trouble, but each time one of us rescued him. I meant to send him some supplies after I returned home, but because of lack of funds I was too slow about it. T.C. got into some toxic substance, and a vet had to put him to sleep a couple of months after I left South Vietnam.

Hoi Chanh was the mascot of the 19th Military History Detachment.

Pets were the rage with most units in South Vietnam. One general kept a 16-foot python in a Conex, and you can imagine that nobody bothered his supplies. Dogs, cats, monkeys, or anything you could name became mascots. Commanders tolerated these pets because they were good for the morale of the troops. It was so popular to adopt exotic pets that some of the soldiers were conned by wily Vietnamese into thinking they had acquired an exotic pet when the coloring of the animal had been doctored. One such case was a lesser leopard that became a simple domesticated cat when the spots disappeared a month or so later.

By the time I was to leave the detachment there had been a complete turnover of personnel in the detachment. My replacement had arrived before I left so I could train him. All the artists from the original crew had also departed. It was easier for me to make friends with the new crop. They were a curious bunch, but I enjoyed their company.

One thing that I knew for certain was that I wanted to finish my Ph.D. Before leaving South Vietnam I sent a letter to my advisor at the University of Iowa indicating that I wanted to continue my graduate work there. Dr. Alan Spitzer informed me that he had a teaching fellowship waiting for me in September 1970. This news reinforced my desire to resume my academic career. After being at the bottom of the military hierarchy for two years, I wanted more in life than just surviving. A side effect of my career in the military was that now I knew what I wanted out of life and I was willing to be aggressive in pursuing that goal. Every soldier had to be interviewed before leaving the army on whether or not he wanted to reenlist in the army. At the time of my short interview I almost laughed in the face of the sergeant. He was used to turn downs and he handled it with good humor.

Among the last tasks that I undertook in South Vietnam was the rounding up of documents that in my estimation would be destroyed when the 9th Infantry Division left South Vietnam. Before the move from Bearcat to Dong Tam there had been a massive destruction of documents because units simply did not want to take the documents with them on the trip. It did not take

Specialist Mike Perrella was my replacement in the Military History Section of the 19th Military History Detachment.

Specialist Rene Evans was an artist in the Combat Art Team, pictured here with me in Dong Tam.

much logic to realize that when the time came the 9th Infantry Division would destroy mountains of documents rather than box them up and take them to an uncertain future in the United States. The historian in me tried to save as many documents as possible. I was able to save only a small percentage of the documents, some of which fragments appear in this book.

My favorite document was the "Form Letter" from the 9th Infantry Division. This letter, actually a piece of dark humor purportedly written by a representative soldier, is reproduced in Appendix K. In some respects its contents are an exaggeration, but it holds elements of truth. Life in a combat zone had changed all of us. Vietnam veterans returned to the United States with a different outlook than what they had when they headed for South Vietnam. In most respects, war was a dehumanizing experience and some soldiers handled it better than others did. Above all the letter calls for the soldier's loved ones to "treat him with kindness, tolerance, an occasional fifth of good liquor, and you will be able to rehabilitate that which was once, and now is a hollow shell of, the happy-go-lucky guy you once knew and loved." It was good advice.

My day for leaving South Vietnam, or DEROS, finally arrived on January 29, 1969, on my twenty-eighth birthday. The trip to Long Binh and the out–processing was nervewracking because rumors were rampant about soldiers being killed or wounded just before flying to the States. Other rumors concerned soldiers with venereal diseases not being allowed to leave South Vietnam until they were cured. My trip to Long Binh turned out to be without incident. As we proceeded to the aircraft, there was a big container where soldiers could dispose of illegal merchandise rather than be arrested stateside. It was crammed with all sorts of paraphernalia. I bet that barrel had everything from drugs to classified materials.

Because of crossing the international dateline, January 29, 1968, was the longest day of my life. I left South Vietnam on January 29 and arrived at Oakland early the same day for separation from the army. When I was finally processed out of the army it was still on the 29th. Enough time was still available for me to catch an airplane to Dallas, Texas, on the same day. It was both the longest day of my life and one of the happiest. Even the theft or loss of my plane ticket at Oakland Airport could not restrain my happiness. I was a civilian again.

Richard Gray arrived as a new member of the Combat Art Team in November 1968.

Conclusion

My ten-month tour of South Vietnam changed few of my political beliefs, but it did turn me into a more aggressive personality. Constant combat and isolation from any type of civilized behavior turned me into a more aggressive soldier than I could ever have anticipated. The risks that I took during firefights were unimaginable before I joined the army. Slowly my friends disappeared as the casualty rates caught up to my unit. Only after leaving my combat unit and becoming a rear-echelon warrior did I have much contact with the outside world. The election of Richard Nixon to the presidency was announced, but it had less impact on me than the St. Louis Cardinals winning the pennant in 1968. While the military newspaper *Stars and Stripes* provided basic news, it was limited in coverage and scope. Only toward the end of my tour did I begin to sustain any interest in American politics, but the world had changed so much in this one year that I felt almost lost when I returned stateside. Illustrating the attitude of Vietnam veterans was that we referred to the United States as the "land of the Big PX."

After I returned to the United States from South Vietnam on January 29, 1969, I found American public opinion was no longer pro-war. It was almost like returning to another country. Moreover, I had an almost two-year gap of knowledge about daily affairs back in the States. My earlier skepticism about the war had turned into outright opposition.

It took several months for me to readjust to civilian life. The humorous document on readjusting to civilian life had much truth in it (see Appendix F). I had learned a new vocabulary in South Vietnam such as di di mau (move quickly), and I had to adjust to not aggressively reacting to loud noises. Veterans like me were sensitive to things that most Americans took for granted, such as certain smells, sounds resembling gunfire, and noises resembling incoming and outgoing artillery rounds. It took my wife several months to adjust to this stranger returning home, but gradually my symptoms drifted away.

The biggest blow after my return to the States, however, was news from South Vietnam that one of my best friends in high school, Alfred Suhr, had been killed in a mortar attack only two weeks after I left South Vietnam. He was a naval copter pilot stationed at Dong Tam. A mortar round hit his copter as he was taking off from a launching pad. I had no idea that Suhr had been stationed at Dong Tam, or else I would have looked him up. We had entered the University of Missouri–Columbia together and at one time considered becoming roommates, but he won a navy academic scholarship. This meant that he had to room on the south side of campus with other scholarship winners.

Members of my family have fought in every war since the American Revolution so my participation in the Vietnam War fit the family pattern. Although I had doubts about the wisdom of fighting a land war in Southeast Asia, I served my country to the best of my ability. It is easier to serve in a cause in which one believes in, but duty calls regardless.

Despite my reservations, the U.S. Army gave me several awards for my military service. It gave me a Bronze Star, an Army Commendation Medal, and a Good Conduct Ribbon while in South Vietnam. None of these awards came from when I was in the infantry. My unit was too busy fighting and patrolling to worry about medals. Nevertheless, I felt then and now that I deserved my medals for my duty there also. My proudest award, however, was my Combat Infantryman Badge. The army awards this badge only to those who have been under fire in combat and have the infantry military occupational specialty of 11 Bravo.

My views on the Vietnam War have been colored by my experiences there. After years of thinking about it, I still believe that 1968 was the pivotal year in the war. If the United States had a chance of winning the war, it was in that year. Viet Cong forces were demoralized in the Mekong Delta and around Saigon. Significant progress was also being made in other regions of the country. In my opinion, two factors mitigated against success: misunderstanding of the political nature of the war and the rivalry between the regular army leaders and Special Forces.

If the only chance to win the war was to "win the hearts and minds of the Vietnamese people," then the United States lost the battle before it started. While the U.S. Army and the marines were successful killing machines, they were not in the same ball game as the National Liberation Front (NLF) with regard to war aims. The leadership of the NLF was willing to fight a hundred years' war suffering defeat after defeat to wear down the resolve of the Americans to continue the war. Moreover, for every asset spent by the 9th Infantry Division on psychological operations, it directed a thousand towards destroying the Viet Cong military machine. My experience on a psychological operation showed me it was more a farce than a serious attempt to win the Vietnamese over to the South Vietnamese government. Perhaps other divisions operated more successful psychological operation programs, but I doubt that much more effort was put into these type operations than by the 9th Infantry Division.

The second reason goes back to internal politics in the U.S. Army. Regular army officers had no use for the Special Forces because they operated outside of the traditional infantry, armor, and artillery umbrella. These officers found the popularity of the Green Berets unacceptable. The Vietnam War alternated between low-intensity combat to the traditional slug it out between regular army units. Viet Cong strategy was to test conditions constantly and adjust its mode of attack. If their commanders found their units at a disadvantage, then they changed tactics. The American commanders on the other hand wanted the war to be a traditional military campaign where superior U.S. firepower could carry the day. In those areas where the Viet Cong used traditional guerrilla tactics, American tactics were like an elephant attacking an ant. While casualties piled up, the problem was whether enemy casualties were Viet Cong or civilians. This dilemma was never solved by American commanders. Meanwhile, the people trained to fight this type of warfare, Special Forces, were stationed in static defense positions and becoming more and more frustrated. They believed, quite rightly, that their expertise and training was being wasted.

Another factor in the lack of success in the Vietnam War was the top-heavy military organization employed in South Vietnam. It was almost as if the war was a make work project for high-ranking officers. Binh Hoa was notorious for the number of generals around there. Traveling through the complex showed row after row of living quarters for high-ranking officers. Feuds between high-ranking officers were common knowledge. The enlisted men were amused by the antics of these officers in their pursuit of promotions and medals, but eventually it became a morale problem. Incidents of troops firing at command copters became more common during my stay in South Vietnam. While I never heard of a case of fragging in the 9th Infantry Division, it may have happened. Fragging was not something that was publicized because it might encourage other attempts. Much of this type of activity took place after I left South Vietnam.

In a top-heavy organization, it meant that in a division of around 15,000 soldiers only about 5,000 were combat troops. The rest were support troops. Yet, my infantry company was in the field for three weeks in May 1968 without relief and without supplies except for food, ammo, and water. My socks rotted off my feet, and my uniform was in tatters. My platoon was down to one cleaning kit for the platoon for nearly two weeks. It took nearly two weeks for supply to deliver my glasses to me after I lost the first glasses in a military operation. For all this large support effort, the combat troops were often the forgotten part of the division. I was bitter about this when I was still in the infantry, and my mood has not changed much over the years.

The Vietnam War was a citizen-soldier war. Approximately 7 million American soldiers passed through South Vietnam during the years of fighting. Because so many soldiers rotated in and out of the war, the quality of the units differed greatly. Although Wilfred Burchett, the Australian communist, hated the American army, his analysis of the quality of American combat units makes some points. He maintained that the first units sent to South Vietnam, the 1st and 3rd Marine Divisions, the 1st and 25th Infantry Divisions, and the 1st Cavalry (Airmobile) Division were top-notch units, but the later units, the 4th and 9th Infantry Divisions, and the 196th and 198th Light Infantry Brigades were inferior in quality. Yet, even these so-called inferior units defeated both the North Vietnamese and Viet Cong in every engagement in which they met. Citizen-soldiers have both strengths and weaknesses, but in the long run, we make good soldiers.

It took me nearly twenty-five years to come to grips with my wartime experiences. While I was not as impressionable as some of the younger soldiers were, my adjustment was easier than most because I returned to a wife and an opportunity to continue my education. There were still a few roadblocks. When I tried to find a job in the winter of 1969 in the Dallas area, nobody would hire me. Businesses told me that they did not want to hire Vietnam veterans. Even when one finally offered me a job they gave it to someone else before I could report to work. I finally found a job as a laborer working on the Fort Worth City Hall building with a contractor who was friends with my father.

When I returned to the University of Iowa in September 1969, it was like going back to a different world. In the autumn of 1970, the anti-war movement was now popular with both the faculty and the students. I decided to join two anti–Vietnam War organizations with differing perspectives: Priorities for National Survival and Vietnam Veterans Against the War. Priorities for National Survival was a small faculty-student study group. Vietnam Veterans Against the War was a national organization of those Vietnam veterans that believed the war had been a mistake. Most of my activities in both organizations involved speaking engagements about my experience in the war. Once I appeared on a Cedar Rapids television station to debate the merits of the war with an ROTC colonel. The association with other like-minded veterans gave me some satisfaction. It did not isolate me from criticism from elements in the anti–Vietnam War movement. One of the leaders of the movement challenged me about killing their heroes the Viet Cong. I shut this person up with the statement that when the Viet Cong started shooting at me then I shot back. My anti-war activities took out some of my frustrations, but this was only a temporary respite.

My GI benefits ran out after a few years so I looked for other sources of income to allow me to write my dissertation. Although I no longer had a military obligation, I joined the Army Reserves in 1973 and became a weekend warrior. Joining the 1st Battalion, 410th Infantry, I was the only Vietnam veteran in the unit. It was comical how unprepared this unit was for military duty. Except for the officers, none of the enlisted men were reupping because they had joined to avoid the war. Now that they had escaped active military service, none of them wanted anything to do with the military. Fortunately, the battalion was never called to active duty. After a promotion to specialist E-6, I left the unit in 1977. Service in this unit helped me adjust to both the civilian and military sides of my life.

In the end, however, I adjusted because I wanted to rid myself forever of the ghosts of the war. My platoon had suffered nearly 40 percent killed, some of whom I called friends. The wounded list was much higher and some of the wounds were permanent. My only wound was cutting my finger opening a beer can. I have always felt guilty about my luck in transferring out of the infantry, but the transfer undoubtedly saved my life. It was not until a visit to the Vietnam Memorial in 1996 that I finally came to grips with my guilt and my feelings towards those who did not come back. It was strange that by then I could not even remember more than a few of their names. I have returned to the memorial several times since then, and it has been more of a healing process each time. It has only been in the last few years that I have erased the ghosts of the past, allowing me to finish the story of my experiences in the Vietnam War.

Appendix A: Captured Viet Cong Attack Plan

General

The following is a plan prepared by the Viet Cong to attack the bridge located at Ben Luc. The plan was captured by the 2nd Battalion, 60th Infantry at Binh Trinh Dong Village (XS653656) on 10 March 1967. This plan is included in this report to show the amount of detail which was normally employed by the Viet Cong prior to initiating any operation of this nature.

Combat Plan

I.   ENEMY SITUATION

The enemy forces camped at Len Luc area is one battalion, consisting of 395 men, commanded by Captain Gian and four US. Officers. They are the 3rd Battalion, 50th regiment, 25th Division, their headquarter is located at the end of the bridge in the direction of Dinh-Nhut.

Weapons: 1 81mm mortar
1 57mm recoilless rifle
4 60mm mortars
4 .50 cal machine guns
26 submarine guns
4 Combat boats armed with 16 machine guns
Individual weapons: rifles

There are local force and popular forces deployed in this zone especially to protect the bridge, four outposts, and a tank at each end of the bridge. There are 6 soldiers deployed to protect each support of the bridge. They are armed. They will shoot on any suspicious object floating close to the bridge. On both ends of the bridge and under the bridge there are four outposts about 250 meters away located near the bank of the river. There are 2 squads in each outpost. There are soldier's barracks on both sides of the bridge. Three men guard each end of the bridge. The generator is located about 30 meters from the bridge on the Binh Nhut side of the river. Combat boats patrol the river every one or two hours from the bridge out to 700 meters. They use searchlights on the river and on both banks. On each span of the bridge are four searchlights. Both sides of the river are also lighted for 250 meters by lamp posts. The bridge is very brightly lighted. When they see something suspicious they also electrify the water around the bridge. This battalion also patrols Binh Nhut and Binh Duc Strategic Hamlets. These forces sometimes attack our perimeter. The four combat boats are docked next to the ridge supports. There is one company stationed in Binh Nhut Strategic Hamlet now.

II.   OUR SITUATION

Both Binh Duc and Binh Nhut are Strategic Hamlets. These are enemy controlled areas. The enemy has firm control of these areas. The houses are crowded very close together. Two-thirds of the people are neutral and one-third are families of Viet Cong and are working for us in propaganda missions. We have a few secret cells in the hamlets but they are weak.

III.   TERRAIN AND TOPOGRAPHY

The Vam Co Dong River begins in Tay Ninh and flows into Vam Lang River which flows into the sea. The river is about 350 meters wide at the bridge, and the current is fast. This river has a bridge at Ben Luc on highway #4. Ben Luc Bridge is about 518 meters long. Maximum load for the bridge is 36 tons. The bridge is strategic for the enemy since the highway links Saigon and the Mekong Delta. This highway is usually patrolled and well guarded. There are ARVN outposts along the highway and Americans are camped from Ben Luc Market to Go Den along the highway. On the Long An side of the bridge there is a road which runs through Binh Duc Village and leads to Ben Da, then runs past the outpost at Ba Bong Stream. Natural obstacles are present on both sides of the river at Binh Nhut Village. There are many coconut trees that can be used for cover and concealment. So movement is very easy.

The Binh Nhut side of the river from Binh Duc to Cho Tao Market is a liberated area. On both sides of the river there are many bushes, but sometimes there are sampans filled with people fishing along the river bank from Binh Chanh to the Ben Luc Bridge, distance of about 150 meters. The natural obstacles will aid us when we approach the objective. On the river there are no sampans, on the banks of the river the enemy has a double barbed wire fence which surrounds the area. This is a heavily populated area; the houses are very close together. There are ruins of a large shrine on the river bank 800 meters from the bridge. Sometimes during the night the enemy sends recon patrols which come to the shrine. There is a river in this area that passes through Binh Chanh and Binh Nhut outpost a distance of 2 kilometers. This river has four small branches that run along the Vam Co Dong River, Rach Dinh Stream and the Rach Tua Stream. The distance from the Thu Doan Canal to the Binh Duc side of the river to Ben Luc Bridge is 5 kilometers. On the river, Ben Luc Bridge to Ba Bong Stream is 300 meters. This area is clear of brush from the Ba Bong Stream to the Thu Doan Canal. The terrain will aid in seizing the objective. The distance from Ong Thong Stream to Ben Luc Bridge is 180 meters on the river bank. There is a new life hamlet along this distance. There are 5 barbed wire entanglements surrounding it. Several houses and gardens and a saw mill, where enemy forces usually camp, are 700 meters from the ridge next to the river bank. In the area of this strategic hamlet thee are 6 small streams which run from the Vam Co Dong River into the rice fields. Cho Moi Canal is 250 meters from the bridge. The Ba Bong Stream is 300 meters from the bridge. On the Saigon side of the river there is a Ben Luc Market that has many people. This side of the stream has good natural concealment. There are sampans of migrating people located 500 meters from the bridge toward An Thanh Village.

IV.   MISSION

Our cell mission is to investigate and study point L. I. (Ben Luc Bridge). Our commander has decided that our cell will raid and destroy point L.I. in order to defeat the enemy's attempt at rural pacification and cut the highway connecting Saigon with the Mekong Delta. When we attack them we will meet many hardships and advantages such as:

A.   Advantages:
1. We have studied the whole enemy situation from the inside.
2. We have kept informed on the enemy's defenses.
3. We know the terrain and natural obstacles well.
4. We are ready to fight.

B.   Disadvantages:
1. Our explosives are very heavy to transport.
2. It is very difficult to transport explosives to the objective because of the bright lights and swift current.
3. In order to seize the objective we must cross many streams and pass through many strategic hamlets and travel across many swamps; this will be very difficult.

V.   RESOLUTION

According to the situation above, our cell will have many advantages and disadvantages. We must try to overcome all obstacles. We must try to affix a pulley on the objective. Even if conditions are difficult we will carry out our mission. We will destroy the L.I. point in order to disrupt the transportation of the enemy who plans an offensive against us in the dry season.

VI.   COORDINATION

A.   *Prior to Combat*
1. The 1st spearhead consists of four elements:
   a. The Destruction Element consists of 2 comrades. Re is in charge of the 1st stage.
   b. The 1st stage Medic Section has four laborers commanded by Rong.
   c. The deployment element is commanded by Sau Minh and is

responsible for the avenues of approach and withdrawal.

   d. The sampan element will transport the explosives and place them in the water. It consists of six comrades commanded by Anh.

  2. The Attack Element Consists of 5 Cells:

    a. 1st Cell — Comrade Nam is #1, Comrade Ie is #2, they will carry 2 pulleys, 1 pistol, and 1 grenade, and will hold the wire from the river bank to the objective.

    b. 2nd Cell — Trang is #3, Anh is #4, they are in charge of playing out the wire from the river bank to the bridge support of the 1st cell.

    c. 3rd Cell — Is comprised of 3 comrades — Van is #5, he will attach the wire to the explosives. Thien is #6, he will play out the electric wire. Xuan is #7, he will play out the electric line at 5 meter intervals.

    d. 4th Cell — It has 2 comrades — Bun is #8, Xien is #9. Their mission is to pull the wire for the 2nd cell after it has been connected to the explosives. The explosive transportation element which will transport the explosives from the departure point to the water position, must be on time.

  3. The 2nd spearhead consist of 2 elements: the support element and the medical service element, which are divided into 3 cells each.

    a. 1st Cell — Thno and Tao, armed with 2 CKC rifles, mission to stand at the mouth of the Ba Bong Stream and observe enemy activity.

    b. 3rd Cell — It is the mortar cell and will be deployed at Ba Su and the medical service element is comprised of one medic and four laborers with 2 sampans. They will be deployed at Ong Pho Stream.

  4. The sabotage device consists of two mines, each one is 1,000 kilograms, 1200 meters of electric wire, 200 batteries, 2 pulleys, 2 (illegible), 600 meters of nylon rope and 400 meters of rope.

B. *During Combat:*

  1. To transport the explosives A element must travel along waterways. They will travel by two motorized sampans to Binh Nhut. There they will turn off the motors. Then they will paddle to the "water position" which is located at the mouth of the Binh Chanh River where there will be men waiting for them. They must arrive at the Binh River at exactly 2000 hrs. The attack will move by land to the water position and wait there for the deployment element to report on the situation. The deployment cell and the medical service must come to the predetermined position, if they come early they must wait for the other elements to deploy.

  2. Numbers 1, 2, 3, and 10 will carry 2 rolls of nylon rope and 2 pul-

leys to the "fire position," numbers 4, 5, 6, 7, 8, 9, and 11 will go to the "water position" and tighten the mines. The end of the rope will be passed from man to man by their numbers. They will push the 2 mines to the "firing position" then wait there. Numbers 3 and 10 will play out the roll of nylon rope to number 1, then number 2 will tie it to the objective. After this has been accomplished number 10 will tighten it to number 3. Then number 3 and number 4 will take the rope and tie it to the bottom of numbers 6 and 7 explosives. Then prepare to play out the electric wire and tie the wire to the bottom of all the explosives. After this has been done numbers 3 and 4 will pull numbers 5 and 6 explosives step by step and play out the rope and wire at the bottom of the explosives coordinating with numbers 7 and 8. Then, they will pull the battery box to the side of the river and wait for orders. Numbers 1 and 2 will seize the objective and tie a rope to it. They will then float something on the river to Ba Bong Stream. Six comrades will go by sampan to the "water position" and give them to the attacking element. Then 5 of them will return to Binh Nhut factory and wait there. The 6th man will join the attack element. If numbers 1 and 2 cannot seize the objective, they must drop number 3 and 4 pulleys. They must then continue their attack in the 2nd stage, and numbers 10 and 11 will play out the rope to numbers 3 and 4 who will take the end of the rope to the objective. They will tie it there, and throw the other end into the water for the current to carry to Ba Bong Stream. They will then contact numbers 1 and 2, and the other members will then carry out their missions as outlined above.

3. B Spearhead: At exactly 2000 hours — The support element carrying 2 CKCs, 1 submachine gun, and 2 machine guns must be in position with foxholes prepared and ready. The mortar cell must be present at a predetermined position, and the medical elements with four laborers must be at Ong Pho Stream. The support cell must seize the river. Thuc and Tao, carrying two CKC must stand at the Ba Bong Stream to watch the activity at enemy cement pillar.

C. *After Combat*

1. A Spearhead: When the explosives blow up, numbers 6 and 7 will draw up the wire and reenroll it, numbers 3 and 4 will draw back the rope, numbers 8 and 9 will tighten the battery box, then elements will withdraw to Binh Nhut factory, check the soldiers and withdraw to a safe area.

2. B Spearhead: After the explosion the support element will not fire and it will withdraw to Ong Pho Stream then with the medic and other elements withdraw to safe areas.

VI.   MEDICAL

A. Element:
   1. One medic and one nurse and four laborers with stretchers, led by Rong are located at Binh Chanh Stream with local cadre men.
   2. B Element: One medic and four laborers with stretchers, led by Phu are located with two sampans and local cadre man at Ong Phu Stream
VII.   WITHDRAWAL
A. Spearhead
   1. A Spearhead — It will reassemble at Binh Nhut Factory to check strength
   2. B Spearhead — It will reassemble at Ong Phu Stream with the machine gun team and recon team and will check their strength

Estimate of the Situation

A. A Spearhead:

When numbers 1 and 2 carry the rope toward the objective, if they are discovered, the CKC cell should open fire at the combat ships in order to signal the machine gun cell. When the CKC cell opens fire this is the signal for the machine gun cell to open fire on the bridge and the mortar team will start firing on the soldiers camped next to the generator in Binh Nhut which is about 80 meters from the bridge. Numbers 1 and 2 must quietly attach the pulleys to the iron pillar, numbers 3 and 4 must quickly attach the explosives then withdraw to the firing point.

B. B Spearhead:

In case they are discovered by the enemy everyone must find another way to get to their positions on time. If the explosives are not blown up, then they should be withdrawn after receiving the order to do so.

C. A and B Spearhead:

If someone is wounded, then they should go to the aid station where medical aid will be available.

D. If the explosives don't blow up, comrade Anh is in charge of recovering them.

E. If the nylon rope gets snagged, a comrade must swim over and free it and put it in the river where the current will carry it to Miss Tu's house where comrade P will see it.

F. If the situation is quiet, then the ship will go down Rach Tao River, turn into Oe Dong River and come to Binh Nhut where there is a dump truck. If the situation is not quiet and there are ships on the river, then we will have to move toward Binh Chanh.

G. Although the Binh Nhut Post is deployed, we will still move to be at the mouth of Vam Dinh Chanh River at exactly 2000 hours.

Appendix B: Battle of Saigon, May 1968

Rumors and fragmentary intelligence reports warned the 9th Infantry Division of a possible offensive by the Viet Cong in early May. Although the Tet Offensive had more political than military results for the Viet Cong, another offensive was thought to be forthcoming to reaffirm the strength of the Viet Cong. Many intelligence officers considered Saigon the likely target and the birthday of Ho Chi Minh on May 9 the possible date.

On May 6, 1968, in response to the tense situation developing in Saigon, the 9th Infantry Division moved a mechanized infantry company up from Long An Province to reinforce the National Police in the area just south of the canal. The division commander also directed that the mechanized battalion commander establish a forward command post to maintain contact with precinct officials. This proved to be a timely move because the Viet Cong had already begun their infiltration into the outskirts of the city.

At first light on the morning of the 7th, a battalion sized enemy force attacked a National Police compound south of the canal between route 5A and the Y bridges. Elements of Company C, 5th Battalion, 60th Infantry were in the vicinity of the two bridges and responded to the call for help from the besieged headquarters. Heavy contact ensued but after an hour, the enemy withdrew to the southwest. Company C pursued and with the help of B Troop, 7th Squadron, 1st Air Cavalry reestablished contact. As the intensity of the conflict grew, the battalion commander made a decision to commit his Company A from Ben Luc. Their arrival at mid-morning "cracked the nut" although contact continued throughout the rest of the day becoming sporadic by 2000. The day's results showed 213 VC KIA (BC) versus 2 US KIA and 45 US WIA.

A serious enemy threat demanded greater response on our part. Reinforcements were brought in to counter Viet Cong activity. The scout platoon from the 2nd Battalion, 47th Infantry, was brought in from the Bearcat area and placed OPCON to the 5th Battalion, 60th Infantry. In addition, the 3rd Battalion, 39th Infantry (minus Company C) was moved to block below the built up area south of the Y Bridge.

New contact with the enemy was made on May 8. At mid-morning, the 3rd Battalion, 39th Infantry, departed their night deployment positions to reconnoiter northward into the built up area near the Y Bridge. The scout platoon, 2nd Battalion, 47th Infantry, worked west from the Y Bridge toward the common objective area. By mid-afternoon all elements were in contact with a Viet Cong reinforced company. Operational control of the 2nd Battalion, 47th Infantry, was given to the 3rd Battalion, 39th Infantry, and together they pushed northeast toward the Y Bridge. The going was slow as it became a house-to-house, street-by-street type of operation. At day's end 115 Viet Cong had been killed as against 4 US KIA and 25 WIA.

Fighting extended on May 9 to three different areas. Elements of the 5th Battalion, 60th Infantry reconnoitered in force to the northwest from their nighttime positions. As they approached the built-up area, near Thien Durong (XS827876), they established contact with an unknown sized enemy force and the fighting lasted for two hours. Near the Y Bridge, the 3rd Battalion, 39th Infantry augmented by Company B, 5th Battalion, 31st Infantry searched throughout the surrounding built up area. Frequent sniper fire was returned by US units. To the northeast, the 2nd Battalion, 47th Infantry, having been sent from Bearcat to recon in force a suburb northeast of the Y Bridge, made contact with the enemy near Highway 231. To the southeast, companies A and C, 6th Battalion, 31st Infantry encountered sporadic contact throughout the afternoon. These four separate actions produced 202 enemy bodies in contrast to 11 US KIA and 66 US WIA.

At the close of the third day in the Battle of Saigon, the 9th Division had five battalions and two air cavalry troops operating in the southern capital military district. Artillery support had been doubled when three more batteries were brought within range of the division's operations. The movement of the 5th Vietnamese Marines into Saigon made the division also responsible for their area of operation.

Fighting continued on May 10. At dawn, a Vietnamese reconnaissance force outpost to the south at Xom Tan Liem (XS815824) came under heavy ground attack from the Viet Cong. It was decided to send B Troop, 7th Squadron, 1st Air Cavalry, to assist the beleaguered government forces. When the air cavalry unit received intense ground fire, the decision was made to commit two companies, A and C, 5th Battalion, 60th Infantry. Company A began to receive fire as it approached within 600 meters of the Vietnamese outpost. Company C supported its fellow company by approaching from the northwest. As these forces closed on the enemy, Company C drew heavy automatic weapons fire from the wood line to the southwest. Because of this resistance, two more companies, A and C, 6th Battalion, 31st Infantry, were airmobiled behind the Viet Cong hitting them from the northwest. Contact ceased around dusk.

Further Viet Cong resistance was encountered near Saigon. At mid-morning, the 3rd Battalion, 39th Infantry, and D Troop, 3rd Battalion, 5th Cavalry, commenced a reconnaissance-in-force operation from their overnight positions in the built-up area near Saigon. Companies A and B, 3rd Battalion, 39th Infantry, were to work in conjunction with D Troop, 3rd Battalion, 5th Cavalry, astride the Ong Nho River with a company on each side of the river. Upon arrival at the river (XS842882), Company B received automatic weapons fire. As contact intensified, Company A was ordered to cross over from the west bank. During the crossing back over the bridge (XS641882), Company received B-40 rocket fire and became heavily engaged against the

Viet Cong. The enemy was of unknown size and well bunkered. Contact subsided at nightfall. These engagements on May 10 resulted in 113 Viet Cong KIA, and 9 US KIA and 57 WIA.

Final mopping up operations were undertaken by the 3rd Brigade on May 12. The five companies under the operation command of the 3rd Battalion, 39th Infantry, began a reconnaissance-in-force in the built-area south of the Y Bridge. By mid-day all companies had established contact with squad sized Viet Cong forces. The enemy fire continued until dusk in degrees varying from sniper shots to sporadic gunfire. Company B, 6th Battalion, 31st Infantry, came into heavy contact with a platoon size enemy force near an abandoned South Vietnamese regional force outpost at 1720. This contact too broke at darkness. The enemy suffered 93 killed with the US losses were 4 KIA and 26 WIA.

The Battle for Saigon lasted from May 7 to May 12. For the next week US military forces pursued an aggressive pursuit of the Viet Cong into their base camp areas south and southeast of Saigon. This pursuit resulted in sporadic contact. The Viet Cong lost 148 KIA (BC) during this eight day period from May 13 to May 20 in contrast to 7 US KIA and 36 WIA.

The fighting during the Battle of Saigon had been difficult particularly in the built-up areas. Air strikes were the only answer to the enemy bunkers along the southern edge of Saigon, and air cavalry gunship supported our forces throughout. At the relatively small cost of 33 US KIA, the enemy lost 852.

Appendix C: After Action Report, Battle of the Plain of Reeds

Department of the Army Headquarters, 19th Military History Detachment. *Combat After Action Interview Report — 4-68*

1. Name and type of operation: TRUONG CONG DINH: The Plain of Reeds

2. Dates of operation: 31 May to 4 June, 1968

3. Location: XS6229 IV, XS6230 III, XS6230 II, XS6130 I, XS6230 IV

4. Control of command headquarters: 1st Brigade, 9th Infantry Division

5. Interviewed personnel: Brigadier General William A. Knowlton, 0-0025436, Assistant Division Commander, 9th Infantry Division; Lieutenant Colonel William L. Leggett, Jr., 0-0066361, Commander, 2nd, 39th Infantry; Lieutenant Colonel James J. Lindsay, 0-0075235, Commander, 2nd,

60th Infantry; Major Frank L. Day, 0–0073661, S-3, 1st Brigade; Major Robert E. Joseph, Jr., 0–0072117, Executive Officer, 2nd, 60th Infantry; Captain William B. Henrich, 0–5312289, Commander, A-411 Special Forces Group, My Phouc Tay, Captain Joseph C. Rischerie, 0–5541353, Surgeon, HHQ, 2nd, 60th Infantry; 1st Lieutenant John G. Griffith, 0–5425396, Artillery Liaison Officer assigned to 2nd Battalion, 60th Infantry from 1st, Battery, 11th Artillery; 1st Lieutenant Gregory D. Hering, 0–5334014, Platoon Leader, J Platoon, Company E, 2nd Battalion, 39th Infantry; 1st Lieutenant Adrian Mitchell, 0–5424033, Forward Observer, Company A, 2nd Battalion, 39th Infantry' 1st Lieutenant Jerome Zamora, 0–5339138, Platoon Leader, Company B, 2nd Battalion, 60th Infantry; 2nd Lieutenant Thomas P. Downey, 0–5342612, Platoon Leader, Company A, 2nd Battalion, 60th Infantry; 2nd Lieutenant Phillip A. Poynter, 0–5341318, Platoon Leader, Company A, 2nd Battalion, 60th Infantry; 2nd Lieutenant William Schmiedecke, 0–5341331, Platoon Leader, Company C, 2nd Battalion, 60th Infantry; 2nd Lieutenant Phil H. Ward, 0–5345841, Platoon Leader, Company A, 2nd, 39th Infantry; Master-Sergeant Peter V. Astalos, RA10812185, Advisor, A-411 Special Forces Group, My Phouc Tay; Master-Sergeant Bobby J. McFarland, RA14456514, Intelligence Sergeant, 2nd Battalion, 60th Infantry; Staff Sergeant Thomas I. Dunnings, RA14773297, Acting Platoon Leader, R Platoon, Company E, 2nd Battalion, 39th Infantry; Staff Sergeant Joe C. T. Guyton, Jr., RA13657215. Advisor, A-411 Special Forces Group, My Phouc Tay; Staff Sergeant William H. Golden, RA12732592, Platoon Sergeant, Company C, 2nd Battalion, 39th Infantry; Staff Sergeant Edwin P. Williams, RA13773098, Acting Platoon Leader, Company C, 2nd Battalion, 39th Infantry; Sergeant Alexander J. Kolego, RA11569835, Squad Leader, Company B, 2nd Battalion, 60th Infantry; Sergeant Roy D. Petty, US54955189, Squad Leader, Company C, 4th Battalion, 47th Infantry; Sergeant Andrew M. Ramsey, RA11748529, Platoon Sergeant, Company A, 2nd Battalion, 39th Infantry; Sergeant Stephen Sifferman, US56958420, Company B, 2nd Battalion, 39th Infantry; Specialist 5 Kenneth R. Petty, US4439997, Medic, Company B, 2nd Battalion, 39th Infantry; Specialist 4 Roger L. Hubbell, RA19815274, Company A, 2nd Battalion, 39th Infantry; Specialist 4 Bobby J. Thomas, US4813252, Mortar Platoon, Company A, 2nd Battalion, 39th Infantry; Specialist Paul Thompson, US54927366, Platoon Leader's RTO, Company C, 2nd Battalion, 60th Infantry; Private First Class Roy E. Drassinger, Rifleman, Company C, 4th Battalion, 47th Infantry; Private First Class John E. Nielson, RA11757247, Rifleman, Company B, 2nd Battalion, 39th Infantry; Private First Class Clarke L. Scherff, US56708102, Medic, Company C, 2nd Battalion, 60th Infantry.

6. Interviewer: Research Assistant, Sergeant Stephen E. Atkins

7. Task organization: 2nd Battalion, 39th Infantry, 2nd Battalion, 60th Infantry, Company C, 4th Battalion, 47 Infantry, and 4th Battalion 39th Infantry

8. Supporting forces: 1st Battery, 11th Artillery, 1st Battery, 84th Artillery,

1st Squadron, 7th Air Cavalry, 191st and 240th Helicopter Companies, 214th Aviation Battalion

9. Background information:

The 1st Brigade had been on Operation Duong Cua Dan (People's Road) since 17 March 1968. The Brigade's mission in Dinh Tuong Province had been to keep QL4 open from the junction of QL4 and LTL (lightly surfaced two lane) 6a to Cai Lay. This portion of QL4 has long been considered the least secure part of the road as it bisects heavily Viet Cong controlled territory. In order to accomplish this mission, the 2nd Battalion, 39th Infantry, 2nd Battalion, 60th Infantry, and Company A, 5th Battalion, 60th Infantry (Mech.) had been attached to the 1st Brigade. These units guarded QL4 by a series of base camps along the road from which patrols sallied forth each evening. By late May, the area adjacent to QL4 had been largely pacified. The 2nd Battalion, 60th Infantry was stationed at Brigade Headquarters at the Pink Palace (XS4049), Companies A and C, 2nd Battalion, 39th Infantry, were at Firebase Moore (XS26450), Company B, 2nd battalion, 39th Infantry, and Company A, 5th Battalion, 60th Infantry (Mech.) were at Firebase Lambert (XS3249), and Company E, 2nd Battalion, 39th Infantry was at Patrol Base Mohawk (XS2450).

The morale of the units of the 1st Brigade on the eve of their operation in the Plain of Reeds was high due to their recent successes along QL4. The men of the 2nd Battalion, 9th Infantry and the 2nd Battalion 60th Infantry had become adept at night work as a result of the constant night patrolling along QL4. In the previous two months, these night patrols had clashed frequently with elements of four Viet Cong battalions in Dinh Tuong Province. Heavy Viet Cong casualties coupled with light U.S. losses contributed to this high state of morale among the units of the 1st Brigade. Another factor that accounted for the high morale of these units was that after each action the units returned to their permanent base camps to clean up and relax.

The 1st Brigade, however, did not restrict its activities solely to Operation DUONG CUA DAN. The brigade participated whenever conditions along QL4 permitted it, in operations outside the limits of Operation DUONG CUA DAN. Anytime the brigade operated outside of an artificial boundary (AO Crackerjack), 3,000 meters on either side of QL4, it became part of Operation TRUONG CON DINH. The mission of units of Operation TRUONG CONG DINH was to purge Dinh Tuong Province and surrounding areas of Viet Cong influence. The mission of the 1st Brigade in the Plain of Reeds, therefore, was a part of Operation TRUONG CONG DINH. For this new operation, Company B, 4th, 39th Infantry, and Company C, 4th, 47th Infantry, were placed temporarily under the operational control of the 1st Brigade. Their role was to guard QL4 while the rest of the 1st Brigade maneuvered in the Plain of Reeds.

The size, the terrain, and the proximity to Cambodia makes the Plain of Reeds a natural haven for the Viet Cong. The Plain of Reeds is an extensive marshland with an interlaced system of rivers, streams and canals. There are broad expanses of open land interspersed with heavy brush and wood lines. These wood lines are often used by the Viet Cong for base camps. The Viet Cong find it easy to build bunkers unobserved, and the bunkers are easily camouflaged. A system of trails from Cambodia provides them with a constant flow of supplies and reinforcements.

The size and terrain of the Plain of Reeds presents special problems for U.S. operations. Large ground sweeps are simply not practical because of the terrain. The tactic usually employed by the 1st Brigade in the Plain of Reeds is the "jitterbug." A "jitterbug" is an airmobile operation in which small groups are inserted to search out suspected Viet Cong positions while another group of similar size units remain in the air to provide reinforcements in case of contact. This approach means that many trouble spots can be checked out in a single day, and, that once the enemy's position is fixed, reinforcements can be airlifted in to encircle and destroy the Viet Cong forces. The secret of the success of this tactic is the availability of air assets, because, if these small groups made contact with a Viet Cong force of any size, there is always the danger that the small unit will be annihilated before adequate help arrives.

Another tactic that is employed on occasions by the 1st Brigade is the "bushmaster." The "bushmaster" was developed to counter the Viet Cong tactics of disappearing during large scale operations only to reappear once U.S. troops left the area. The theory is to deceive the enemy by a false or partial extraction of U.S. units. Those units left on the ground would then proceed to a new position for the night. Company, platoon, or squad size ambushes would be established at strategic points in the area. There are endless possible variations of this tactic, but all of them depend upon deception. This tactic has met with moderate success in that it is difficult to hide large scale movement of U.S. forces from the Viet Cong.

Support bases for artillery are a problem in the Plain of Reeds. Special Forces camps are so widely scattered throughout the Plain of Reeds that there is always the possibility that the situation will necessitate operations outside of the range of the artillery. To solve this problem, provisions have been made in emergencies for rapid displacement of artillery on short notice to new firing positions, but again the key to success is the availability of air assets.

10. Intelligence:

Intelligence reports had reached the 1st Brigade Headquarters during the month of May of heavy enemy activity in the Plain of Reeds area. Information gathered for over seven months had indicated that two Viet Cong staging areas existed in southeastern Cambodia (coordinates XS2696 and XS2996) from which the Viet Cong in the Plain of Reeds were receiving reinforcements and supplies. (See Inclosure 1) At various times in the month of May, large groups of Viet Cong had been spotted in the northern part of the Plain of Reeds. These units had been identified as the 261A MF (Main Force), the 261B MF, the D800 (or AKA C800) MF, and 504 LF (Local Force), the 506

LF, and the 514C LF battalions. Several smaller groups had also been noted, and they were identified as mainly sapper units. All of these units had large base camps in the northern Plain of Reeds in which they received their supplies, and in which they trained their reinforcements. Moreover, information from prisoners of war indicated that in the same general area as these base camps the Viet Cong had several medical training centers, a hospital, two prisoner of war holding stations, several replacement points and a central command post. On 29 May a prisoner of war revealed that the 514B LF Battalion was to rendezvous shortly with the 261A MF and the 261B MF battalions in the tree line vicinity XS345685.[1] This activity and information from agents led the 1st brigade to conclude that the Viet Cong were reorganizing for an extended campaign in the 1st Brigade's area of responsibility. Finally, an escaped prisoner of war provided S-2 with several sets of coordinates where Viet Cong battalion base camps were supposed to be located. This was the intelligence picture which led the 1st Brigade to decide on a large scale operation in the northern Plain of Reeds (See Inclosure 2).

11. Mission:

The 2nd Battalion, 39th Infantry and the 2nd Battalion, 60th Infantry with support from 1st Battery, 11th Artillery, 1st Battery, 84th Artillery, and 1st Squadron, 7th Air Cavalry were by a series of air mobile operations to search out and destroy suspected Viet Cong base camps in the northern Plain of Reeds area.

12. a. Concept of Operation:

Operating on intelligence data that indicated two large Viet Cong base camps at coordinates XS2685 and XS2984, elements of the 2nd Battalion, 39th Infantry and the 2nd Battalion, 60th Infantry were to investigate these sites. The 2nd Battalion, 60th Infantry was to proceed by air to the vicinity of coordinates XS2685 to discover and destroy the Viet Cong base camp at that location. In the meantime, the 2nd Battalion, 39th Infantry was to secure an old French fort (XS337846) so that A Battery, 1st Battery, 11th Artillery could provide support for the operation. The 2nd Battalion, 39th Infantry was then to proceed on foot to coordinates XS2984 to locate and destroy the Viet Cong base camp there. With these two large base camps destroyed, the 1st Brigade hoped to cripple Viet Cong activity in the Plain of Reeds for

---

[1] A prisoner of war, Nguyen Thanh Mau, the former XO of the 2nd Regional Forces Company of Cai Lay District, stated on June 11, 1968, that until January 1968, the 514 LF Battalion and the Dinh Tuong Provincial unit covered both Dinh Tuong and Go Cong areas. In January, the 514 Battalion was predesignated the 514A Battalion and grouped with the 261A and 261B MF Battalions to form the 1st Battle Group. A 514B Battalion was created to serve as the Dinh Tuong Provincial unit but it was reassigned to Go Cong Province. Because of the need for experienced troops, the cadre from several district units were transferred to the new battalion. In early May, a 514C Battalion was organized to provide a provincial unit for Dinh Tuong Province. Great difficulty was experienced in manning this battalion and it was necessary to take personnel form hamlet level guerrilla units to fill command positions.

months. A side goal was to locate the Viet Cong medical facilities and any other Viet Cong installations in the northern Plain of Reeds. To provide support, C Battery, 1st Battery, 11th Artillery's AN/T.S.-25 and 1st Battery, 11th Artillery's AN/MEQ-4A were placed at the Special Forces camp at They Dong on 29 May to select and fire on targets of opportunity. Their instructions stated that, prior to 31 May, they were not to fire on radar sightings unless the Viet Cong were in groups of 100 or more and appeared to be leaving the area.

12. b. Execution:

On 30 May, the 2nd Battalion, 39th Infantry and the 2nd Battalion, 60th Infantry received orders for an airmobile operation in the northern sector of the Plain of Reeds. After some scattered activity in the northern Plain of reeds on 30 May, the 2nd Battalion, 39th Infantry landed early in the morning of 31 May to establish a base camp and guard A Battery, 1st Battery, 11th Artillery at an old French fort (XS337846). In the afternoon, the companies of the 2nd Battalion, 39th Infantry moved from their new base camp on foot to widely dispersed destinations for night operations. The 2nd Battalion, 60th Infantry conducted several "jitterbug" operations on 31 May in an area bordered by grid lines 34–38 east-west and 81–78 north-south hoping to find a reported Viet Cong camp, but this base camp was never located. That night, the companies of both the 2nd Battalion, 39th Infantry and 2nd Battalion, 60th Infantry conducted "bushmaster" operations near Cambodia. There was no enemy contact that day or night for either battalion.

Early on the morning of 1 June, the 1st Brigade commander, Colonel Henry Emerson in his command ship noticed a trail leading through the Plain of Reeds. He ordered C Troop, 7th Squadron, 1st Air Cavalry, to investigate. At 0940, elements of the 1st Air Cavalry spotted an enemy mortar tube and several running Viet Cong soldiers at coordinates XS382718, and a possible ammo cache at coordinates XS394700. Half of Company C, 2nd Battalion, 39th Infantry, with Captain Peck in command, were inserted (XS385716) at 1240 to pick up the mortar and the body of one of the Viet Cong soldiers, and the other half of the company, with 1st Lieutenant Nonte in charge, landed (XS395701) approximately 1,500 away to search for the ammo cache. Almost as soon as the northern most group started to move through the bushes point elements stumbled into a bunker complex from which the Viet Cong delivered heavy small arms and automatic weapons fire. The initial enemy gunfire was so heavy and effective that the men of Company C were unable to move from behind initial protective cover.

The terrain had been difficult to move through because of the mud and the thick underbrush. This underbrush with some reeds as tall as ten feet and thick undergrowth, forced U.S. soldiers to use well-worn trails. Enemy bunkers were built low to the ground, and the Viet Cong had all the trails covered by fields of fire. Point elements of Company C had moved with five meters of the bunkers without knowing of their existence before the Viet Cong opened fire. Their initial burst of firing wounded five U.S. soldiers. Later, some of the others units, forewarned of enemy contact, came as close as 15 meters before the Viet Cong opened fire. The Viet Cong had their bunker situated at junctions of the trails so that any movement down the trails was suicidal. Booby-traps were visible hanging in the bushes off the trails so as to discourage any attempts to flank the bunkers.

Noting heavy contact, Colonel Emerson request Lieutenant-Colonel Leggett, commander of the 2nd Battalion, 39th Infantry to send reinforcement. Leggett ordered Company A, 2nd Battalion, 39th Infantry into the battle. Company A landed south of Company C (XS390710) at 1400, but as Company A attempted to link up with Company C it ran into gunfire and booby-traps. Both units soon realized that the Viet Cong were between the two companies, and this made it difficult for the men to return fire without endangering U.S. troops. This dilemma was partially solved by throwing hand grenades. These grenades did little actual damage to the Viet Cong, however, as the Viet Cong positions were too close to U.S. troops. The grenades merely sailed over the Viet Cong bunkers and exploded harmlessly. Meanwhile, the accuracy of Viet Cong fire made maneuvering by U.S. forces almost impossible.

From 1500 to 1600, Companies A and C, 2nd Battalion, 60th Infantry were inserted (XS383705) to deny the Viet Cong an escape route to the west. The mission of these companies was to move northeast from their landing zone to positions on the western flank of the Viet Cong bunkers. Initial enemy contact at the landing zone and the difficulty of movement through the bush resulted in Lieutenant Colonel Lindsay, commander of the 2nd Battalion, 60th Infantry, assuming ground command. The two companies marched in single file for almost 1,000 meters to their blocking positions on the western flank of the Viet Cong positions.

Throughout the afternoon and early evening U.S. troops maneuvered to encircle the enemy. By 1600, after a forced march through knee deep mud and water, the other half of Company C, 2nd Battalion, 39th Infantry moved up and joined Company A, 2nd Battalion, 39th Infantry. At 1935, Company B, 2nd Battalion, 39th Infantry was inserted (XS396717) with the mission to flank the enemy to the north and complete the encirclement. The heavy concentration of Viet Cong fire, booby-traps, and darkness, however, prevented the complete encirclement of the enemy. A gap between Companies A and B, 2nd Battalion, 39th Infantry on the eastern side was never closed before contact with the Viet Cong ceased at approximately 2130.[2] Night ambushes were placed in strategic positions, but the Viet Cong were still able to escape during the night with relatively light losses.

Because of the confusion about the location of friendly units and the close

---

[2]2nd Lieutenant Phil Ward, Platoon Leader in Company A, 2nd Battalion, 39th Infantry, claims that his unit never had a chance to close the gap as Viet Cong fire was so heavy that it would have been suicide for the men to move forward. Moreover, the confusion was such that nobody knew exactly where the Viet Cong positions were located.

proximity of U.S. troops to the Viet Cong bunkers, fire support was not as heavy nor as effective as is the normal case. The only artillery support available on 1 June was A Battery, 1st Battery, 11th Artillery with only six 105mm Howitzers. Moreover, there were difficulties displacing A Battery from the old French fort to near Ap Bac Dong (XS476702), which resulted in no artillery support until approximately 1630. (See Inclosure #3)[3] Five TAC air strikes, gun ships and Spookie filled in the void until the battery had been placed in its new firing location, but the bunkers were simply too close to U.S. troops for them to be effective.

From documents captured at the scene of the battle, it is known that the battle on 1 June was with the 261 A and 261 B Main force Viet Cong Battalions. The intensity of the fire from the bunkers indicated that the Viet Cong were well-equipped with small and heavy caliber weapons. They also had an elaborate bunker system at this location. Subsequent examination showed that the bunker system had no discernable pattern except that each bunker could cover a trail junction of interlocking trails. The bunkers were mutually supporting with U.S. communication equipment providing the communications between the bunkers. This area was probably a major area base. Witnesses mentioned hearing the voices of women and children and the banging of utensils during the night as the Viet Cong infiltrated through U.S. lines.

A sweep the next day revealed that the Viet Cong had escaped. U.S. forces did find 41 Viet Cong bodies, 10 small arms, 2 radios, and 1 M-60 machine gun. Observation and "people sniffer" teams were able, however, to reestablish contact with Viet Cong elements. These teams trailed the Viet Cong to a wood line (XS429688), but a detailed search of this area revealed only traces of recent enemy occupation. Company E, 2nd Battalion, 39th Infantry, and a CIDG Company from My Dien Special Forces Camp established multiple checkerboard ambushes southwest of previous contact, but the two enemy battalions slipped through without detection. On 3 June, another trail was detected and it was followed to the southwest until aerial spotters noticed enemy activity around coordinates XS 275582. Company A, 2nd Battalion, 39th Infantry was ordered to investigate this activity. Company A was inserted by airlift at 1000 (XS254584) in an area known as the "Triangle."[4] This area had long been known for its pro-Viet Cong tendencies.

[3]For some reason, a request to move A Battery was denied initially by the commanding officer, 9th Infantry Division Artillery. This delay meant that no artillery support was available for a key three and a half hour period during which the 2nd Battalion, 39th Infantry was heavily engaged.

[4]There is a natural confusion about the locations of units during any battle. This was also the case on 3 June. Much of the confusion was ended by Lieutenant Colonel Leggett. On the afternoon of 2 September 1968, Leggett made an aerial reconnaissance of the area. He is positive of the location as the battlefield was marked by two large white crypts. He had used one of them as cover on the evening of 3 June. TheDinh Mot Canal (XS257588), which runs north and south, points right at the crypt behind which Leggett took cover at XS257583. He reconstructed a map of the action. (See Inclosure #4)

Airships dropped Company A, 2nd Battalion, 39th Infantry in a rice paddy south of a heavily wood lined canal. The officers and men had little idea what to expect as they had been informed that only about 70 Viet Cong had been spotted earlier in this area. Moreover, the company had not been completely resupplied the previous night as the men were low on water and ammunition.[5] Company A had been ordered to land west of the reported enemy contact in order to outflank the Viet Cong positions from the west. The company landed only about 1000 meters from the wood line, and, as the men moved north toward the wood line, they received intense heavy automatic and semi-automatic fire from the front and both sides.[6] Some sporadic fire also came from some hooches to the rear. Heavy initial casualties were inflicted on Company A by the superior accuracy and fire discipline of the Viet Cong. Although Viet Cong bunkers were identified on a dike in front of the wood line, fire was so intense that the men were rarely able to discover the exact location of the bunkers. From the wood line on the right, snipers with scopes mounted on their rifles kept U.S. troops pinned down with extremely accurate fire. Survivors recount that any movement on the part of men of Company A resulted in a hit or near miss. It was this fire that accounts for the large number of fatal head wounds suffered by Company A in this engagement. Little fire support was available for Company A as only

[5]Lieutenant Colonel Leggett claims that this statement is erroneous. He maintains that "Company A, 2nd Battalion, 39th Infantry had in effect stood down on the night of 2 June at the My Dien Special Forces Camp. Except for the listening posts, the entire company was within the camp and did receive water, ammo and food. This can be substantiated by the officers of the Company A, 2nd Battalion, 39th Infantry." I based this statement upon information given to me by the enlisted soldiers in Company A, 2nd Battalion, 39th Infantry. According to them, the officers and men understood that they were to be airlifted back their permanent base camp on the morning of 3 June. A water trailer was provided for Company A, but when members of the company went to fill their canteens on the morning of 3 June the water trailer was empty. Consequently, many members of Company A went into action on 3 June with an insufficient supply of water. While there was ammunition and food, my sources state that they did not have their standard load of ammunition. None of them worried about food, because Company A was returning to base camp that morning. Lieutenant Ward stated in an interview on October 7, 1968, that his company was resupplied, but he also agreed about the shortage of water. He added, however, that there would have been a water problem during the battle even if the men had sufficient water at the base camp on the morning of 3 June. His most serious problem was that his unit did not receive a resupply of smoke grenades. Consequently, he had difficulty in indicating his position for air and gun ship strikes on 3 June.

[6]Lieutenant Colonel Leggett also disputes this statement. "The company landed at least 200 meters from the wood line. The ships received no fire. This can be verified by Major Cal Griggs, 191st Airmobile Company. Thinking back, I cannot ever remember landing troops within 200 meters of a wood line that was not already occupied by U.S. forces. The men came under fire between 50–100 meters from bunkers along the wood line. This was at least 5–10 minutes after the insertion." Lieutenant Ward maintains that the landings were 150 to 200 meters from the wood line, but in his opinion this is still much too close to the wood line for safety. Yet, most of the men interviewed from Company A immediately after the battle were convinced that they had landed within 100 meters of the wood line.

one battery of six 105mm howitzers at the Special Forces Camp at My Dien II was ready to support them and this battery was firing at its maximum range.

Efforts were made to reinforce Company A and block a possible enemy retreat. Within an hour of first contact, Company E, 2nd Battalion, 39th Infantry was inserted approximately 100 meters to the south of Company A in order to sweep a wood line on the right of Company A from which heavy enemy fire was raking Company A.[7] Soon Company E was also pinned down by Viet Cong fire. Companies A and E had to stay in a hot rice paddy the rest of the day, and, besides heavy enemy inflicted casualties, both companies suffered numerous cases of heat exhaustion. By the time additional reinforcements arrived, these units were no longer combat effective.[8]

The Brigade commander, Colonel Emerson, overhead in his command ship, recognized the seriousness of the situation, and he called for further reinforcements. At 1400, Company A and Company B, 2nd Battalion, 60th Infantry were inserted west of contact at XS244585 and XS244587 respectively. Their mission was to sweep toward contact and roll over the flanks of the Viet Cong positions. In a methodical sweep, Company B eliminated over 60 bunkers as the men used World War II tactics of knocking out one bunker at a time with grenades, M-7 rounds, and LAWS (Light Anti-Tank Weapon). Movement through the wood line was slow, because of enemy resistance and

---

[7]According to Lieutenant Ward, who replaced 1st Lieutenant O'Reilly as commander of Company A after O'Reilly's death in the first few minutes of the battle, Company E was dropped in the wrong place. Company E should have landed 500 to 600 meters to the east of where the company landed. Eventually Task Force Joseph carried out Company E's mission.

[8]Lieutenant Colonel Leggett also disagrees with this statement. He says, "I was up over these units all afternoon and had communications with them. I landed around 1800 in the afternoon and saw from the ground how effective they were. It is true that both companies suffered from heat and mental strain. It is also true that some of the men fainted. However, I observed return of fire throughout and received reports of enemy movement. Enemy movement was observed first to the west and then back to the east as the 2nd Battalion, 60th Infantry came up on our left flank and taken under fire with small arms with good effect. Captain Dent and 2nd Lieutenant Ward, who controlled the two companies were in constant communications with me and assisted in brining in air strikes, helicopter gun ships and artillery throughout the day. As a matter of fact by the time reinforcements arrived, it was late in the afternoon, cooler, and both companies were no longer suffering form the heat. When I landed at 1800, the 2nd Battalion, 60th Infantry had not yet come up on the flank. Heavy firing was still going on and both A and E companies were returning more than they received. It should be mentioned that the company commander of Company A (1st Lieutenant O'Reilly) was killed early in the battle, and this may have caused an emotional effect and added to mental stress." In his interview on 7 October, Lieutenant Ward stated that he told Lieutenant-Colonel Leggett on 3 June that by mid-day his company was no longer combat effective. Several members of Company A mentioned that they were terrified that the Viet Cong would launch a final attack and butcher them. The men of companies A and B, 2nd Battalion, 60th Infantry, who relieved Company A, agreed that Company A was in little condition to fight when they relieved them in early evening.

the numerous bunkers. Company A met less resistance, but, in order to keep in contact with Company B, it was also forced to move slowly.

Another unit called into action was Task Force Joseph. Task Force Joseph, which was comprised of Company C, 4th Battalion, 47th Infantry, and Company C, 2nd Battalion, 60th Infantry landed at XS260579 and XS260582 respectively at 1600 southeast of the positions of Companies A and E, 2nd Battalion, 39th Infantry to seal off the eastern flank of the Viet Cong bunker system.[9] Commanded by Major Joseph, executive officer of the 2nd Battalion, 60th Infantry, Task Force Joseph's mission was to advance north to the main canal (King Tong Doc Loc). Numerous heavily defended bunkers and effective sniper fire made progress slow. Pinned down most of the evening, Company C, 2nd Battalion, 60th Infantry and Company C, 4th Battalion, 47th Infantry, finally accomplished their mission shortly after midnight when an assault finally carried the eastern wood line.[10]

To complete the encirclement, Colonel Emerson requested assistance from the Special Forces Camp at My Phuoc Tay. The mission of the CIDG group was to arrive at positions north of the main canal (King Tong Doc Loc) and prevent the Viet Cong from escaping the trap by crossing the river. Arriving at their designated position (XS253589) by 1920, this force had only moderate success.[11] While the CIDG force killed only four Viet Cong, it did capture 2 .45 caliber pistols, web gear and assorted documents.

Throughout the afternoon and night, airships, tactical aircraft, and artillery pounded enemy positions. The artillery was especially effective as early evening five batteries were available for fire support missions. These batteries were B and D Batteries, 1st Battery, 84th Artillery, and A and B Batteries, 1st Battery, 11th Artillery at FSPB Moore, and C Battery, 1st Battery, 11th Artillery at Ap My Dien. Seventeen air strikes also helped destroy enemy bunkers and accounted for the high body count. Colonel credited 89 percent of the Viet Cong body count on 3 June to artillery and air strikes.

---

[9]I used Major Joseph's reconstruction of troop movements rather than the official coordinates. Since a disagreement on location exists of about 1000 meters, I felt that the commander's reconstruction was more accurate than official documents. Lieutenant Colonel Leggett agrees with the approximate position of Task Force Joseph with Joseph's account.

[10]This assault was initially carried out by a force of from 16 to 20 men from Company C, 2nd Battalion, 60th Infantry as the soldiers of Company C, 4th Battalion, 47th Infantry refused to assault. Most of the soldiers of Company C, 4th Battalion, 47th Infantry that I talked to considered the assault as a suicide mission. Even the officers agreed and no charges for disobedience under fire were ever lodged. Luckily for those engaged in the assault, the Viet Cong were more intent in escaping than fighting at this stage of the battle.

[11]The Special Forces advisors were unanimous in their belief that the 80 soldiers present on 3 June were insufficient to block the Viet Cong escape across the river. Noises were heard of escaping Viet Cong throughout the night, but little could be done with the limited forces available for this mission. The tape of their interview was unfortunately destroyed, but Master Sergeant Peter Astalos and Staff Sergeant Joe Guyton stated on 12 June that the "Triangle" area had long been a Viet Cong stronghold. They had long believed that the hooches in this area housed dependents of the Viet Cong.

Enemy casualties were heavy. In the sweep the next morning, U.S. forces found 192 bodies and 47 individual and 9 crew served weapons. Airships also noted several trails leading away from Viet Cong positions. Company B, 4th Battalion, 39th Infantry, was brought in to reestablish contact. Elements of the 1st Air Cavalry and Company B, 4th Battalion, 39th Infantry made several light contacts during 4 June, which added 17 more to the Viet Cong body count.

The exact identification of enemy units is difficult, but from prisoners it is known that there were elements of three Viet Cong battalions. These battalions were the 261A MF, 261B MF, and 514B LF.[12] While the strengths of these are not certain, intelligence reports indicate that together these battalions constituted a formidable fight force. On 29 May, a prisoner of war had stated that the 514B LF Battalion had a strength of 45 men. This figure is probably on the high side, and the 261A and the 261B MF Battalions were much smaller, especially after the 1 June battle.

From a roster captured at the scene of the battle, intelligence learned that the Viet Cong units had recently been reequipped with new ChiCom weapons. The Viet Cong in the Plain of Reeds area had new AK47s, sniper rifles, RPG-2 and RPG-7s, light and heavy machine guns, and a few mortars. Moreover, these Viet Cong knew how to handle these weapons as almost all the U.S. soldiers remarked about the accuracy and the extraordinary fire discipline of the Viet Cong units. Special comments were made about the deadly nature of the Viet Cong snipers.

13. Statistics:
    a. U.S. Losses[13]:

1 June 1968	3 June 1968
12 KIA	24 KIA
26 WIA	35 WIA

TOTALS: 36 KIA; 61 WIA

---

[12]Intelligence sources agreed about the presence of the 261A MF and the 261B M Battalions, but the 514B was originally identified as the 514C LF Battalion. U.S. participants interviewed several days after the battle on 3 June were still under (continued next page) the impression that they had made contact with the 514C LF. Two prisoners of war, Nguyen Van Tien and Nguyen Can Chi, however, stated on 6 and 8 June respectively that their battalion, the 514B LF, was present at the battle on 3 June.

[13]A controversy has developed over the official casualty figure. The above statistics have been called the official figures by the 9th Infantry Division, but the journals of the 1st Brigade and the 2nd Battalion, 39th Infantry give different totals. I have attempted to reconcile these figures without much success. Nobody seems to know the exact figures While I suspect that the official figures are too low, I distrust the journal's figures almost as much for reasons stated in Inclosure #4. The following casualty statistics are my best attempt to give the correct breakdown on U.S. losses.

1 June 1968

2nd Battalion, 39th Infantry			2nd Battalion, 60th Infantry		
Co. A	5 KIA	18 WIA	Co. A.	1 KIA	1 WIA
Co. B	2 KIA		Co. B	2 WIA	

b. Viet Cong Losses[14]:

1 June, 1968	3 June, 1968
41 KIA (Body count)	192 KIA (Body count)
10 Small arms	47 Small arms
2 Radios	9 Crew served weapons
1 M-60 machine gun	

TOTALS: 233 KIA (Body count)
57 Small arms
9 Crew served weapons
2 Radios
1 M-60 Machine guns

14. Analysis:

The most significant aspect of this five day operation is that the 1st Brigade displayed the full potential of the "jitterbug" tactic. The philosophy behind the "jitterbug" is that by the continuous insertion of troops near potential Viet Cong strongholds constant contact can be achieved with the enemy. Once contact is made, fresh reinforcements are airlifted in to encircle the Viet Cong forces. This part of the technique is often referred to as "piling on." With the Viet Cong boxed in all sides, massive air strikes and artillery fire are used to destroy the enemy. On 1 June, the 2nd Battalion, 39th Infantry made con-

(continued)

2nd Battalion, 39th Infantry		2nd Battalion, 60th Infantry	
Co. C	4 KIA 12 WIA	Co. C	2 KIA 6 WIA
	1 KIA (Dog handler)		
Totals	**12 KIA 30 WIA**		**3 KIA 9 WIA**

TOTALS FOR 1 JUNE: 15 KIA; 39 WIA

3 June 1968

2nd Battalion, 39th Infantry		2nd Battalion, 60th Infantry			4th Battalion, 47th Infantry	
Co. A	13 KIA 25 WIA	HHQ	1 KIA (medic)		Co.C	1 KIA 13 WIA
Co. E	7 KIA 14 WIA	Co.B	1 KIA	7 WIA		
		Co.C	3 KIA	14 WIA		
Totals	**20 KIA 39 WIA**		**5 KIA**	**21 WIA**	**1 KIA 13 WIA**	

TOTAL FOR 3 JUNE: 26 KIA; 73 WIA
(1 KIA Tiger Scout, Co. a, 2nd Battalion, 60th Infantry)
GRAND TOTAL OF ALL U.S. CASUALTIES; 41 KIA; 112 WIA; 1 KIA (Tiger Scout)

[14]The official Viet Cong body court for the engagement on 3 June was 192. Information from prisoners of war, however, has led to the claim that Viet Cong casualties on 3 June may have totaled as high as 474. I was told on 7 June in an interview with Major Day, 1st Brigade, that he had received information that the Viet Cong casualties were 174 KIA, 100 WIA, and 200 MIA. On 6 June, a prisoner of war, Nguyen Van Tien, 3rd Company, 514 LF Battalion, stated that there had been 174 KIA, 2000 WIA, and 100 MIA. Another prisoner of war , Nguyen Can Chi, a survivor of the same battalion, maintained that the 514B sustained 250 KIA and 60 WIA. He believed that the 261 Battalions had lost 200 casualties. Finally, Nguyen Van Tiep, a former member of the 261A, mentioned on 12 June that the 261A had lost only 10 KIA. Whatever the actual figures, the three Viet Cong Battalions were seriously crippled after their confrontation with the 1st Brigade on 1 and 3 June.

tact, but, because of the nature of the terrain and enemy resistance, the encirclement was never completed. Moreover, the delay in receiving artillery support hindered effectiveness. These two failures allowed the Viet Cong to escape relatively unscathed.[15] This was not the case on 3 June. Although some difficulty was experienced in reinforcing the units in contact, the enemy positions were encircled and by the effective utilization of artillery and air support assets the Viet Cong suffered heavy casualties. The result is that after this engagement three Viet Cong battalions were no longer combat effective. It was the weakness of the blocking force across the canal and the delay in sealing off of the Viet Cong's eastern escape route that were the only reasons preventing the total annihilation of the three Viet Cong battalions.

Another significant feature of this battle was that it demonstrates the benefits in keeping in close contact with the enemy. In this regard, the air cavalry and "people sniffer" teams proved to be invaluable. It is standard operating procedure for the Viet Cong to break down into small groups and infiltrate out of any trap, and the engagements of 1 and 3 June were no exceptions. However, it is always advantageous to reestablish contact as soon as possible before the Viet Cong have an opportunity to reorganize and disappear into the countryside. What helped after the battle on 1 June was the nature of the terrain. As Major Day, S-3 of 1st Brigade, explained it, at certain times of the year troop movements through the marshland of the Plain of Reeds will leave green trails which can be readily seen from the air. Colonel Emerson, commander of 1st Brigade, spotted such trails on 1 and 3 June from his command airship. "People sniffer" teams confirmed that there were sizeable concentrations of possible enemy troops in these localities. Then, air cavalry ships made low level observation runs before U.S. troops were committed into action. The result was contact was made in two out of three insertions.

This operation again proves the importance of artillery support. On 1 June, four companies had two Viet Cong battalions isolated, but, because of difficulties moving an artillery battery, the Viet Cong were able to escape before suffering crippling casualties. On 3 June, three Viet Cong battalions were trapped, but this time five batteries were available to inflict heavy casualties on the Viet Cong before they could infiltrate out of the trap. The differences in body count and in the number of weapons captured between the two engagements reinforces the importance of artillery support.

Communication was the most serious problem encountered in this oper-

[15]Lieutenant Colonel Leggett again disagreed. He claimed that reinforcements arrived as soon as it was possible to deploy them. "Company C was inserted at 1240. I got word of contact at 1300. Company A was inserted at 1400. Companies A and C, 2nd Battalion, 60th Infantry were inserted at 1500 and 1600. Each took pressure off Company C, which after the initial contact when it took the majority of casualties held its own in good fashion." In other words, initial contact was made at 1240, but it was not until almost three hours later that the bulk of the of the US forces arrived on the field of battle.

ation. Interviews with forward observers, platoon leaders, and RTO's reveal that they all had difficulties with communication. They attributed their difficulties to the fact that the nets had too many people on them. It took as long as 30 minutes for requests for artillery and gun ships to reach their destination. This delay in fluid battle-field situations hindered combat operations on both 1 and 3 June as the Viet Cong reacted swiftly to US movements. This lag in communication also led to some difficulties with unit movements as commanders were unable to ascertain the location of other friendly units. Finally, there exists a need to waterproof hand sets as almost all the radio failures can be attributed to wet hand sets. Almost all the RTOs had placed plastic bags around the hand sets, but rice paddy water still seeped in to render the radios useless.

A complaint voiced by both the platoon leaders and the enlisted men was that the commanders were ordering insertions of troops too close to the danger areas. They expressed concern that, if a wood line or heavy bush line was occupied by a large Viet Cong force as was the case on 1 and 3 June, they had little chance to survive. Company C, 2nd Battalion, 39th Infantry, and Company A, 2nd Battalion, 39th Infantry on 3 June were inserted close to danger areas. Both these units suffered heavy casualties almost as soon as they left the landing zone. The platoon leaders suggested that troops be dropped several hundred meters from areas of potential danger so that security and dispersion can be obtained before contact.

Another problem was resupply. Water is a precious commodity in the Plain of Reeds, because the lack of population means that US troops cannot resupply themselves with rain water from Vietnamese hooches. Three or four canteens are not enough for troops marching long distances through mud and water in the head of the day. Because of the weight, most of the soldiers in the 2nd Battalion, 39th Infantry and 2nd Battalion, 60th Infantry operated with only two or three canteens. This lack of water led to a large number of heat casualties. Most of the troops survived because they drank rice paddy water. During the battle on 3 June, several survivors remarked that they had fainted for periods up to two hours. There appears to have been some difficulty about salt tablets as the normal practice was to have the medics carry the salt tablets, but the medics were unable to distribute them during the fire fight contributing to the number of heat casualties as much as the lack of water.

Another problem was the tardiness of reinforcements. Reinforcements from Company C, 4th Battalion, 47th Infantry, on 3 June waited almost six hours before they were picked up to be inserted into the battle. This was at a time when Company A and Company E, 2nd Battalion, 39th Infantry were in dire need of support. This same problem existed on 1 June when it took several hours, after initial contact, to provide reinforcements for Company C, 2nd Battalion, 39th Infantry. Part of the problem had to do with the availability of air assets, but some method must be devised to bring reinforcements to the battlefield more quickly.

Another problem was the slowness of troops to respond to the cover provided by fire support. Major Joseph, XO of 2nd Battalion, 60th Infantry and commander of Task Force Joseph during this operation, remarked that it was 30 minutes after an artillery barrage before his troops advanced toward the wood line during the Task Force Joseph's midnight assault on 3 June. The result was that the assault lost the advantage of what cover the artillery barrage could provide.

Finally, the 1st Brigade experimented with sending a medical doctor, Captain Ritscherie, 2nd Battalion, 60th Infantry surgeon, to the field to deal with emergency cases on both 1 and 3 June. Captain Ritscherie concluded that there is little more a doctor can do in the field than can be done by a good medic. On both occasions, he was pinned down most of the time, and the medics had a tendency to depend upon him too much instead of doing their jobs. He does feel that medics should have available for field use life preserving fluids. He believes that these fluids might substantially reduce US deaths in the field.

Note on Journals

There are numerous inaccuracies in the journals of the 1st Brigade, 2nd Battalion, 39th Infantry, and 2nd Battalion, 60th Infantry. The journals were compiled from fragmentary notes several days or even weeks after the events of 1 and 3 June. This accounts for the gaps as well as the inaccuracies. When I left the Pink Palace on 14 June, none of the journals had been worked on by any of the units. I was told that the journals would be incomplete because much of the action was out of the radio range of those who normally compile the journals. A member of the 2nd Battalion, 39th Infantry informed me in late July that the 2nd Battalion, 39th Infantry compiled their journal from information gathered from the journal of the 1st Brigade. I assume that the 2nd Battalion, 60th Infantry may have done the same. Consequently, none of the journals are reliable. In fact, especially inaccurate are the map coordinates. I have attempted to reconstruct troop movements as accurately as possible from eyewitness accounts.

INCLOSURE 1: JOURNAL EXTRACT FOR PERIOD 31 MAY–4 JUNE (PLAIN OF REED) (2ND BATTALION, 39TH INFANTRY, 9TH INFANTRY DIVISION)

On 30 May 2nd Battalion, 39th Infantry moved into the Plain of Reeds, vicinity XS338846 to attempt to locate enemy forces in that area. On 30 May it conducted reconnaissance in force. Bushmaster operations with A, B and C companies were conducted on the night of the 30th. There was negative contact on 30 May. On 31 May, Eagle Flights and Bushmaster operations were conducted again with negative contact.

The Battalion then moved to the south of the initial area of operations to react to intelligence that the enemy might be in that area. At approximately 1200 hours on 1 June and element of C Company, C6 element, was inserted at XS385716. At the same time another element of C Company, C5 element, was inserted at XS395701. Immediately upon landing, C6 element encountered heavy enemy fire in a bunker system within 100 meters of where they landed. C6 element was immediately pinned down and begun to sustain heavy casualties. The Battalion Commander directed C5 element to move north to come to the assistance of C6 element. At 1400 hours, A Company was inserted at XS382710 in an attempt to flank the enemy and come to the assistance of C6 element. A Company began to move north and they also were pinned by heavy enemy fire. It was then clear that the enemy was in a large bunker complex of at least Battalion size. The next move was to insert elements of the 2nd Battalion, 60th Infantry to the west of the area of contact. They were inserted at approximately 1500 hours at XS380710 and began to move northeast to relieve the pressure on A and C Companies. At approximately 1600 hours C5 element closed with A Company which was attempting to relieve C6 element from the south. The enemy persisted in his defense and we were unable to break his lines. At approximately 1930 hours B Company was inserted at XS390720 in an attempt to flank the enemy to the north and to seal off all avenues of escape. B Company moved to the southwest and closed upon the rear of C6 element. These were the dispositions which remained in effect throughout most of the action, with B Company and C6 element at XS385716, A Company at XS385712, and elements of 2nd Battalion, 60th Infantry at XS382712. Throughout the night there were air strikes and artillery placed on the enemy. Contact continued throughout the night with the 2nd Battalion, 39th Infantry sustaining a number of casualties.

The following morning a sweep of the battle field revealed that the enemy had sustained a heavy amount of casualties and that the bunker complex was an important one with permanent type structures. On the morning of 2 June, it was determined that the enemy had fled to the southeast to a treeline extending from XS430685 to XS442675. Brigade decided to employ 2 Battalions on line along the north side of this treeline while blocking the escape route with air and artillery. B and C Companies of the 2nd Battalion, 60th Infantry were placed on line from the western edge of this treeline down to XS440680. At approximately 1500 hours B Company 2nd Battalion, 39th Infantry was inserted on the east flank of the 2nd Battalion, 60th Infantry and E Company was inserted to their left flank. This action produced negative contact. The enemy had moved out. That night B Company came under operations control of the 2nd Battalion, 60th Infantry and A Company of 2nd Battalion, 39th Infantry went to the My Dien Special Forces camp to provide security. C Company 2nd Battalion, 39th Infantry moved to XS476470 to provide security for direct fire artillery.

The action on 3 June developed when a Company 2nd Battalion, 39th

Infantry was inserted at XS250584 at approximately 1030 hours. It advanced toward the canal to the north and came under extreme heavy automatic weapons fire and RPG fire as well as heavy sniper fire from the hooches in the open area to the south. The company was soon pinned down and sustaining casualties. By this time it was apparent that a large enemy force was entrenched along the east-west canal to the north of A and E Companies. Brigade then inserted 2 companies of the 2nd Battalion, 60th Infantry. B Company 2nd Battalion, 60th Infantry was inserted at XS242586 and moved north and reached the canal thus flanking the enemy on the west. C Company 2nd Battalion, 60th Infantry was inserted behind them and both companies began a sweep to the east in an attempt to flank the enemy and to relieve the pressure on our A and E Companies. These insertions were made at approximately 1400 hours. At 1600 hours an additional element of the 2nd Battalion, 60th Infantry plus 1 unit from an additional Battalion was inserted to the west at approximately XS258583 in an attempt to flank the enemy on that side. During the day they were unable to move forward and had to make a night attack at midnight. This attack broke the enemy's east flank. These were the dispositions for the remainder of the night. On the north bank the CIDG from My Phuoc Tay Special Forces Camp screened to prevent enemy movement across the river.

We held these positions and pounded the enemy with air strikes and artillery until the morning of 4 June. The battle field was swept on the morning of 4 June. Companies A and E, 2nd Battalion, 39th Infantry moved to the north sweeping to the canal line and then to the east to join the units of the 2nd Battalion, 60th Infantry which were sweeping to the west from that direction. Additionally the forces on our left of the 2nd Battalion, 60th Infantry swept to the east.. Once the sweep of the battle field was completed the operation was terminated and the elements were extracted and returned to base camp.

INCLOSURE 2: 1ST BATTALION, 11TH ARTILLERY OPERATION, 28 MAY TO 5 JUNE 1968

1. During the period 1 June–4 June 1968, the 1st Brigade conducted operations in the Plain of Reeds between the Special Forces camps at My Dien II and Thuy Dong and then progressed into the triangle area east of My Phuoc Tay. The purpose of this letter is to inform you of the 1/11 Artillery operations in support of the 1st Brigade during that period.

2. Task Organization:

A 1/11th	Priority of fires to 2/30th Infantry
C 1/11th	Priority of fires to 2/60th Infantry
B 1/84th	GSR 1/11th (3–5 June)
C 1/84th	GSR 1/11th (1–2 June)
D 1/84th (2 tubes)	GSR 1/11th (1–5)

3. Sequence of Events: The operation was originally planned to begin

26 May. However it was slipped 24 hours at a time requiring repeated cancellation of air assets for the artillery. Detailed air reconnaissance had been made by the artillery. Detailed air reconnaissance had been made by the artillery. On the morning of 29 May, C 1/11th, the AN/TPS 25, and the 1/11th's AN/MPQ-4A were airlifted to Thy Dong, the battery being laid and ready to fire at 1015 hours. Again the operation was delayed. In the two days that elapsed before the operation began, Division Artillery therefore directed only us not to fire on radar sightings unless there were groups of 100 personnel or more and appeared to be leaving the area. The AN/TPS 25 gathered intelligence data which was given to both maneuver battalions and the brigade. On the morning of 31 May, both maneuver battalions and 1 1/11th airlifted into the Thuy Dong area. The first lift of the battery was at 0720 hours and they were laid and ready to fire at 1850 hours. On the morning of 1 June, air reconnaissance detected a large cache at XS395700. At 1030 hours, a combat emergency was declared by the 1st Brigade to move A 1/11th to a position from which this area could be covered. For unknown reasons, the request was denied initially by CO 9th Division Artillery. The 1st Brigade, anxious to react to current intelligence, moved in at 1400 hours without artillery support and by 1430 hours, the 2nd, 39th Infantry was in heavy contact in the vicinity of XS403700 and XS382718. The first lift for a 1/11th did not arrive until 1455 hours. One of the helicopters had mechanical difficulties and was unable to carry howitzers. It was therefore 3½ hours before six guns were laid and ready to fire. This action resulted in 19 US KIA compared to 41 VC KIA. To support A 1/11th and to give wider coverage to planned operations, C 1/84th (at Tan An) and D 1/84th were assigned the mission of GSR 1/11th. D Battery moving from Dong Tam to the Tan An airstrip. On 2 June, the infantry worked south towards My Dien II. To help support this, a combat emergency was declared at 1510 hours to move C, 1/11th to My Dien II. Response was quicker than the previous experience; the air assets arriving at 1630 hours and the battery was laid and ready to fire at 1850 hours. The move was completed at 1945 hours. On 3 June, the 2nd Battalion, 39th Infantry moved west into the "triangle" and made contact at XS275585. An extensive shift of artillery followed: B, 1/84th from Ben Luc to FSPB Moore; three howitzers of B, 1/11th from FSPB Lambert to FSPB Moore; A 1/11th to FSPB Moore; and D 1/84th to FSPB Moore. on 4 June, C 1/11th was moved to My Phuoc Tay to support an intended operation north of My Phuoc Tay. However, infantry elements were not committed. Contact was broken on 5 June and all elements returned to flag locations. Of the 187 VC body count, the 1st Brigade Commander credited artillery and air with approximately 80 percent.

    5. Commander's Evaluation: The operation as a whole must be regarded as a highly successful and dynamic one, primarily due to the magnitude of the artillery moves. This was extremely beneficial from a training standpoint. Despite the delay in a battery's air mobile displacement on 1 June, the operation impressed upon the ground commanders the responsiveness of artillery

to changing situations. Of course, the operation highlighted again several problems which need attention:

a. There is a need, not only during air movement, but on a continuing basis, for a more thorough exchange of information between airmobile companies and artillery units. For example, during airmobile training conducted by the 9th Aviation Battalion for all our batteries on 19 May 1968, batteries were informed that A-22 bags could be lifted out of the bed of a 2½ ton truck. When A 1/11th moved on 31 May, the pilots refused to pick up the bags out of the trucks. The bags had to be pulled out of the beds of trucks by other vehicles, bags breaking open in the process, requiring repacking and a considerable delay. During the same move, a pathfinder from the airmobile company re-rigged one howitzer because a strap was frayed. The pilot then refused to move the howitzer because it was improperly rigged.

b. A truly smooth operation demands prior planning, particularly where air movement of several batteries is involved. Combat emergency (CE) air assets cannot be depended upon. In this operation dependence upon CE assets resulted in the infantry maneuvering outside of artillery range on 1 June. Air assets requested at 1030 hours did not arrive until 1455 hours. When the aircraft did arrive, one CH-47 had only one engine and could not lift howitzers. With only every other sortie being a howitzer, A 1/11th did not have six howitzers layed and ready to fire until 1825 hours. In the meantime, the infantry had been in heavy contact since 1430 hours. Again on 030830 hours June, CE assets were requested to move A 1/11th to FSPB Moore. These assets did not arrive until 1440 hours. Two CH-47's had been anticipated, but one CH-54 arrived. For a unit in the middle of the Plain of Reeds without extensive rigging material, this presented problems. Ammunition sorties that had been rigged for CH-47 (two A22 bags on doughnut slings) had to be shuttled into groups of two by the CH-54 (which normally carries four A22 bags on different rigging). This re-rigging represented a considerable delay. Two CH-47's arrived an hour and a half later. As a result of these delays, four sorties and six artillery personnel along with about one platoon of infantry were left behind. At 1920 hours, this stay-behind force came under ground attack resulting in one slight WIA. A larger attack could have been catastrophic.

c. The necessity for combat emergency requests for air movement of artillery is subject to doubt if the request goes through artillery channels only. The individual on the spot who can properly declare combat emergency is the brigade commander. Hence, it would seem more proper to submit all combat emergency requests through the supported commander.

d. During the operation there were 15 check fires imposed for a total of over 18 hours without artillery support (see Tab A). On at least one occasion, there is evidence that this resulted in further loss of US lives. The primary cause of check fires is airstrikes. This as has been emphasized repeatedly, is unnecessary and undesirable. One solution is for the ground commander to require the FAC to work on the direct support artillery fire direction net. This enforces coordination between the FAC and the LNO and places this extension of fire support firmly on the shoulders of the fire support coordinator. Any checkfire should also be coordinated through the forward observer to ensure that artillery is not stopped due to mistaking hostile rounds falling into friendly positions for friendly artillery. Checkfires due to command and control ships are unnecessary since an artillery liaison officer is habitually on boards.

Clarence D. Little
CPR, Arty
Ass't Adjutant

TAB A: CHECK FIRES

Date	Time	Reason
1 June	1000–1230	People Sniffer
	1545–1830	Friendly location unknown and gunships
	1850–2230	C&C Ship in area
	0100–0130	One round too close to 2nd Battalion, 39th Infantry
2 June	1351–1420	Slicks and gunships coming in
3 June	1040–1220	Air strikes and gunships
	1345–1417	Gunships
	1530–1602	Air Strikes
	1610–1630	Air Strikes
	1642–1643	Air Strikes
	1645–1745	Gunships, insertion, and air strike (in contact area)
	1743–1822	Air Strikes
	1850–1927	Air Strikes
	2130–0035	Resupply of infantry
4 June	0525–0535	Too close to Special Forces

Appendix D: Evaluation of Intimate Psychological Warfare

1. *Background:* The 9th Division has been tasked to test and evaluate the concept of conducing Intimate Psychological Warfare (INPSYWAR) to induce small unit defections from the enemy ranks. The INPSYWAR concept was developed based upon indications that small VC/NVA units, plagued by deteriorating morale, loss of faith in their leadership, and lack of public

support, may be talked into surrendering if properly approached under the correct circumstances.

2. *Purpose:* The purpose of this evaluation is to determine the operational feasibility of the INPSYWAR concept and to evaluate the suitability of the AN/PIQ5A portable loudspeaker system in this application.

3. *Concept:* In essence, INPSYWAR envisions making a timely appeal to small VC/NVA units which have been pinned down and/or surrounded by friendly troops, with the purpose of inducing them to surrender. The entire effort is conducted at platoon level supervised by the platoon leader and executed by a Tiger, Kit Carson Scout, Vietnamese interpreter or specially trained soldier using preplanned messages and when contact is made. A heavy volume of friendly fires is alternated by periodic cease fires during which the appropriate surrender message, selected by the platoon leader, is transmitted to the enemy guaranteeing his fair treatment and medical care if he will surrender and certain death if he continues to resist or tries to escape. The INPSYWAR concept used in conjunction with the Recondo Checkerboard tactical concept is discussed Tab A.

4. *Material:*

   a. Description: AN/PIQ5A

      (1) Power requirements: batteries: B30

      (2) Power output: 25 watts

      (3) Weight: (To be determined)

      (4) Dimensions: (To be determined)

      (5) Estimated battery life: (To be determined)

   b. Procurement: 100 ea AN/PIQ5A loudspeakers have been requisitioned by HQ USARV for use by 9th Inf Div in this evaluation. Authorization to requisition was granted in accordance with AR 310–34 by HQ DA, ACofS Force Development on 23 Feb by TWX CITE DA 852593. Retention of equipment is authorized for a period not to exceed one year.

5. *Objectives:* The objectives of the INPSYWAR evaluation are as follows:

   a. Objective 1: To determine the effectiveness of INPSYWAR through a study of the circumstances under which it was employed and in terms of the number of enemy soldiers who surrendered as compared with the estimated number exposed.

   b. Objective 2: To ascertain what doctrinal changes could improve INPSYWAR operations.

   c. Objective 3: To evaluate the effectiveness of the AN/PIQ5 in INPSYWAR and to ascertain any changes, modifications or improvements which may be necessary.

   d. Objective 4: To determine the requirements to adequately train selected personnel in INPSYWAR techniques.

6. *Evaluation Design:* The evaluation of the INPSYWAR concept will be

conducted by the 1st Brigade, 9th Inf Div. Units to participate should include the combined reconnaissance intelligence platoons, aerorifle platoon, and elements of the 1st Brigade as directed by CO 1st Brigade. The evaluation will be conducted in two phases.

    a. Phase I (Training and Orientation) will commence upon receipt of equipment and run for period of approximately 30 days. During Phase I an orientation will be conducted in which platoon leaders, company and battalion commanders will be advised on the concept of INPSYWAR. Personnel will be selected from each participating platoon and will be trained to operated the equipment, receive detailed instruction in the concept and conduct of INPSYWAR and, if they are non–Vietnamese speakers, trained to satisfactorily pronounce the prepared messages and contingency phrases. Phase I will also include a field evaluation of the AN/PIQ5A to determine the maximum effective range of the speaker under battle field conditions. Phase I will terminate with the issue of equipment and the return of the trained personnel to their units.

    b. Phase II consists of the field evaluation and testing of the INPSYWAR concept and is expected to run approximately 6 months. As part of the evaluation, participating units will report progress on a continuing basis recommending appropriate changes of improvements in the operational concept.

    7. *Reports:* A total of three reports will be submitted to CG, 9th Inf Div. ATTN: AVDE-GC pursuant to the objectives listed in paragraph 5 above.

    a. The first report will be submitted following the completion of Phase I and will include the following:

        (1) A analysis of the capabilities of the AN/PIQ5A together with any appropriate recommendations and comments as to its capabilities or limitations.

        (2) An outline of the criteria established for the selection of personnel, to include retainability, education, language aptitude, etc.

        (3) A narrative description of the training administered to personnel to include the duration of training, skill level attained and recommendations for future training

        (4) A copy of the implementing directive or plan for the conduct of Phase II.

    b. The second report will be due midway through phase II and include the following:

        (1) INPSYWAR statistics, including, but not necessarily limited to the information listed below:

            (a) Total number of engagements by participating units.

            (b) Total number of engagements where INPSYWAR was employed.

     (c) Time duration of such contact, where INPSYWAR was employed.

     (d) Time lapsed from the initial contact to first use of INPSYWAR and the number of appeals made.

     (e) Number of surrenders attained.

     (f) Estimated total size of enemy unit.

     (g) Relative, language fluency of the operator.

  (2) A narrative description of each incident when INPSYWAR was employed to include the tactical situation, the mission, enemy situation, weather, terrain, problems encountered and recommended changes in doctrine.

  c. The final report will be similar in format to the 2d report except that it will include a final recommendation as to whether the INPSYWAR concept is recommended for implementation throughout the division and/or for implementation by other US forces. The final report will be submitted with 30 days following the completion of phase II.

Tab A — A description of the Recondo Checkerboard concept at Battalion Level and the concept of Intimate Psychological Warfare.

Tab B — A detailed description of Psychological Warfare Ground Action on 11 November 1967.

Tab C — A current PSYOP estimate of the situation with respect to Intimate Psychological Warfare.

Appendix E: Recondo Checkerboard Concept

The objective of the Recondo Checkerboard concept is to find, fix, and destroy enemy forces. The battalion saturates an area approximately 10 to 15 kilometers on a side with platoon sized units dispersed in a "checkerboard" configuration. The checkerboard concept is not meant to convey assignment of platoons to a fixed area of operation in a precise geometric pattern. Moving by stealth, normally under the cover of darkness, the company commanders shift their platoons from area to area in search of likely ambush positions from which to destroy the enemy and disrupt his movement. It is through this procedure, with each platoon concentrating its efforts in promising target areas, that guerrilla type operations are conducted to beat the enemy at is own game. When necessary, based on the size of the enemy force detected and fixed, platoons are moved from their ambush positions to block the enemy's escape from the area, and to converge on and destroy him. One company is normally designated as an airmobile reaction force to assist in the enemy's complete destruction as required. Until employed as the reaction force, the unit can conduct limited checkerboard operations.

The concept is passive in the sense that units move covertly in their search for successive ambush areas from which to intercept enemy movement. No attempt is made to clear or sweep the area. However, once the enemy is located or intercepted, immediate overt action is taken to destroy or capture him. As success depends upon the continuous search for the enemy, an ambush position is normally occupied for no longer than 24 hours.

The key to this concept is clandestine night operations with emphasis on platoon and reinforced squad ambushes and patrol of opportunity. All elements of the battalion move by air or surface to areas adjacent to or within the battalion area of operations during the hours of darkness and proceed to their assigned areas. No artillery or air preparations are fired, there are no H&I fires, aerial reconnaissance, LZ preparation or other activities conducted that would reveal the units' presence in the area. Platoons are kept on the move throughout their assigned areas conducting ambushes, and collecting and reporting information. Control is decentralized to the platoon leader permitting the platoon to destroy enemy forces and facilities within its capabilities. The primary direction from battalion headquarters is the assignment of operational areas to each company in which the platoons concentrate their efforts. (Experiences of 2nd Brigade, 50th Infantry, and 1st Brigade, 101 Airborne Division have shown that decentralized execution tends to foster maximum ingenuity, initiative and guile on the part of the small unit leader and capitalizes on his imagination, aggressiveness and motivation. As a result this unit was able to take advantage of the traditional American genius for improvisation and best the cunning enemy at his own game.) When the company commander is satisfied that no lucrative target remain in a platoon's area, he moves it to another area repeating the procedure for all his platoons until the entire company area has been covered, or until contact with a superior enemy force is made. When platoons encounter superior enemy forces, the clandestine nature of the operation ceases and control becomes centralized. While the unit in contact fixes the enemy force, battalion headquarters maneuvers various adjacent units to blocking positions along likely, avenues of escape and directs others to converge on the target. Frequently the airmobile reaction force is committed to finish the enemy force. Brigade and division reserves may be committed if additional forces are required. When destruction of the enemy is completed, the battalion again undertakes checkerboard operations taking care not to establish predictable patterns or move into locations that may have been compromised. This does not preclude returning to an ambush site if this tactic will catch the enemy off guard or intercept a moving enemy unit.

In heavily vegetated areas platoons normally use trails for stealthy night movement to discover signs of likely enemy movement. During this movement between successive positions, the platoons are particularly alert for meeting engagements with the enemy since he too, uses the trails at night for resupply and relocation of his forces. Experience has shown the enemy to be careless in the execution of his night moves and, therefore, vulnerable to attack or hasty ambush by an alert platoon that is searching for the enemy in a stealthy manner. The use of night vision devices gives the platoon a decided advantage in engagements of this nature. Use of trails also leads units to enemy base camps, way stations and assembly areas, and increases chances of locating and ambushing enemy forces, as the enemy also relies on trails for mobility. (Experience in the 2nd Battalion, 502 Infantry revealed that enemy forces were most active from 1800–2200 and 0500 to 0900 daily. As a result, friendly forces normally maintained a 100 percent alert in ambush positions during those periods. Units would move to a new ambush position between the hours of approximately 2200 to 0500 and remain in position until the following night. Between the hours of 0900 to 1800, a 30 percent alert was maintained to allow platoon members to rest and eat. Although areas with extremely dense foliage would permit some daylight movement, 75 to 80 percent of the time platoons moved during the appropriate hours of darkness making maximum use of night vision devices.)

Platoons participating in a checkerboard operation are lightly equipped for maximum mobility. Mortars and antitank weapons are held at battalion level for immediate airlift to units making contact with a sizeable enemy force. The weapons platoon can be re-equipped to acct as a fourth rifle platoon. Sufficient rations and ammunition are carried to sustain the unit for a five day period. (To reduce the weight each individual carried in the 2nd Battalion, 502nd Infantry, two wet "c" rations were issued and the remainder was rice. At the end of the five day period companies are assembled, fed a hot meal, resupplied and given a day's rest prior to resuming checkerboard operations. Normally, a battalion should not be committed to checkerboard operations for more than 15 or 20 days without a reasonable break in the routine to preclude reducing the combat effectiveness of the unit.

To avoid compromising unit locations, supporting supply and maintenance functions are deferred until units have completed five days of operations or until contact with enemy forces requires resupply. Emergency requests should be made only to the ground commander, subject to the battalion commander's approval.

Prior to commencement of a checkerboard operation, all individuals are given a thorough physical examination and those that are not considered fit for the five day period are screened out. Troops are indoctrinated to be physically and mentally tough so that they will continue to operate in spite of minor injuries or ailments. Evacuation of sick or wounded by medevac helicopter is accomplished only when absolutely necessary during each five day period to preclude compromising the operation. The ground commander makes the determination in each individual case, based on the advice of the medic, as to the necessity for evacuation. Replacements to the battalion are handled in the normal manner. However, they are not physically assigned to a company while that unit is conducting a checkerboard operation.

Another feature of the checkerboard concept is the great stress that is placed on the use of psychological operations at the platoon level. The enemy soldier endures many hardships, whether it be while moving down to infiltration routes from North Vietnam or while constantly trying to avoid contact with allied forces in South Vietnam. An ironclad indoctrination program steels them to accept these hardships. There is little question that they are told they will be mistreated if they fall into our hands. Therefore, every effort must be exerted to convince the individual enemy soldier that if captured, he will receive humane and kind treatment. This completely unexpected friendly treatment will frequently be disarming and give prisoners a sense of relief. Consequently, they can be expected to talk more freely, without any coercion, and readily reveal information about themselves and their units.

A platoon conducting checkerboard operations has the enemy in the best position to exploit this psychological vulnerability. At this level of operation, removed from the direct influence of their political advisors, the individual enemy soldier is more susceptible to an appeal to surrender. While he has been indoctrinated to expect mistreatment from US Forces and that he should never surrender no matter how severe the hardship, this indoctrination can be overcome if he is approached while in direct contact with US Forces with an appeal emphasizing the advantages to surrender.

An interpreter with each platoon and a power megaphone would enable the unit to conduct "intimate" psychological operations immediately upon making contact with the enemy. This radically new concept, unlike the present centrally controlled psychological warfare effort which depends primarily upon leaflets, airborne loudspeakers, etc. and often fails to reach the individual enemy soldier, would serve to counteract his strong indoctrination by reaching him at a time when he is most vulnerable and should produce immediate results. Recognizing that a qualified interpreter will not be available for each platoon, it will be necessary to utilize locally available military personnel such as RVN, RF, PF or CIDG who have limited, and perhaps even no, English capability.

To insure that the proper appeal is made, prepared "pitches" in the form of small laminated cards should be available to each platoon leader for use as the situation dictates. The theme should be simple and directed toward counteracting the enemy's indoctrination that he will be mistreated if captured; the appeal should emphasize humane treatment, the availability of food, water, cigarettes, etc. plus the opportunity for rest from the hardships of war. At least three different themes (cards) would be required as follows:

    a. The first card, based on a close range fire fight, should point out that, while the enemy is currently being subjected to only locally available firepower, he will subsequently be the victim of both an artillery and air bombardment. In lieu of this however, we would prefer to pause for a short period of time in order to permit him to surrender; if he chooses not to surrender, then destruction is certain. The procedure for surrendering should be specified.

b. The second card should be based on a situation where the enemy is surrounded. The appeal would emphasize the futility of continuing to fight and the advantages of surrendering.

c. The third card should contain a theme appropriate for transmittal by a captured enemy soldier, preferable a leader, who, based on the kind treatment he has received, is willing to explain to his contemporaries the benefits of surrendering.

These "theme cards" should be prepared in both English and Vietnamese to enable US personnel to select the theme to be presented based on the situation. The reverse side of the card should contain a reduced version of the "pitch" spelled out phonetically for use by US personnel when no interpreter is available; through proper training and practice US personnel can achieve the degree of proficiency necessary to be effective.

Achievement of psychological success and the surrender of enemy soldiers at the platoon level could well be the catalyst necessary to spark surrender by enemy units, which unlike in previous wars, has not yet occurred in Vietnam in spite of all the factors present (unsophisticated logistical system, poor medical care, hardships of war, etc.) which should lead to surrender by units. Once a battalion size or comparable unit does surrender, the psychological warfare opportunities become unlimited. Using this unit as an example of the good faith and kind treatment by US Forces, other enemy units would then be enticed to surrender — once started, the trend could become perpetual.

Appendix F: Psychological Warfare Ground Action, 11 November 1966

Early on the morning of 11 November the 1st Brigade, 101st Airborne Division Psychological Warfare Team was airlifted from the CP of the 2nd Battalion (Airborne) 502nd Infantry to an LZ close to the point where the 2nd Battalion, 502nd Infantry was engaged with the 5th Battalion, 95th NVA Regiment. The Psy War Team moved to the forward positions and placed speakers in a nearby tree. The latest enemy intelligence was obtained and molded into an appeal to fit the existing situation by deliberately capitalizing on the enemy's weak position and low morale. After approximately 20 minutes, the first NVA soldier walked directly to the speakers, following instructions explicitly, and surrendered with his weapon. After the prisoner was fed, the psychological warfare team convinced him that the Government of Vietnam and its American allies did not want to harm him and that his comrades' senseless struggle could only end in death. An appeal was devised with the concurrence of the prisoner to urge his fellow soldiers to surrender. Current intelligence was acquired from the prisoner and used to make the basic appeal more personalized and meaningful. Shortly thereafter, five more NVA soldiers walked in. At this time it was learned that the executive officer of the opposing enemy battalion was killed. This information was immediately incorporated into the appeals and more soldiers chose "to rally to the GVN with honor than to continue to fight and be killed and buried in an unknown grave." Approximately one hour later, the battalion commander of the 2nd Battalion, 502nd Infantry directed the team to move to his vantage point, a tall tree located on the crest of the hill, and continued the mission. From this location appeals were broadcasted and several more NVA soldiers surrendered. It was during these broadcasts that an intense fire fight broke out in the A Company area. The Psychological Warfare Team was immediately displaced forward to this position, the speakers were set up during the first lull in the fire fight and broadcasting was begun "face-to-face" with the enemy. The team emphasized that the "soldiers of the Screaming Eagle were everywhere, that the NVA cause was lost and that death was soon to be their only honor." Greater impact was gained by using a wounded NVA soldier lying nearby. Five more "hard core" soldiers chose life rather than death.

By 100 hours, the enemy's position had been overrun, and the Psych War team returned to the battalion CP. During the day's action 18 prisoners were used in live broadcasts, four special personalized appeals were made and a total of 9 hours of speaker time was recorded. These appeals were modified as fresh intelligence and changing battle conditions dictated. The 2nd Battalion, 502nd Infantry captured a total of 35 prisoners.

It should be pointed out that it is most likely that the results achieved would not have been possible, had it not been for the constant pressure placed on the surrounding enemy by the 2nd Battalion, 502nd Infantry. In this case Psychological Warfare had the unique advantage of being in the right place, at the right time, with the right appeals. The enemy was under great pressure from the Infantry, and Psychological Warfare offered an "honorable" way out. The choice was theirs — life or death.

Lessons Learned

Many critical lessons were learned which stress the fact that Psychological Warfare is most effectively utilized on the ground in direct support of the ground troops. Briefly they are:

1. In jungle-terrain the enemy often finds it easy to detach himself from air appeals since the aircraft is often hidden from view by the thick foliage and the message is sometimes garbled by aircraft and atmos-

pheric conditions. However, when made on the ground the appeal is direct and personal and is not distorted by the jungle canopy. The sound appears to reverberate off the ground and the jungle canopy achieving a surprising range.

2. On the ground the appeal can be instantly molded to fit ever-changing battle conditions, and it can employ spontaneous prisoner appeals.

3. A loudspeaker appeal on the ground during a lull in intense fire fights helps to stress the magnitude of American technology and has a definite demoralizing effect on the enemy.

4. It was also noted that although leaflets were on the ground, many were inaccessible due to thick vegetation. Trails seem to be the most profitable target for leaflet dissemination.

5. During lulls in ground contact psychological warfare is most effectively employed by using aircraft for broadcasts and leaflet dissemination. However, once significant contact with the enemy is made, the Psychological Warfare effort should be on the ground with the units in contact.

Special Appeals

- SOLDIERS OF THE 5TH BATTALION, 95TH NORTH VIETNAMESE ARMY REGIMENT

The government of Vietnam and its allies are your friends and do not want to harm you. We give you a choice—life or death. If you come in now you will have life. Is it not better to rally now to the government of Vietnam with honor than to continue to fight and be buried in an unknown grave (and have your soul wander the earth forever)? This choice is yours—life or death. Your family and your loved ones want no harm to come to you. They need you. The choice is yours. Life or death.

- SOLDIERS OF THE 5TH BATTALION, 95TH NORTH VIETNAMESE ARMY REGIMENT

Do you want to be buried in an unmarked grave? That is the only honor you will have if you continue your senseless fight. Do you think that's right? The soldiers of the Strike Force Airborne Division are everywhere. Approach the Americans with your hands above your head. Wave something white. Have your weapon muzzle down and you will not be harmed. Wave something white. This is your last chance and only hope. Life or death — the choice is yours.

- SOLDIERS OF THE 5TH BATTALION, 95TH NORTH VIETNAMESE ARMY REGIMENT

Your life is about to end! Are you ready to die? The soldiers with the eagle on their shoulders are everywhere. They are closing in. This is your last chance. If you do not come in now you will be killed without mercy. Wave something white, have your hands up, bring your weapons with you, muzzle down. This is your last chance. This is your last chance.

Comrades, this is _____ of _____
                              (name)   (unit)

I have come in to the Americans and they did not lie. I am being well treated. They gave me food, water, and treated my wounds. The American do not want to hurt us. I am being treated very well! I urge you _____
to come in.   (name if known)

They will not hurt you if you come in now. Have your hands up. Come in, come in now before it's too late.

Appendix G: Psyop Estimate of INPSYWAR

1. There have been increasing reports through intelligence channels that due to the heavy losses incurred by main force Viet Cong units, Viet Cong cadreman and military proselytizing sections within the Viet Cong Infrastructure have been forced to recruit not only guerrillas but civilians including women and children to serve in combat and combat support units. It is becoming increasingly evident that low morale and severe disillusionment plague many Viet Cong units. The failures of the TET Offensive, the staggering losses sustained, the non-arrival of promised reinforcements and "super weapons" have all contributed to further lowering the morale of the Viet Cong soldier. Perhaps most significant among the many failures of the TET Offensive was the utter lack of public support engendered by the VC/NLF movement. The Viet Cong in pre–TET propaganda targeted at their troops made much of the anticipated uprising of the people and the supposed rallying of public support behind the Viet Cong movement. As the Viet Cong made their attacks against the Provincial and District capital it had been expected that a general uprising of the population would follow heralding the Viet Cong and the NLF as the liberators of South Vietnam.

2. Similarly, there is considerable evidence of deteriorating morale on the part of North Vietnamese soldiers infiltrated into the south to participate in what they were told would be the coup de grace. The winter-spring offensive was to have achieved fantastic success, and NVA soldiers were supposedly needed only to finish off isolated pockets of resistance and then would ride forward on the crest of the waves of victory into the welcoming arms of the liberated people of South Vietnam. Their disillusionment has been profound.

3. In recent policy guidance received from the Joint United States Public Affairs Office, a country wide program of psychological operations targeted

at Viet Cong and NVA units has been outlined and is being currently implemented, to fully exploit the failures of the Viet Cong TET Offensive, and the many other PSYOP vulnerabilities which are now in evidence. In leaflet and loudspeaker propaganda the enemy is told of the failures of the winter-spring offensive, and of the inevitable defeat of the Viet Cong and NVA forces. The enemy is also told of the Chieu Hoi Program and is encouraged to rally to the Government of South Vietnam as his only hope for survival. Yet statistics indicate a record low in the number of ralliers to come into the program since the beginning of the offensive. While it may be expected that these statistics will improve as the winter-spring offensive loses momentum the fact remains that for the present the Viet Cong or NVA soldiers are being kept too busy to make escape possible or feasible in most cases, regardless of how much he may desire to do so. Whereas the nationwide campaign of PSYWAR presently being implements in accordance with current JUSPAO guidance may well engender the desire to surrender or rally to the GVN, the campaign does not afford the enemy the opportunity. As psychologically correct as the moment might be, events have precluded him from acting. It would appear that in consideration of this, a deliberate plan to provide an otherwise doomed enemy with the opportunity to surrender could well achieve a good measure of success.

Appendix H: Air Cushion Vehicle Report

After Action Report, 1–5 July 1968

1. General

a. The Air Cushion Vehicle Unit was attached to the 3rd Infantry Brigade, 9th Infantry Division during the period 1–5 July for operation in the Plain of Reeds. The primary missions assigned to the unit were reconnaissance-in-force and blocking force roles. Troops from the 3rd Brigade and the My Phouc Tay Special Forces CIDG were made available for the unit's use, as was the continuous use of one H-23 helicopter.

b. The base of operations for the period was the My Phouc Tay Special Forces Camp, XS201600. Supplies and equipment required were air transported to the camp on a daily basis. Direct communications between the unit and the Brigade rear at Dong Tam were maintained with PPRC-25 and VRC-47 radios.

c. During the operation, enemy contact resulting in an exchange of fire

was made three times. Twelve detainees were evacuated to Dong Tam, several
of whom were identified as POWs. The total confirmed body count for the
operation was eleven; however, the battle area of 3 July was not searched so
total enemy casualties inflicted by the unit were not determined.

2. Movement to the base camp and operations — 1 July

a. *Operations:* The unit departed Dong Tam Base Camp 1 July for the
My Phouc Tay Special Forces (SF) Camp. About ten miles from Dong Tam,
eighteen 3rd Brigade infantrymen were picked up to ride the side decks. The
initial plan was to carry 24 troops, but the weight proved to be too great. The
movement to the initial area of operations was delayed several times while waiting for additional air assets to be made available. One H-23 helicopter was
made available for the ACV commander to control the operation. The first
area the unit was assigned consisted of a large populated triangular shaped
rice bowl about five miles east of the SF camp. According to the Vietnamese
Camp Commander, the area was completely Viet Cong controlled and earlier in the year the Special Forces had lost 200 CIDG and 8 advisors in the
triangle. A detailed house-to-house search was made of the area resulting in
eleven detainees, most of whom were identified as prisoners of war. The vehicles were deployed generally on line in the sweep through the area. Key houses
were occupied for short periods of time to insure that the vehicle would not
be ambushed, not caught in a cross fire, or not be able to mutually support one
another. After completing the sweep of the triangle, the unit moved directly
to the Special Forces camp to set up the base. Supplies were brought in and
coordination made with the Camp Commander for security and fire support.

b. *Terrain.* The terrain for the day's operation varied from the open water
of the My Tho River to very rough and confined tree line breaks. The first
25 kilometers of the operation consisted of moving up the Xang Canal at high
speed. The canal is about 100 feet wide and averages about 15 feet deep and
no particular problems were encountered. At the triangle, some searching was
necessary to find a place to get through the tree line. The gap found had 2–3
foot banks and very high grass and brush; the vehicles easily jumped the bank
and brush. The tree line immediately opened up to a large open space covered with a 3–4 foot elephant grass. Once again a search was necessary to find
a gap in the tree line separating the elephant grass area from the rice fields of
the objective. This time it was necessary to knock down several small trees
and jump a small canal, all of which was accomplished with delay. The rice
paddy village, which was the objective area, was about 6 kilometers long and
4 kilometers at the widest. The paddies had 4–8 inches of water and new
growth rice. The dikes were spaced about 100 meters apart. Approximately
every 1000 meters, a small canal had to be traversed. Except where trees obviously blocked the canals, they could be crossed at will. ACV #902 was hung
up once trying to cross an area where two of the larger canals intersected. The
H-23 had returned for refueling and the size of the canals and their banks
was not apparent from the ground. The vehicles had been moving slowly to

keep generally online with the undersigned warning them of large dikes or canals, in which case the driver would pick up power to get across. If such warning had been given, the vehicle would not have been hung up. It was pulled free using ACV #903. The only access from the western end of the triangle to the Special Forces camp was through two heavy tree lines and up two medium sized canals. No breaks in the first tree line had been apparent on an earlier air reconnaissance; therefore, the Air Force FAC was asked to try several bomb strikes on the trees in hopes of blowing though a hole. Two gaps were made, one using a large bomb which cleared the trees, but left too large a crater (it will fill with water in time and be usable). The other was made with several smaller bombs, which left a rougher place, but at the time more usable. The gap was negotiated without major problem; the first vehicle had to finish knocking over a large tree which caused a small dent (no repair necessary). The remainder of the 5 miles to the Special Forces camp was accomplished without incident, except that ACV #902 could not overcome hump drag in the two shallow canals. Each appeared to be about 5–8 feet deep. This was one of several times that the relative lower SHP of ACV has been noticeable. The other two vehicles had no trouble accelerating over hump drag. The base area was an old French outpost that has long since disappeared. In the middle of June, a small engineer force was moved to the outpost with two small dozers by CH-54 helicopters. The area was leveled and three parking pads constructed using rubber fabric cloth and MB steel matting. The area had baked hard enough so that dust was not a problem, and the hardstand assisted in keeping the crews out of the mud during the daily monsoon downpour.

     c. *Logistics:* In addition to the engineer effort previously accomplished, the following logistical support was required: JP-4 fuel, fresh water, ammunition, and C-rations. A four day load of rations and ammunition and enough fuel and water for two days was air supplied. An R&D gpm fuel service was issued for use with standard 500 gallon fuel bladders. Water was transported in a standard 400 gallon water trailer. Three complete basic loads of ammunition were moved along with 4 days rations. The small airmobile shop that has been loaded with parts, tools, and equipment was also moved up. A total of five CH-47 Chinook sorties were used. The prime objective was to get minimum essential support moved to the base and to keep the logistical support as simple and flexible as possible. The only problem encountered was finding enough people to prepare and hook up supplies at Dong Tam, and to unhook and distribute them at the forward base. The S-4, 3rd Brigade, finally came to the rescue and provided a five man detail, a rigger, and a 2½ ton truck with driver. The success of the entire logistical support far exceeded expectations and conclusively proved that the unit can operate for extended periods in the field without elaborate of costly support packages. The only shortcoming experienced was the fact that the vehicles had to return to the base to refuel. Each day's operation involved a well planned move to an operational area some distance from the base. The additional round trip to the base for refueling would have unduly placed the vehicles in jeopardy of ambush. The problem was "solved" by carefully pacing the vehicles to stretch the fuel: this economy resulted in on-station times in excess of six hours. However, if the unit had been required to continuously move at moderate or higher speeds, the time would have been cut by a third or more.

3. Operations — 2 July

a. *Operations.* The ACV unit was scheduled to conduct a reconnaissance-in-force mission in a 40 square kilometer area of operations. For the mission 24 Vietnamese CIDG troops and 2 American Advisors were attached. Shortly after leaving the base, ACV #90 hit a high canal dike attempting to get out of the Muoi Hai canal. The banks of the canal were very high and steep; after several unsuccessful attempts to get out, a low spot was found that appeared to be negotiable; however, the place was narrow and the driver misjudged the slope catching the right side deck on the high side of the hole. The vehicle spun in tearing a 20 foot section of skirt off and denting the buoyancy tank. The remainder of the morning was consumed in stripping the vehicle, having the sling brought up from Dong Tam, transporting the equipment off ACV #901 out by CH-54. At 1300 hours the mission was again resumed with the two vehicles, but without the CIDG. Four 3rd Brigade troops were carried on each vehicle. The afternoon mission was uneventful except as an opportune test of the vehicles' mobility in high, thick grass, scrub brush, and in crossing deteriorated canal banks. Numerous houses, bunkers, etc. were checked out without incident. Four large bunkers were destroyed.

b. *Terrain.* The Muoi Hai Canal is a large and well traveled route between Cai Lai and Moc Hoa. The banks are unusually high and steep, possibly as a result of the constant boat traffic. At times there is a four foot tide in the canal, but it is not predictable using current tide tables. If operations in the future require the vehicles to traverse the canal, attempts will be made to knock down ramp areas using Air Force bombs or demolitions. The open areas, the Plain of Reeds proper, are ideal for the ACV; at times the H-23 could not keep up with the vehicles. At the present time the grass is about a foot high and the ground covered with 3–4 inches of water, as a result the air escaping out the front of the skirts slicks down the green grass and the ACV becomes faster than at the best water conditions. At first, stopping was a problem for the drivers; however, it was discovered that low speed "plough-ins" were as smooth as on the water and that reverse pitch had more effect than over water. Many of the driver techniques required to operate over ice have proven helpful in the grass. (Ice operations were experienced during the training period at Aberdeen Proving Grounds).

c. *Logistics.* No problems encountered. The CH-54 was on station less than two hours after requested. At Dong Tam the pilot released the sling before it was lowered to the deck knocking a two inch hole in the bondolite deck.

4. Operations — 3 July

a. *Operations.* Two US Battalions and a Vietnamese CIDG company conducted an air assault into a triangle area bounded on three sides by medium canals (So Muoi, Phy Nuyen, Tong Doc Loc) nine miles to the west of My Phouc Tay. The ACV unit was assigned the mission of establishing a blocking force along the east side of the So Muoi Canal. Fifteen Vietnamese CIDG and two American Advisors were attached to the unit and rode the side decks. A direct route to the objective area was not available; therefore, the length of the route was about 1 mile due to the circumnavigation of the heavy tree lines. The trip was made at maximum speed and without incident. All suspicious areas were reconned-by-fire and a couple of narrow passage ways checked out by dismounting the troops. Once visual contact was established with the infantry battalions, the unit began a wide zone reconnaissance along the canal. The speed of the vehicles allowed the unit to range up to 4 kilometers from the assigned axis and still maintain an adequate blocking force. During the day over 60 houses were investigated, 26 bunkers destroyed, and 1 confirmed prisoner-of-war apprehended. At 1100 hours one Viet Cong was observed running from the approaching vehicles by the crew of #902. He was fired upon and was seen to tumble off the dike on which he was running. Since the area was fairly heavily wooded the CIDG were reluctant to go into the area to get their weapons as they feared an ambush. About an hour later both vehicles were fired upon with small arms from a tree line. After thoroughly saturating the area with machine gun and 40mm grenade fire the CIDG were sent in to check over the area. Two bodies were found with web-gear and weapons. The unit remained on-station over six hours and was released about 1700 hours to return to the base camp. A route different from the one used in the morning was selected and again traversed at high speed using recon-by-fire techniques. Approximately 4 miles from the base several VC were spotted running along a tree line and were immediately engaged. This action touched off a violent fire fight with an enemy force dug into the tree line. The VC force was dressed in blue shirts, black pants, and had a white band around their heads. Weapons used included caliber .50 machine guns, AK-47s, M1 riles, carbines, and a number of other unidentified automatic weapons. Indications were that the VC unit was taken by surprise. Many of the VC were fighting from open bunkers, one of the .50 machine guns had so little overhead cover that it was blown off with the M5 40mm grenade launcher, and no recoilless weapons were used. At times during the battle the vehicles were as close as 100 feet and one VC was run over by ACV #902 instantly killing him. The vehicles, crews, and weapons (except the minigun) all performed extremely well. Contact was held as long as possible waiting for an airmobile assault to finish up the fight; however, the infantry units had already moved in RON positions and were not immediately available. Before the infantry unit could be moved the ACV unit had to break contact as the vehicles had taken so many hits, two men were seriously wounded, the engine on #903 had a hole in the power stage, and the hydraulic system of #902 had been shot out. The vehicles moved clear of the area to make temporary battle patches, evacuate the wounded (the H-23 was used), and to maintain visual observation of the area. After a few minutes, mortar rounds began to fall around the vehicles and it was necessary to move further away. Eight VC bodies were counted laying in the open, but the airmobile assault never materialized so the total VC casualties are unknown. The vehicles were driven the remaining 3 miles to the base with some difficulty. ACV #903 lost all oil pressure just as it pulled up on the pad and ACV #902 was moved up on the pad; it had come part of the way down the canal and had to cut off its power. In each case when the enemy contact had been made during the day, helicopters had had been working the area, the H-23 C&C and air cavalry scout LOH's. In none of the cases had the aircraft spotted any of the activity until the vehicles were engaged. This is an excellent example of the necessity to control the ground and have something occupying terrain, neither of which can be accomplished by aircraft. It also points out the limitations of aerial observation when working in heavy foliage areas.

b. *Terrain.* The terrain was mostly very level, with a few small canals. The only dikes encountered were around the built-up areas. The larger tree lines proved to be more difficult to get through than anticipated; one tree line ran for over 4 miles with only two small breaks in it. Due to the very flat ground and excellent observation, reconnaissance-by-fire techniques paid handsome dividends especially when making high speed runs to move from one area of interest to another.

c. *Logistics.* Fuel almost became a problem as the vehicles each averaged over seven hours of operation by the time they returned to base. An air transportable refueling system would have been useful. The critical damage to ACV #902 was repaired with the tools and parts in the small maintenance shop, thus paying for itself in one day.

5. Operations-4 July

The decision was made by the 3rd Brigade to fly both vehicles back to Dong Tam by CH-54. The vehicles were stripped and the items loaded in A-22 containers. the excess fuel and ammunition were moved into the Special Forces camp proper for future use. The vehicles, shop, water trailer, and A-22 containers were air lifted back to Dong Tam without incident or problem.

6. Lessons Learned:

a. The ACV can be operated and maintained for extended periods away from the permanent base camp.

b. The best type of terrain for the ACV is the Plain of Reeds or areas very similar to it.

c. The commander of the ACV unit must be provided a Light Observation Helicopter (LOH) for command and control. The only time the vehicles were stuck or lost was when the H-23 had returned for fuel.

d. An air transportable refueling capability must be devised/constructed.

e. The ACV can find the enemy, make contact, and maintain the contact for short periods of time. More vehicles are an absolute necessity if any extensive operations are anticipated or if it is envisioned that the vehicles do more than make contact, stage a brief fight and then retire from the battlefield for 2–3 weeks for repairs. At present there is no hope of the unit fighting to a satisfactory conclusion in any large engagement.

f. The ACV contributes to the battlefield a combat vehicle that can fight and hold terrain in areas impassable to tanks or wheeled vehicles. This is a capability not possessed by any other item in the Army inventory.

David G Moore • MAG, Armor • Commanding

Appendix I: Viet Cong Strength and Combat Effectiveness, 1 August 1968

Unit	Estimated Strength	Combat Effectiveness
9th VC Division	6,420	Combat effective
1st Regiment	760	Not combat effective
271st Regiment	1,450	Marginally combat effective
272nd Regiment	1,450	Marginally combat effective
273rd Regiment	1,400	Marginally combat effective
274th Regiment	950	Not combat effective
Doan 10	180	Marginally combat effective
Dong Thap I Regiment	940	Not combat effective
K3 NVA Battalion	350	Combat effective
K34 Artillery Battalion	250	Combat effective
Phu Loi II	300	Combat effective
2nd Independent Battalion	80	Not combat effective
5th Nha Be Battalion	60	Not combat effective
6th Battalion	100	Not combat effective
16th Battalion	250	Marginally combat effective
261A Battalion	150	Not combat effective
261B Battalion	200	Marginally combat effective
263rd Battalion	200	Marginally combat effective
265th Battalion	200	Not combat effective
267th Battalion	325	Marginally combat effective
267B Battalion	300	Marginally combat effective
269 Battalion	300	Marginally combat effective

Unit	Estimated Strength	Combat Effectiveness
294th Battalion	275	Marginally combat effective
504th Battalion	300	Marginally combat effective
506th Battalion	270	Marginally combat effective
514A Battalion	230	Marginally combat effective
514B Battalion	100	Not combat effective
516th Battalion	300	Combat effective
518th Battalion	250	Marginally combat effective

Number of Units	Estimated Strength	Combat Effectiveness
29	18,340	5 — Combat effective
		15 — Marginally combat effective
		9 — Not combat effective

Appendix J: Viet Cong Order of Battle (9th Infantry Division's Area), September 1968

Units	Type of Unit	Subordinate To	Location (Prov.)	Strength
HQs, 5th Div.	VC (MF)	COSVN	Long Khanh	500
274th Regiment	VC (MF)	5th VC Div.	Long Khanh — Phuoc Tuy	2,000
275th Regiment	VC (MF)	5th VC Div.	Long Khanh — Phuoc Tuy	2,000
24th Artillery Gp.	VC/NVA (MF)	5th VC Div.	Long Khanh — Phuoc Tuy	400
Doan 84 (Gp. 84)	Rear Service	COSVN	Long Khanh — Bien Hoa — Phuoc Tuy	1,352
Doan 10 (T-10)	VC (MF)	COSVN	Rung Sat Special Zone	1,000
D445 Battalion	Provincial Bn.	Ba Bien Province	Phuoc Tuy	500

Units	Type of Unit	Subordinate To	Location (Prov.)	Strength
C240 Company	District CP	Long Thanh — Ba Bien Provinces	Long Thanh — Ba Bien	120
C245 Company	Unknown	Unknown	Nhon Trach Dist. — Bien Hoa	100
C207 Platoon	Unknown	Long Thanh Dist. Labor Com — Ba Bien	Long Thanh Dist. — Bien Hoa	35
4th Battalion	VC (MF)	Thu Duc Dist., Military Region IV	Long Thanh Dist. — Bien Hoa	150
506th Battalion	Provincial Bn.	Long An	Duc Hoa Dist. — Hai Nhia	330
2nd Battalion	Provincial Bn.	Long An	Can Duoc — Tan Tru Districts — Long An	250
C75 RR Co.	Provincial Combat Support	Long An	Unlocated	100
C2 Company	Provincial Infantry Co.	Long An	Unlocated	100
U/I Sapper Co.	Provincial Combat Support Co.	Long An	Unlocated	100
C312 Company	District Infantry Co.	Ben Thu Dist.	Ben Luc — Thu Thua Districts — Long An	120
C313 Company	District Infantry Co.	Chau Thanh Dist.	Binh Phuoc District — Long An	120
C314 Company	District Infantry Co.	Tan Tru Dist —. Long An	Tan Tru Dist. — Long An	120
C315	District Infantry Co.	Can Duoc Dist. — Long An	Can Duoc Dist. — Long An	70

Units	Type of Unit	Subordinate To	Location (Prov.)	Strength
5th Battalion	VC (MF)	Nha Be Dist.— Military Region IV	Thanh Duoc Dist.— Long An	175+
6th Battalion Dist.—	VC (MF) 200+	Binh Tan Dist.— Military Region IV	Long An	Ben Lu
261st Battalion	Regional Force	Military Region II	Dinh Tuong	550
263rd Battalion	Regional Force	Military Region II	Dinh Tuong	550
514th Battalion	Provincial Bn.	My Tho	Dinh Tuong	350
C212 Sapper	Provincial Combat Support Co.	My Tho	Dinh Tuong	90
C207th Company	Provincial Infantry Co.	My Tho	Dinh Tuong	80
Cai Lay Company	District Inf. Co.	Cai Lay Dist.— My Tho	Khiem Ich Dist.— Dinh Tuong	80
Cai Be Company	District Inf. Co.	Cai Be Dist.— My Tho	Kien Binh Dist.— Dinh Tuong	80
Cho Gao Co. Dist.—	District 80 Inf. Co.	Cho Gao Dist.— My Tho	Dinh Tuong	Cho Ga
Chau Thanh Co.	District Inf. Co.	Chau Thanh Dist.— My Tho	Long Dinh Dist.— Dinh Tuong	80
Estimated Strength of All Enemy Forces				11,782

Notes

1. The D445 Battalion could be used to reinforce district units with Bien Hoa and Long Thanh Provinces as well as in Phuoc Tuy Province.
2. The 4th Battalion frequently crosses into Bien Hoa Province to avoid operations by allied/US Forces in its own area.
3. The 5th Battalion operates in Nha Be District, Military Region IV, but is based in Thanh Duoc District, Long An province, to avoid allied/US operations in Nha Be District, Gia Dinh Province.
4. The 6th Battalion operates in Binh Tan District, Military Region IV, but is based in Ben Luc District, Long An Province to avoid allied/US operations in Binh Chanh-Tan Binh Districts, Gia Dinh Province.

Appendix K: "Form Letter" from the 9th Infantry Division

Dear Family, Friends, Civilians, and Draft Dodgers:

In the very near future the undersigned will once more be in your midst, dehydrated and demoralized, to take his place again as a human being with the well-known forms of freedom and justice for all, engage in life, liberty and the somewhat delayed pursuit of happiness. In making your joyous preparations to welcome him back into organized society you might take certain steps to make allowances for the crude environment which has been his miserable lot for the past twelve months. In other words, he might be a little Asiatic from Vietnamesitis and overseasities and should be handled with care. Do not be alarmed if he is infected with all forms of rare tropical diseases. A little time in the "land of the big PX" will cure this malady.

Therefore, show no alarm if he insists on carrying a weapon to the dinner table, looks around for his steel pot when offered a chair, or wakes you up in the middle of the night for guard duty. Keep cool when he pours gravy on his dessert or mixes peaches with his Seagram's VO. Pretend not to notice if he eats with his fingers instead of silverware and prefers C-rations to steak. Take it with a smile when he insists on digging up the garden to fill sandbags for the bunker he is building. Be tolerant when he takes his blanket off the bed (and leaves the sheet) and puts it on the floor to sleep on.

Abstain from saying anything about powdered eggs, dehydrated potatoes, fried rice, fresh milk, or ice cream. Do not be alarmed if he should jump up from the dinner table and rush to the garbage can to wash his dish with a toilet brush. After all, this has been his standard. Also, if it should start to rain, pay no attention to him if he pulls off his clothes, grabs a bar of soap and towel and runs outdoors for a shower.

When in his daily conversation he utters such things as "xin loi" and "choi oi" just be patient. Simply leave quickly and calmly if by some chance he utters "di di" with an irritated look on his face, because it means no less than "get the hell out of here." Do not let it shake you if he picks up the phone and yells "Reliable, sir," or says "roger out" for goodbye, or simply shouts "working."

Never ask why the Jones' son held a higher rank than he did, and by no means mention the term "extend." Pretend not to notice if at a restaurant he calls the waitress "numbah one girl" and uses his hat for an ashtray. He will probably keep listening for "Homeward bound" to sound off over ARVN; if he does, comfort him, for he is still reminiscing. Be watchful when he is in the presence of a woman — especially a beautiful woman.

Above all, keep in mind that beneath that tanned and rugged exterior there is a heart of gold, the only thing of value he has left. Treat him with kindness, tolerance, an occasional fifth of good liquor, and you will be able to rehabilitate that which was once, and now is a hollow shell of, the happy-go-lucky guy you once knew and loved.

Last, but by no means least, send no more mail to the APO, fill the refrigerator with beer, get the civies out of the mothballs, fill the car with gas, and get the women and children off the streets ... *because the kid is coming home*!!!!!

Index

Abrams, Gen. 102
Advanced Individual Training (AIT) 6, 13
African Americans 6, 30, 127, 134
Agent Orange 43
Agnew, Spiro 133
Aio di dresses 28
Air cavalry 120, 124
Air cushioned vehicle 116–117, 196–202
Air Cushioned Vehicle Unit 196
Air Force aircraft 25
Air Force FAC 198
Air mattresses 39
Air mobile operations 34, 51, 93, 168, 189
Air strikes 172, 175
AK-47 41, 69–70, 146, 176, 200
Alcohol 98
Ambush Alley 136
Ambush patrols 1, 52–53, 66, 147, 172, 189–190
Americal Division 11, 23
American casualties 99, 101, 120, 147–148, 163–165, 176–177
American propaganda leaflets 77
An Nhut Tan (SV) 121
An Phu Hamlet 56
AN/PIQ5A portable loudspeaker system 186–187
Anniston (AL) 6–7
Anti-war demonstrations 5
AO Crackerjeck 167
Ap Bac Dong 172
Ap Cam-Chau Rubber Plantation 37
Ap My Dien (FSB) 175
APC (armed propelled rocket) 50
Armed Forces Radio 78
Armored personnel carriers (APCS) 50, 70, 119
Army Commendation Medal 139, 153

Army Reserves 5–7
Artillery ear 143
Artillery fire support bases (FSB) 95
Artillery support 178
ARVN see South Vietnamese Army
Astalos, Peter 175
Atkins, Jordan 3
Atkins, Stephanie 3
Atkins, Susan 8
Attack Element Against the Ben Luc; Bridge 160
Audrain County (Mo.) 5

Ba Bien (province) 204
Ba Bong Stream 158–159, 161
Ba VC Secret Zone 75
Badminton matches 82
Ban Long (village) 147
Bang Long Village (5V) 56
Bangkok (TH) 105, 130
Base Camp Smokey 47
Bataan (PH) 12
Battery A, 1st Battery, 11th Artillery 169, 172, 175, 182–184
Battery B, 1st Battery, 11th Artillery 175, 183
Battery B, 1st Battery, 84th Artillery 175, 182
Battery C, 1st Battery, 11th Artillery 175, 182–183
Battery C, 1st Battery, 84th Artillery 182
Battery D, 1st Battery, 84th Artillery 175, 182–183
Battle of Britain 98
Battle of Saigon 42, 62–63, 67, 95, 101, 163–165
Battle of the Plain of Reeds 90, 93, 98, 101, 105–106, 127, 163, 165

Battlefield (movie) 16
Bearcat 23, 25–28, 31, 33–37, 44, 51,
    59–61, 79–80, 82, 90–91, 101–102, 107,
    109, 112, 113, 126, 143, 149, 163
Beer allocation 78
Bellingham (WA) 22
Ben Da 158
Ben Luc (district) 205
Ben Luc (town) 101, 163, 183, 205
Ben Luc Bridge 45–46, 157–159
Ben Luc Market 158–159
Bien Chanh (district) 47, 51, 67
Bien Dinh (province) 108
Bien Duc Train (village) 57, 158
Bien Hoa (province) 103, 204–205
Bien Hoa Air Force Base 25
Bien Hoa Complex 154
Bien Long (province) 115
Binh Chanh (village) 162
Binh Chanh River 160–162
Binh Duc Strategic Hamlet 158
Binh Minh (district) 115
Binh, Nguyen This 135
Binh Nhut Strategic Hamlet 158, 160–162
Binh Phuoc (district) 204
Binh Phuoc (town) 108
Binh Tan (district) 205
Binh Trinh Dong (village) 157
Black Angus Restaurant 8
Black market 29, 126–127
Black Panthers (Thai) 102
Bo Bo Canel 56–57
Bob Hope Show 144, 145
Body count 98
Bombing of North Vietnam 126
Booby-traps 30–31, 41–47, 71, 171
Bowden, Ed 24
Bragg, Robert Gordon 22
Bronze Star 153
Brown, James 78
Bubbles helicopter 120
Bunkers 2, 52, 168, 170–172, 174, 199
Burchett, Wilford 59, 63, 155
Bushmaster operations 168, 180

C2 Company (VC) 204
C-4 18, 40
C75 RR Company (VC) 204
C207 Platoon (VC) 204–205
C212 Sapper (VC) 205
C240 Compny (VC) 204
C312 Company (VC) 204
C313 Company (VC) 204
C314 Company (VC) 204
C315 Company (VC) 204

Cai Be (town) 142, 147
Cai Be Company (VC) 204
Cai Lay (district) 167, 169
Cai Lay (village) 199
Cai Lay Company 205
Calley, Lt. 15
Cambodia 55–58, 94, 107, 134, 170
Campbell, Sp-4 59
Can Duoc (district) 204
Can Giouc (SV) 55
Can Tho (town) 139, 147
Canadian Broadcasting Corporation
    (CBC) 63
Cannon, Gerald 47
Catholic Church 26, 106, 136
Cayuses Helicopter 120
Cedar Rapids Television Station 156
Central Highlands 1
CH-47 Chinook 184, 108
CH-54 Chinook 199, 201
Chau Thanh (district) 205
Chau Thanh Company 205
Chawalit, Lt. Col. 103
Checked fire (Artillery) 184
Checkerboard ambush 172
Chesterfield cigarettes 39
Chi, Nguyen Can 176
Chicago (IL) 87–88
Chien, Cmdr. 147
Chieu Hoi Program 54, 67–68, 109, 141–
    142
Chikuma, Don 20, 43, 51
China 12
Chinh, Nguyen Van 147
Cho Gao (district) 205
Cho Gao Company 205
Cho Moi Canal 159
Cho Tai Market 158
Cholon (VN) 1
Cholon Y Bridge 163–165
Chu Lai (VN) 11, 23
CIA-front airline 23
CIDG (Vietnamese government irregulari-
    ties) 175, 181, 196, 199–200
Civil rights demonstrations 30
Claymores 41–42
Cleaning kits (M-16) 60
Cobra gunships 120–122, 125
Columbus (GA) 8
Combat Art Team 85–86, 130, 143, 150,
    151
Combat Infantry Badge 153
Command and control 47, 189, 201
Communications 178–179, 194
Communism 6

Company A, 2nd Battalion, 39th Infantry 96, 167, 171–174, 178–180
Company A, 2nd Battalion, 60th Infantry 98, 171, 174–175, 178, 182
Company A, 3rd Battalion, 39th Infantry 164
Company A, 5th Battalion, 60th Infantry 164, 167
Company A, 6th Battalion, 31st Infantry 164
Company B, 2nd Battalion, 39th Infantry 171, 180–181
Company B, 2nd Battalion, 60th Infantry 174–175, 181–182
Company B, 3rd Battalion, 39th Infantry 164
Company B, 4th Battalion, 39th Infantry 167, 176
Company B, 6th Battalion, 31st Infantry 164–165
Company C, 2nd Battalion, 39th Infantry 110, 167, 171, 178–81
Company C, 2nd Battalion, 60th Infantry 171, 175, 178, 181
Company C, 3rd Battalion, 39th Infantry 147, 175
Company C, 4th Battalion, 39th Infantry 146
Company C, 4th Battalion, 47th Infantry 166–167, 175, 179
Company C, 5th Battalion, 60th Infantry 163–164
Company C, 6th Battalion, 31st Infantry 11–12, 15, 17, 23, 35, 52, 54, 64, 66, 70–71, 102, 111, 164
Company D, 2nd Battalion, 39th Infantry 147
Company E, 2nd Battalion, 39th Infanty 167, 172, 174, 179, 181–182
Conex boxes 129, 141, 148
Congressional Inquire Team 69
Continental Hotel 109
Cook, Maj. 2, 79, 91, 109
Cooke, Sgt. 96
Copter in the Sky syndrome 97
Court-martial 21, 129, 141
COSVAN HQ 145
C-rations 39, 48, 51, 64, 66, 78, 82, 198
Criminal Investigation Division (CID) 141
C315 Local Force Regiment (VC) 48
Curran, Major 139

D445 Battalion (VC) 203, 205
D800 Battalion (VC) 55
Da Kho Creek 74

Da Phuoc Village 67, 70–71, 109
Dallas (TX) 151–155
Day, Maj. 178
DeAngelis, Joe 20
Demilitarized zone 11
Demolitions 2, 18
Dent, Capt. 174
Department of Defense 2, 80, 83–84, 97
Deployment Element Against Ben Luc Bridge 159
Destruction Element Against Ben Luc Bridge (VC) 159
Di Di mau 152, 206
Diarrhea 78, 82
Diem, Pres. Ngo Dinh 131
Dinh, Sa 146
Dinh Mot Canal 172
Dinh Nhur 157
Dinh Tuong (province) 55–56, 92, 94, 105, 116, 141, 147, 167, 169, 205
Distinguished Service Cross 21, 22
Do Son (NVN) 108
Doan 10 (VC) 203
Doan 84 (VC) 203
Doan Tharp 1 Regiment (VC) 202
Doi Creek 74
Dominquez, Sgt. 72
Dong Hoa Orphanage 136, 143, 144
Dong Nai (309th Infiltration Group) 55, 75
Dong Tam Base Camp 56, 90–92, 109–116, 118, 125–126, 128, 130–132, 134, 136, 138, 144, 147–150, 153, 196–199, 201
Dong Thap (village) 118
Draft boards 5
Duc Hoa (district) 204
Duc Ton (district) 116

Eagle flights 51–52} 180
8th Battalion (AKA IG309B) (NV) 55
8th Company, 3rd Artillery Battalion 134
8th Infantry Regiment 12
84th Regiment, 5th Region Binh Dinh (VC) 108
11B MOS 48
Emerson, Col. Henry (gunfighter) 93, 170, 174–175, 178
Evangelisto, Maj. 106
Evans, Rene 150
Ewell, Julian J. 24, 27, 47, 63, 92, 98, 102, 106, 127

Facial hair 29
Fatty four-eyes 6
15th Infantry Regiment 12

5th Battalion, 12th Infantry 13, 25
5th Battalion, 60th Infantry 163–164
5th Battalion, 95th NVA Regiment 192, 205
5th Nhe Be Battalion (VC) 202
5th Vietnamese Marines 164
50th North Vietnamese Army Regiment 108
Firebase Lambert 167, 183
Firebase Mohawk 106
Firebase Moore 167, 175, 183–184
1st Battalion, 410th Infantry (Reserves) 156
1st Battery, 11th Artillery 166, 169, 170
1st Battery, 79th Artillery 139
1st Battery, 84th Arillery 166, 169
1st Brigade, 9th Infantry Division 92, 95–96, 98, 165–169, 170, 180–183, 187
1st Brigade, 101st Airborne 189
1st Cavalry (Airmobile Division) 155
1st Infantry Division 155
1st Marine Division 155
1st Regiment (VC) 202
1st Squad, 3rd Platoon, 263 Mortar Company 147
1st Squadron, 7th Air Cavalry 167, 169
1st VC Regiment 118
504th Local Force (VC) 168, 203
514th Battalion (VC) 55–56, 142, 169, 203, 205
514B Local Force (VC) 169, 176, 203
514C Local Force (VC) 169
517th Battalion (VC) 203
506th Local Force (VC) 168–169, 203–204
516th Battalion (VC) 203
568th Regiment, 330 Division (NV) 55
Form letter 150, 206–207
Fort Benning (GA) 8, 13, 110
Fort Dix (NJ) 6, 13, 110
Fort Leavenworth (KA) 78
Fort Lewis (WA) 11, 16, 19, 20, 22, 25, 30, 33, 38, 43, 102
Fort McClellan (AL) 6–7
Fort Worth (TX) 82, 155
4th Battalion (VC) 204
4th Battalion, 39th Infantry 139–141, 166
4th Company, 7th Battalion (NVA) 108
4th Infantry Division 129, 155
Fragging 154
France 3, 24, 108, 127, 131
Free-fire zone 4

Geneva (Swit.) 6
Geneva Accords 131
Georgia 60, 80
German Army 85

GI benefits 156
Gia Dinh (province) 205
Gia Dinh (town) 145
Gian, Capt. 157
Go Cong (province) 55, 169
Go Den (village) 158
Goldfarb, Lt. 104
Good Conduct Ribbon 153
Gray, Richard 151
Green Berets 154
The Green Berets 8
Green pineapples 51, 82
Greene, Graham 109
Griggs, Cal 173
Guam 23
Guerrilla warfare 1
Guyton, Joe 175

Hai Bo Van 142
Hai Company (VC) 75
Hai Hai Van 67
Hai Nhia (district) 204
Hai Phong (province-NVN) 108
Hanna, Donald 21, 41–43
Hanoi (NVN) 131
Hawaii 23
Helicopter damage 124
Helicopter gunships 25, 37, 70
Helicopter supply system 125
Hiep Duc (village) 142
Highway 5a 55, 163
Highway LTL2 158
Highway LTL6 167
Highway QL4 14, 45, 47, 59, 92, 158, 167
Hilo Airport 23
Ho Chi Minh 49, 58, 163
Ho Chi Minh Trail 58
Hoeng Sau 56
Honey trap 129
Hong Kong 130
Hooper, Maj. 127, 140
Hoover, Pres. Herbert 77
Hoover Institute 77
Hope, Bob 148
Hot landing zone 37–38, 111
HQ Battalion, 5th Division (NV) 55, 203
Huey (UH-1D) (slicks) 34, 48, 51–52, 60, 70, 95, 120–121, 123, 196–197, 201
Human waste disposal 29
Humphrey, Hubert 133
Hung Long (village) 108
Hunt, Ira A. 24, 47, 114, 125, 129

Inchon Landing 12
Intelligence (U.S.) 49, 53, 59

International Hotel 51
Intimate Psychological Warfare (INPSY-WAR) 99, 185–196
Intrenching tool 39
Iowa City (IA) 5

Japan 12, 38
J.C. Penney's 22
Jeep stolen 141
Jitterbug 168, 177
Johnson, Lyndon 4, 12, 22, 136
Joint United States Public Affairs Office (JUSPAO) 195–196
Joseph, Maj. 180
Jungle fatigues 64–65
Jungle fighting 1
Jungle rot 98

K1 Battalion (NV) 55
K2 Battalion (NV) 55
K3 Battalion (NV) 55, 202
K54 Artillery Battalion (NA) 202
Kait snakes 54
Keeley, Maj. 146
Kennedy, Robert 100
Khe Sanh (VN) 11, 108
Kheim Ich (district) 205
Kien Binh (district) 205
Kien Dong Canal 62
Kien Hoa (province) 56
Killed in action (KIA) 73, 98–99, 103, 109, 113
King, Martin Luther 30, 100
King Cobra 54
King Thong Doc Loc Canal 175
Kinh Nuoc Mon Canal 76
Kit Carson Scout Program 54, 186
Kitchen police (KP) 17
Knapsacks 72
Korea 12
Korean War 12–13, 39, 83, 126
Krosky, Stan 20, 67
Kutscheid, Lt. 103
Ky, Gen. 131

L-shaped ambush 52
Landing zone (LZ) 21, 43
Landing Zone Grasshopper 37
Laurence, Vicky 100
Le Be Canal 75
Leeches 38–39
Leggett, Lt. Col. 96–97, 171–175, 178
Lehman, Ray 71
Leica camera 110
LeMay, Gen. Curtis 127

Lien Luc (Area) 157
Local force guerrillas 2
Locust helicopter 121–123
LOH (Light Observation Helicopter) 201
Long An (province) 28, 44–47, 53–57, 76, 92, 108, 158, 163, 204–205
Long Binh Complex 25, 120, 123, 125, 136, 150
Long Dinh (district) 56, 144, 205
Long Thanh (hamlet) 26, 34, 37, 56
Long Thanh (province) 205
Long Thuan A Hamlet 147
Looting 63
Low-intensity warfare 2, 18, 96, 154
LSD 21
Luc, Bay 147
Lucky Strike cigarettes 39
Ly, Suy 75
Ly Nhut (village) 76

M-14 19, 38, 61, 69
M-16 38, 42, 60, 69–70, 73, 136, 138, 146
M-60 machine gun 38, 61, 73
M-72 (LAWS) light anti-tank weapon system 62, 174
M-79 grenade launcher 35, 69
Maine University 136
Malaria 29, 98, 108, 134
Marijuana 33
Marshall, Gen. S.L.A. 83
Mascots 148
Mason, Sgt. 6
Massachusetts Institute of Technology (MIT) 5
Mau, Nguyen Thanh 169
McCord Air Force Base 11, 23
McNamara's 100,000 16
Mechanized infantry units 43, 50
Medic Section Against Ben Luc Bridge 159
Medical evacuation helicopter (MEDVAC) 42, 72, 190
Medics 38, 41–43, 189–191
Medivac helicopter pilots 72
Mekong Delta 1–2, 24, 26–27, 31, 44–46, 49–51, 55, 58, 64, 66, 69, 71, 77, 80, 86, 90, 92, 94–95, 99, 113, 117, 125, 135, 147, 153, 158–159
Mekong River 113, 116, 121, 128
Mendes-France, Pierre 6
Mess hall (Dong Tam) 130
Mexico (MO) 5
Military convoys 45
Military driver's license 101
Military History Office 83–84, 97

Military occupational specialty (MOS) 2, 13, 48, 80, 89
Military pay script (MPS) 29/ 126–127
Military Police 11, 23, 66, 101, 141, 143
Missouri School for the Blind 5
Mobile Riverine operations 661 80
Moe Hoa (village) 199
Moore, Specialist 112
Moore, David B. 202
Mortars 56, 61, 78, 114–115, 125, 147, 153, 161
Motor track 119
Mount Rainer 11, 16
Muoi Hai Canal 199
Mustaches 29
Mutiny in 6th Battalion, 31st Infantry 122
My Dien Special Forces Camp 172–174, 181–183
My Hanh Trung (village) 56
My Hoa (hamlet) 56
My Lai 15
My Phoc Tay Special Forces Camp 175, 182–183, 196–198
My Tho (city) 114, 128, 130, 131, 147
My Tho (province) 56, 205
My Tho River 197

National Guard 5–7
National Liberation Front 133, 135, 145, 153
National Police 163
NCO Club 77, 91
Nelson, Larry 21, 22, 63
New York City 6
Nganh, Sau 142
Ngoc Maum 53
Nho Be (district) 108–109, 205
Nhon Trach (district) 204
Night ambush patrols 33, 51, 189–190
19th Military History Detachment 2, 35, 79–80, 82, 85–86, 109–110, 113–114, 129, 132, 149
Nikon camera 110
1932 Shanghai Incident 12
1923 Earthquake (Japan) 12
90th Replacement Unit 136
9th Aviation Battalion 123, 184
9th Battalion (AKA IG309A) (VC) 55, 202
9th Division Artillery 183
9th Infantry Division 1–3, 23–28, 30–31, 34, 44, 47, 50–51, 55, 63, 65–67, 74, 77, 90–92, 94, 96, 98–99, 101–102, 107, 113, 116–119, 127–129, 131, 139, 142, 144,

149–150, 154–155, 163–164, 176, 185–186
Nixon, Richard M. 4, 133, 136, 152
Non-commission officers (NCOs) 8, 13, 30, 32, 77–78
Nonte, 1st Lt. 170
North Korea 12, 20
North Vietnam 55, 59, 107–108, 126, 142; regulars 2, 36–37, 43, 55, 63, 94, 109, 133–134, 185–186, 192–193, 195–196
Northey, Private 43
Novocain 134

Oakland (CA) 151
Octofol 63
Oe Dong River 162
Officer Training School (NVN) 108
Officer Candidate School (OCS) 5, 7–8, 13–15
Old Reliable Academy 30–31, 54
105 Howitzers 172
101st Airborne 99, 192–194
198th Light Infantry Brigade 120, 155
165th Regiment Training Headquarters (VC) 108
191 Airmobile Company 167, 173
196th Light Infantry Brigade, American Division 11, 155
Ong Nhut River 164
Ong Phu Stream 162
Ong Thong Stream 159, 161
Open latrines 29
Operation Duong Cua Dan (People's Road) 167
Operation Truong Can Dinh 167
Operational Report of Lessons Learned (ORLL) 107
O'Reilly, 1st Lt. 174
Owen, William 14

Palo Alto (CA) 77
Paris Peace Talk 30, 135, 142, 145
Parrot's Beak 58, 94–95
Patlan, Specialist 85
Patton, George 93
Peck, Captain 170
Pentagon 83–84, 107
People sniffing team 95–96, 120–121, 172, 178
Perrela, Mike 149
Petri FT camera 110
Phan, Dr. 76
Philippines 12
Phu Hoa Dong (NVN) 59
Phu Loi II Battalion (NV) 55, 202

Phu Tho Hoa 75
Phuoc Tay (province) 119, 203, 205
Phuoc Vinh Dong (village) 76
Phy Nuyen Cana 200
Physical profile 7
Pilots (helicopters) 123–124
Pink Palace 92–93, 94, 98–100, 167, 180
Plain of Reeds 2, 98, 167, 180, 182, 184, 196, 199, 201
Point man 1, 18, 20, 31, 38, 47, 61, 70
Poker 88
Polar bear 12
Pork Chop Hill 12
Post Exchange (PX) 28
POWS 197
Presidential Unit Citation 103–104
Pretner, Allen 111
Priorities for National Survival 155–156
Prostitution 28, 50–51
Psychological warfare leaflets 109
Psychological Warfare Team 192–193
Psyops team 99
Pueblo (USS) 20
Punji states 30
Python 54, 148

Q762 (aka 272nd Regiment), 9th VC Division 59
Queen's Cobras (Thailand) 27, 102–105
The Quiet American 109

Rach Dinh Stream 158
Rach La Canal 76
Rach Sa Mieu Canal 57
Rach Tao Stream 158, 162
Rauber, Pvt. 43
Ray, Also 8
Rear-echelon service 83
Recon-by-fire 200
Recondo Checkerboard tactical concept 99, 186, 188–191
Red ants 40, 44
Refueling ACV 198–199
Republicans 22
Reserve Officer Training Corps (ROTC) 15, 87, 118, 136
Rest and Relaxation Leave (R&R) 88
Ritscherie, Cpt. 180
rock and roll music 78
Rocket Propelled Grenade (RPG) 70, 73–74, 119, 146, 176, 182
Rohrback, Specialist 87
Rotation policy 130
RTO operators 38, 179
Rung Sat Special Zone 58–59, 75, 94, 203

Russell, Sen. 60, 64
Russian Civil War 12

Sa Dec (province) 116
Saigon 2, 25–26, 28, 44–47, 51, 53, 57–60, 63–68, 74–76, 94–95, 101, 107–109, 129, 134, 136, 153, 158–159, 163–165; bar girls 134–135
St. Louis, Mo. 5
St. Louis Cardinals 23, 152
Salt tablets 179
Sampan Element Against Ben Luc Bridge 160–161
Sampans 57, 122, 123, 159–160
Sanan, Col. 103
Sanchez, Sgt. 17–18, 43
Sau, Hai 142
Savacool, Paul 111
Schneider, Sgt. 42–43, 48
Schumacher, Specialist 84, 97
Scout Platoon, 2nd Battalion, 47th Infantry 163
2nd Battalion, 39th Infantry 166–167, 169–171, 180, 183
2nd Battalion, 47th Infantry (Mech) 65–66, 105, 143
2nd Battalion, 60th Infantry 121, 123, 157, 166–167, 169–170, 179–181
2nd Battalion, 502nd Infantry (NVN) 190, 192–193, 204
2nd Brigade, 9th Infantry Division 167, 180
2nd Brigade, 50th Infantry 189
2nd Company, 6th Battalion (VC) 67
2nd Independent Battalion (VC) 55, 108
2nd Regional Forces Command (VC) 169
Self-inflicted wound 39
Senegal 127
Seton Hall University 111
7th Battalion (AKAIG309D) 55
Shalek, Lieutenant 142
Sharpening the Edge: The Use of Analysis to Reinforce Military Judgment 24, 47, 92
Simpson, Pvt. 43, 51
16th Battalion (VC) 202
6th Battalion (VC) 202, 205
6th Infantry Battalion 3, 13, 77, 127–128
67ers 15–16
Smoke grenades 173
Snakes 54
Snatch operation 139–141
Snatch trap 143
Sniper 1, 18, 32, 60–61, 96
Snow White and the Seven Dwarfs 99
So Muoi Canal 200

Son, La Than 134
Son Tay (province-NVN) 108
Song Van Co Tay 57
South Korea 12, 20
South Vietnam 1, 3–4, 6–7, 9, 11–13,
    17–18, 20–26, 28–31, 33, 36–37, 42–43,
    48, 51, 54–55, 59, 66, 69, 78, 80–81,
    82–85, 93, 95, 97, 99–102, 105,
    107–108, 110–111, 117, 119, 125, 129–130,
    134, 142–143, 145–146, 148–155, 191;
    government 47, 53, 64, 99, 106,
    130–131, 136, 145–146, 154, 193
South Vietnamese Army (ARVN) 4, 25,
    47, 64, 66, 71, 77, 94, 105, 128–129, 131,
    133–134, 136, 141, 146, 158
Special Forces 153–154, 174; advisors 106;
    camps 105–106, 168, 175
Spitzer, Alan 149
Spookie 172
The Sporting News 23
Standard operating procedure (SOP) 31,
    72, 98
Starlight scope 32, 39–40, 190
Stevens, Sgt. 89, 90
Stolen weapons 141
Stoner, Gen. 129
Street fighting 1
Suhr, Alfred 153
Syracuse (NY) 3

Tacoma (WA) 17–22
Tactical officers (TACS) 15, 110
Tan An (City) 55, 107, 120–123
Tan Nhut (village) 75
Tan Ninh (province) 108, 158
Tan Phuoc Tay (village) 108–109
Tan Quoi (village) 115
Tan Tru (district) 108–109, 204
Tan Tru (village) 121, 123
Tank mines 119
Tanks 119
Task Force Joseph 98, 174–175, 180
Team A Assassination Squad (VC) 146
Tennis 83
TET Offensive 11, 25, 36, 58, 63, 66, 113,
    133, 147, 163, 195–196
Texas A&M University Libraries 3
Thai Army 102
Thai Binh (province) 107
Thai Quan Division (Ve) 107
Thailand 27, 102, 105
Thais, VC 103–105
Than, Huyuh Ngoc 75
Thanh Duoc (district) 205
They Dong Special Forces Camp 170

Thieu, Gen. 131, 136
3rd Battalion, 5th Cavalry 119
3rd Battalion, 39th Infantry, 9th Infantry
    Division 163–164
3rd Battalion, 50th Regiment, 25th Divi-
    sion (ARVN) 157
3rd Brigade, 9th Infantry Division 28,
    196–197, 199, 201
3rd Infantry Division 153
3rd Platoon, Company C, 6th Battalion,
    31st Infantry, 9th Infantry Division 1,
    9
13th Infantry Regiment 12
31st Infantry 12
Thu Dau Mot (province) 55
Thu Doan Canal 159
Thu Thua (district) 204
Thuan Battalion (VC) 109
Thy Dong 183
Tien, Durong 163
Tien, Nguyen Van 176
Tiet, Mia 132, 133
Tiger Scout 54, 186
Tom Cat (TC) 148
Tong Doc Loc Canal 200
Trans-International 23
Transister radio 78
Trans-Siberian Railroad 12
"The Triangle" 106, 116, 172, 175, 183,
    197–198
Triple canopy jungle 42
Troop A, 3rd-17th Air Cavalry 120–125
Troop B, 7th Squadron, 1st Air Cavalry
    164
Troop C, 7th Squadron, 1st Air Cavalry
    170
Troop D, 3rd Battalion, 5th Air Cavalry
    164
Troug, Pham 108–109
Truong Son Mountains 108
Tu Do Street 66, 109, 134–135
Turnover of personnel 128
25th Division (ARVN) 4, 47
25th Infantry Division 155
24th Artillery Group (VC) 203
240th Helicopter Company 167
214th Aviation Battalion 167
294th Battalion (VC) 202
275th Regiment (VC) 203
271st Regiment (VC) 202
274th Regiment (VC) 113, 202–203
272nd Regiment (VC) 202
273rd Regiment (VC) 202
265th Main Force Battalion (VC) 49
261st Battalion (VC) 142

261A Main Force Battalion, 1st Regiment (VC) 118, 168–169, 172, 176, 202, 205
261stB Main Force Battalion, 1st Regiment (VC) 168–169, 171, 176, 202
269th Battalion (VC) 202
267th Main Force Battalion, 1st Regiment (VC) 118, 202
267B Main Force Battalion, 1st Regiment (VC) 202
263rd Battalion (V) 202, 205
U/I Sapper Company (VC) 204
Uniform Code of Military Justice 7
United States 21, 30, 100
U.S. Army: command 93; engineers 46; National Match Rifle Team 18, 19; recruiter 5
U.S. Navy 66
University of Illinois at Urbana-Champaign 3
University of Iowa 3, 5–6, 77, 149, 155
University of Kansas 119
University of Michigan 5
University of Missouri-Columbia 5, 83, 118–119, 153
University of Virginia 87
University of Wisconsin 5

Vam Co Dong River 45
Vam Dinh Chanh River 162
Vam Lang River 158
Van Duesen 197
Van Set River 75
Vancouver (BC) 22
Venereal disease 28, 66. 76
Viet Cong 2, 4, 24–27, 30–31, 33–35, 37, 40–47, 51–65, 69–71, 73–76, 78, 81, 92, 94–99, 105–108, 113, 116–118, 120–121, 125, 129–131, 133–135, 138–139, 141–143, 145–148, 153–154, 156–157, 163, 167–173, 185–186, 195–197, 200; ambush 41; and Battle of the Plains of Reeds 167–185; bunkers 81, 168, 173; casualties 74–75, 98–99, 120, 163–165, 172, 175, 183, 197, 201; and

drugs 33; Main Force 94; Military Hospital 75–76, 169; Military Region II 56; POWS 64, 94, 115, 169; snipers 173, 182; tax collecting 135
Viet Minh 6, 24, 108, 131
Vietnam Veterans Against the War 155–156
Vietnam War 1–2, 5, 12, 22, 24, 70, 93, 120, 127, 153–156; veterans 1–3, 150, 152, 155–156
Vietnam War Memorial 3, 156
Vietnamese 31–31, 105, 127, 130–133, 135, 145, 143–154; narcotics 33
Vietnamization 4
Village in Vietnam 47
Vinh Hoa (village) 146
Vinh Kim (village) 141, 146
Vinh Long (province) 115
Vinh Long Viet Cong Prisoner of War Camp #6 115
Virginia Tech 5

War College 127
War Zone D 23, 55
Ward, Phil 171, 173–174
Washington (state) 16–17
Washington, D.C. 3, 84, 98
Water discipline 36, 178
Water trailor 173
Wayne, John 8
We Will Win 59, 63
West Point 15
Westmoreland, Gen. William 4, 24, 107
Williams, Sgt. 6, 110
Wilson, David 27
World War II 16, 83, 85, 126

Xa Khanh Canal 115
Xang Canal 197
Xam Tan Liem 164
Xuan Loc (VN) 37

Yoodhana, Corporal 104–105